Gnucash 2.4 Small Business Accounting

Beginner's Guide

Manage your accounts with this desktop financial management application

Ashok Ramachandran

[PACKT] open source✷
PUBLISHING   community experience distilled

BIRMINGHAM - MUMBAI

Gnucash 2.4 Small Business Accounting
Beginner's Guide

First published: February 2011

Production Reference: 1040211

Published by Packt Publishing Ltd.
32 Lincoln Road
Olton
Birmingham, B27 6PA, UK.

ISBN 978-1-849513-86-9

www.packtpub.com

Cover Image by Faiz Fattohi (faizfattohi@gmail.com)

Credits

Author

Ashok Ramachandran

Reviewers

Fabrice Estiévenart

Christian Stimming

Acquisition Editor

Usha Iyer

Development Editor

Susmita Panda

Technical Editor

Gauri Iyer

Indexers

Tejal Daruwale

Hemangini Bari

Editorial Team Leader

Mithun Sehgal

Project Team Leader

Priya Mukherji

Project Coordinator

Jovita Pinto

Proofreader

Kevin McGowan

Graphics

Nilesh R Mohite

Production Coordinator

Adline Swetha Jesuthas

Cover Work

Adline Swetha Jesuthas

About the Author

Ashok Ramachandran is a graduate in Mechanical Engineering and has a Masters in Business Management from the Indian Institute of Technology (IIT) Madras. He started with an engineering career, including the running of two small businesses, and then made a mid-career switch to Information Technology (IT). Currently, he is a senior IT executive in the Washington DC area. His penchant for explaining technology to non-technical users and interest in writing culminated in this book. For other open source software suitable for small medium businesses, you can refer to his website `http://smb-soft.com`.

I would like to thank the open source GnuCash team - the developers, the documenters, the people who keep the `gnucash.org` website and related infrastructure up and running and, especially, the people who answer user questions tirelessly on the mailing list. I would also like to thank my technical reviewers, Christian Stimming and Fabrice Estiévenart, for helping to catch my mistakes and providing valuable suggestions for improving my text. I would also like to thank the Packt team, especially my Acquisition Editor Usha Iyer for providing early feedback and channelling my ideas on the right track as well as my Project Coordinator Jovita Pinto, Development Editor Susmita Panda, and the Technical Editor Gauri Iyer for all their painstaking work in getting this book to print.

About the Reviewers

Fabrice Estiévenart is addicted to web and open-source technologies with a specific focus on web frameworks (Symfony, Pylons, Ruby on Rails), search engines (Lucene, Sphinx, Nutch, Solr), and database modelisation/abstraction (Doctrine, SQLAlchemy, Active Record). His favorite programming languages are PHP, Python, and Ruby.

He has initiated or contributed to several open-source projects such as SimPic (a lightweight PHP photo gallery), DocAlchemy (a 'Doctrine to SQLAlchemy' converter), DocRails (a 'Doctrine to Active Record' converter), CatCash (a rule-based transaction classifier in GnuCash) and Retroweb (a visual web-wrapping application).

Besides these initiatives, he is the developer and webmaster of several different web sites ranging from musical news portals (http://www.guitareacoustique.com) to personal blogs (http://www.destinationlibre.org, http://www.fabrisss.com).

Christian Stimming lives in Hamburg, Germany, working with SICK AG on research and C++ software development of real-time signal processing for industrial and automotive sensor applications. He learnt the benefits of Open Source software during his studies in Electrical Engineering at Hamburg University in the 1990s, started to contribute to the GnuCash project in 2000, and has been working with the GnuCash developer team since that time. Recently, he started a consulting business for users of GnuCash, successfully offering customization and training for small and home-office business customers in Germany. While reviewing this remarkably helpful book, his third child was born and Christian is happy to report all is well with his family and the new-born daughter in Hamburg.

www.PacktPub.com

Support files, eBooks, discount offers and more

You might want to visit www.PacktPub.com for support files and downloads related to your book.

Did you know that Packt offers eBook versions of every book published, with PDF and ePub files available? You can upgrade to the eBook version at www.PacktPub.com and as a print book customer, you are entitled to a discount on the eBook copy. Get in touch with us at service@packtpub.com for more details.

At www.PacktPub.com, you can also read a collection of free technical articles, sign up for a range of free newsletters and receive exclusive discounts and offers on Packt books and eBooks.

http://PacktLib.PacktPub.com

Do you need instant solutions to your IT questions? PacktLib is Packt's online digital book library. Here, you can access, read and search across Packt's entire library of books.

Why Subscribe?

- Fully searchable across every book published by Packt
- Copy and paste, print and bookmark content
- On demand and accessible via web browser

Free Access for Packt account holders

If you have an account with Packt at www.PacktPub.com, you can use this to access PacktLib today and view nine entirely free books. Simply use your login credentials for immediate access.

Table of Contents

Preface

Attention, small business owners! Stop tax-day stress. Stop procrastinating with a shoebox full of receipts. Stop reinventing the wheel with a spreadsheet. Stop making decisions simply on a hunch. Stop wasting money on software that is overkill. Start by downloading GnuCash and getting your accounts in order. Designed to be easy to use, yet powerful and flexible, GnuCash allows you to track bank accounts, income, and expenses. As quick and intuitive to use as a checkbook register, it is based on professional accounting principles to ensure balanced books and accurate reports. You can do it and Gnucash 2.4 Small Business Accounting Beginner's Guide will help you get up and running with maintaining your accounts.

Gnucash 2.4 Small Business Accounting Beginner's Guide speaks business language, not accountant-speak, because it is written by a former small business owner. It helps you to use GnuCash from scratch with step-by-step tutorials without jargon, pointing out the gotchas to avoid with lots of tips. It will teach you to work on routine business transactions while migrating transaction data from other applications gradually. It will teach you to work on routine business transactions as well as migrate transaction data from other applications.

Beyond Chapter 3, it is up to you how far you want to go. Reconcile with your bank and credit card statements. Charge and pay sales tax. Do invoicing. Track payments due. Set up reminders for bills. Avoid stress at tax time. Print checks. Capture expenses using your mobile phone.

Gnucash 2.4 Small Business Accounting Beginner's Guide gives you the power. Know your numbers. Make decisions with confidence. Drive your business to its full potential.

Get your accounts in order and avoid tax-day stress with this hands-on guide to GnuCash, the best free accounts software in the world.

What this book covers

Chapter 1, Getting Started with GnuCash: Before you can start using GnuCash you have to install it. Therefore, the first chapter starts with the detailed steps to install GnuCash on a Windows PC. Then, using the built-in template in GnuCash, you will practice creating the set of accounts (also known as categories) needed for a small business. You will also see how to enter opening balances. You will then learn how to make additions, changes, and deletions to the list of accounts to suit your needs. You will see how to output that to a spreadsheet, in case you want to ship it to your accountant for review. You will also quickly review the strengths and limitations of GnuCash.

Chapter 2, Transactions – the Lifeblood of a Business: Having created the accounts in Chapter 1, you will be ready to jump into the core task of bookkeeping, namely, entering transactions. You will learn a couple of different ways to enter simple transactions in GnuCash. Then you can move on to entering more complex transactions, called split transactions. You will also learn how to tweak these transactions by editing, canceling, or deleting them, as needed.

With that under your belt, you will go on to learn several tricks to make you spend less time and be more productive in doing these repetitive tasks. Duplicating transactions will allow you to reuse them and shortcuts will let you do them with minimal effort. Then navigation, views, sorting and filtering will all let you go where you want to go quickly and find what you need.

Chapter 3, Fun and Eye-opening Part - Reports and Charts: In this chapter, you will get familiar with the available standard reports and charts so that you can find them when you need them. Then you will learn how to customize them to suit your needs and how to save these customized reports for repeated use. You will also practice creating custom stylesheets and applying them to reports. You will then walk through the steps to export reports in standard formats that can be used by popular spreadsheet applications, such as MS Excel or OpenOffice.org Calc, for further formatting and printing.

Chapter 4, How Not to Get Lost in the Transactions Jungle: Here you will practice how to cross-check your entries using your bank and credit card statements. You can do this reconciliation by hand if you get printed monthly statements in the mail. Or you can automate it if you are able to download electronic statements. You will also learn why it is not a good idea to change or delete reconciled transactions. We will caution you why it is important in GnuCash to make sure that you select the right account to import into the first time you import into an account. However, if you pointed to the wrong account, we will show you how you can recover from that.

Chapter 5, Repetitive Work? Let GnuCash do it: Bookkeeping often feels repetitive - entering the same or similar transactions every day, week, or month. Here you will learn how to set them up as scheduled transactions and let GnuCash take care of them. You will learn how to convert a regular transaction into a scheduled transaction or set up several in one go. Also you will learn how to keep an eye on them as well as how to edit or delete them.

Chapter 6, Business Mantra: Buy Now, Pay Later: You will practice adding new customers to your business database and creating invoices as well as learn how to keep track of payments due as well as how to process payments when you receive them. Similarly, you will learn how to add vendors to your database as well as how to enter bills as and when you receive them. You will also practice creating reports that will help you to follow up on payments due to be paid to you as well as payments you owe. Even though GnuCash doesn't provide a means for you to set the starting invoice number, we will share an insider tip to editing the GnuCash accounts file directly.

Chapter 7, *Budget: Trip Planner for your Business:* You will learn how budgets help you to set up a Trip Plan to reach your business goals and practice creating budgets and generating reports showing budget vs. actual comparison. You will also learn the limitations of GnuCash budget reports and how to overcome them by exporting to spreadsheets.

In addition, in this chapter you will learn how payroll accounting is complex because of the many deductions and the company's contributions. We will show you how to enter them and how to use the Duplicate Transaction capability of GnuCash to reuse them. Also, tax law allows capital purchases such as office machines and furniture to be written off over a period of time. We will show you how to account for the allowed monthly depreciation. Furthermore, US tax law doesn't allow owners to draw a salary as a business expense. So, owners have to pay themselves through owner's draw. We will show you how to account for that and remind you that, in addition to income tax, you have to provide for self employment tax as well.

Chapter 8, Making Tax Times Less Stressful: You will set up GnuCash accounts to help you run and control your business on a day-to-day basis effectively. However, at tax time, you need to be able to create the tax returns quickly. You will practice how to map your accounts to Schedule C of US Internal Revenue Service (IRS) Form 1040. We will show you how to get the numbers needed for the tax return in a report that can be entered into your tax return software manually. Even better, if your tax return software supports it, you can also export this data in a standard format and import it into your tax return software.

Next, we will show you different ways of setting up sales tax tables to follow the law in different jurisdictions. You will practice how to apply all these sales taxes on your invoice. You will also practice creating reports to attach to your sales tax returns.

Chapter 9, Printing Checks and Finding Transactions: Sorting is often the first step to finding transactions and you will learn how to do sorting. Then you will go on to filtering out transactions that you are not interested in so that you can home in on the ones that you do want. Finally, you will study various ways to search for that needle-in-the-haystack elusive transaction.

You will practice printing checks in standard formats including how to print address and memo on the checks as well as how to print multiple checks in one go. You will also briefly see how to create and save a custom format, if the standard check formats don't work for you.

You will learn why you might want to give numbers to your accounts and how to go about doing that. You will also see how to check and fix transactions, if some of the splits are accidentally not imported or deleted. Finally you will learn how to use the custom calculator provided by GnuCash for calculating loan and mortgage payments.

Chapter 10, Adapting GnuCash for Non-profits and Personalizing: Non-profits have special needs to maintain funding as well as expenses, separately for each program, project, or event. You will learn how you can stretch the features of GnuCash to meet these needs.

You will also practice setting preferences in GnuCash so that you can arrange the environment to suit your needs. You will learn how to back-up and restore data as well as options available for password protection.

Chapter 11, Data Import/Export: Use your Phone to Enter Expenses: You will learn how to save transactions in your smart phone, sync it to your PC, and then import it into GnuCash. If you are using a feature phone, you will see how to use a third-party expense tracking service to send transactions and then import it into GnuCash.

You will become familiar with the various formats and processes available to migrate from other accounting software to GnuCash. You will also learn how to export transactions out of GnuCash.

Chapter 12, Application Integration and Other Advanced Topics: You will learn the benefits of saving data in a SQL database. You will practice connecting from MS Excel and OpenOffice.org to query this data as well as creating custom reports and charts. You will also learn how to use this queried data for integration with other applications that your business uses.

You will practice foreign exchange transactions and how to handle them in GnuCash. You will also learn how you can get reports at the contract level for the same customer by utilizing the Jobs feature of GnuCash. You will practice two different ways to undo a transaction, if that becomes necessary at a later point in time. You will also learn ways to deal with the year-end closing of books. Though GnuCash doesn't have support for inventory management and mileage tracking, we will clue you into some ways to work around these limitations.

What you need for this book

You need a computer that runs Windows XP, Vista, or 7 with about 350 MB of free disk space. You can use a computer running Mac or Linux for GnuCash. However, for these computers you need to get the installation instructions from the GnuCash website. To do some of the tutorials that show how to export data from GnuCash and manipulate it in a spreadsheet, you need MS Excel or OpenOffice.org software. For Chapter 12, you need to download an ODBC driver and install it as per the instructions provided in the book.

Who this book is for

This book is written for you – the self-employed, the start-up, the entrepreneur, the owner, partner, or leader of micro enterprises, home business, part-time business and side businesses, Small Office/Home Office (SOHO) and other small businesses to help you maintain your books of accounts using free GnuCash business accounting software. This book is also for you – the office bearer of non-profits and students who want to learn accounting hands-on. If you are currently using a spreadsheet to maintain your business books and wasting time, or if you are handing over a shoe box full of receipts to your high-priced accountant and wasting money or you are using another accounting application, that is overkill for a small business, and wasting both, get this book and download GnuCash.

Conventions

In this book, you will find several headings appearing frequently.

To give clear instructions of how to complete a procedure or task, we use:

Time for action – heading

1. Action 1
2. Action 2
3. Action 3

Instructions often need some extra explanation so that they make sense, so they are followed with:

What just happened?

This heading explains the working of tasks or instructions that you have just completed.

You will also find some other learning aids in the book, including:

Pop quiz – heading

These are short multiple choice questions intended to help you test your own understanding.

Have a go hero – heading

These set practical challenges and give you ideas for experimenting with what you have learned.

You will also find a number of styles of text that distinguish between different kinds of information. Here are some examples of these styles, and an explanation of their meaning.

New terms and **important words** are shown in bold. Words that you see on the screen, in menus or dialog boxes for example, appear in the text like this: "Enter **Acme** in the value field".

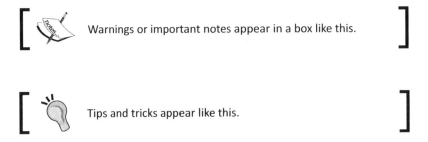

Warnings or important notes appear in a box like this.

Tips and tricks appear like this.

Reader feedback

Feedback from our readers is always welcome. Let us know what you think about this book—what you liked or may have disliked. Reader feedback is important for us to develop titles that you really get the most out of.

To send us general feedback, simply send an e-mail to feedback@packtpub.com, and mention the book title via the subject of your message.

If there is a book that you need and would like to see us publish, please send us a note in the **SUGGEST A TITLE** form on www.packtpub.com or e-mail suggest@packtpub.com.

If there is a topic that you have expertise in and you are interested in either writing or contributing to a book, see our author guide on www.packtpub.com/authors.

Customer support

Now that you are the proud owner of a Packt book, we have a number of things to help you to get the most from your purchase.

Errata

Although we have taken every care to ensure the accuracy of our content, mistakes do happen. If you find a mistake in one of our books—maybe a mistake in the text or the tutorial—we would be grateful if you would report this to us. By doing so, you can save other readers from frustration and help us improve subsequent versions of this book. If you find any errata, please report them by visiting http://www.packtpub.com/support, selecting your book, clicking on the **errata submission form** link, and entering the details of your errata. Once your errata are verified, your submission will be accepted and the errata will be uploaded on our website, or added to any list of existing errata, under the Errata section of that title. Any existing errata can be viewed by selecting your title from http://www.packtpub.com/support.

Piracy

Piracy of copyright material on the Internet is an ongoing problem across all media. At Packt, we take the protection of our copyright and licenses very seriously. If you come across any illegal copies of our works, in any form, on the Internet, please provide us with the location address or website name immediately so that we can pursue a remedy.

Please contact us at copyright@packtpub.com with a link to the suspected pirated material.

We appreciate your help in protecting our authors, and our ability to bring you valuable content.

Questions

You can contact us at questions@packtpub.com if you are having a problem with any aspect of the book, and we will do our best to address it.

1
Getting Started with GnuCash

"For years I've used a spreadsheet to manage my finances. Last November, I discovered GnuCash. I learned rather quickly that I was reinventing the wheel with my spreadsheet."—extracts from the blog of a new user of GnuCash.

GnuCash is a personal and small business bookkeeping and accounting software. In this book, we address the needs of self-employed, micro enterprises, home businesses, **Small Office/Home Office (SOHO)**, and other small businesses. We also include a chapter on how non-profits could use GnuCash for bookkeeping and accounting.

As a small business owner, partner, or leader, here is what you can do with GnuCash:

◆ Maintain your accounts using an interface that has the familiar look and feel of a check register

◆ Use canned reports and charts or customize and save them for reuse

◆ Use your bank and credit card statements to double check your entries through smart reconciliation

◆ Automate repetitive work by setting up scheduled transactions

◆ Create a Trip Planner to reach your business goals using GnuCash budgets

◆ Map GnuCash accounts to your income tax schedules to make tax times less stressful

◆ Create invoices for credit sales and keep track of unpaid invoices

◆ Get reminders for vendor bills when due as well as process employee expense vouchers

◆ Print 3-on-a-page and voucher checks, with memos as well

- Charge state, county, and local sales tax and print statements to attach to payments
- Use your mobile phone to capture expenses while on the go
- Migrate transaction data from other accounting applications
- Avoid redundant data entry by integrating with other applications
- Create your own reports and charts using popular spreadsheet software
- Account for foreign currency transactions
- Maintain accounts of non-profits

This should give you a taste of what is to come before you dive deep into the chapters in this book.

The core function of accounting software is to allow you to keep track of your business transactions in an orderly manner. Accountants call this **bookkeeping**. In plain English, bookkeeping is nothing but keeping a meticulous record of all the financial **transactions** of a business. But before you can record the transactions of a business, you need proper places to record them. In other words, you need to set up accounts to enter the transactions into. "Account" is a term used by GnuCash for grouping a set of similar transactions. For example, you can have an account named "Office Supplies" to record all transactions related to buying stationery. Some other accounting applications call this a "Category". So, our first task is to get started with creating the accounts. We are going to use a built-in template provided by GnuCash to set up an **account tree**.

Why does a small business need an account tree? Think of the account tree as the table of contents of a book. A book is generally organized into chapters, sections, and subsections. With the help of a table of contents, you can find what you are looking for easily in a large book. In a similar manner, your business might have many thousands of transactions in a year. If you organize your accounts in a convenient tree, you can find transactions when needed as well as create reports on different kinds of expenses and so on.

In this chapter, we will:

- Walk through the steps to install GnuCash on a Windows PC
- Quickly create the "Table of contents" for the accounts of a typical small business
- Learn how to tweak this "Table of contents" further to suit the needs of your specific business
- Enter account opening balances
- Output this "Table of contents" to send to your accountant for review
- Review the strengths and limitations of GnuCash

How do I pronounce GnuCash?

Some people use the proper "Guh-noo-cash" and others prefer the easier "NewCash". Go by whatever works for you.

Installing GnuCash on Windows

Before you can use GnuCash, you have to install it. We will walk you through the steps needed to get it installed successfully on your Windows PC, whether you have Windows 7, Vista, or XP.

Time for action – installing GnuCash on Windows

Let us go through the steps for downloading and installing GnuCash:

1. GnuCash is an open source software developed by volunteers, often for their own use, and shared with the community. It can be downloaded for free. Download the latest stable release of the installer for Microsoft Windows XP/Vista/7 from the www.gnucash.org website. The file should have a name like gnucash-2.4.1-setup.exe. The size of the file should be about 90MB. Save the file to a convenient location on your PC, such as the Temp folder in your C drive.

    The GnuCash website will also have other development versions of the software. These are unstable and are for testing purposes only. These are not suitable for business use. Make sure you download the stable release.

2. Launch the GnuCash setup program by double-clicking this file in Windows Explorer.

    Windows security might pop a message like **The publisher could not be verified. Are you sure you want to run this software?** or **Do you want to allow the following program from an unknown publisher to make changes to this computer?**. Click **Run** or **Yes** to continue.

3. The language selection dialog will appear with **English** already selected. Click **OK** to continue.

4. The **Welcome** screen of the GnuCash setup wizard will appear. Close any other application that may be running and click **Next**.

5. The **License Agreement** will appear. Select **I accept the agreement** and click **Next**.

6. The location dialog will show that GnuCash will be installed in C:\Program Files \ gnucash. It will also tell you how much free space is required on your hard disk for installing the program (about 350 MB). Make sure you have the required free space and click **Next**.

 On Windows 7, the default location will be C:\Program Files (x86)\gnucash.

7. The next screen will show that a **Full Installation** will be done. Click **Next** to continue.

8. The next screen will show that a **GnuCash** folder will be created for the menu items. Click **Next** to continue.

9. The next screen will show that a desktop icon and a start menu link will be created. Click **Next** to continue.

10. The next screen is simply a recap of all the selections made by you so far. Click **Install** to start the installation. This may take several minutes, giving you time for a coffee break.

11. When the installation is completed successfully, you should see a window with the title **Information**. Click **Next** to continue.

12. Next, the **Completing the GnuCash Setup Wizard** window will appear. The **Run GnuCash now** box will be checked. Click **Finish** to complete the installation. The **GnuCash Tip of the Day** will pop up. You can close this.

13. You should see the **Welcome to GnuCash** window with **Create a new set of accounts** checked. We are going to do that soon. But for now, click **Cancel**.

14. Say **No** to the **Display Welcome Dialog Again?** question. You should see the **Unsaved book – GnuCash** window:

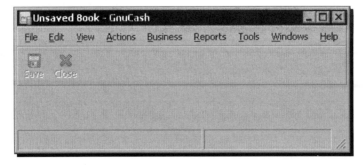

What just happened?

Congratulations! You have just installed GnuCash successfully and you are ready to start learning, hands-on, how to use it.

Other operating systems

In addition to Windows, GnuCash runs on Mac OS X (on the newer Intel as well as the older Power PC) and several flavors of Linux. If you have one of those operating systems, you can download the install package and get installation instructions for those operating systems from the GnuCash.org website.

Other download locations

In addition to the GnuCash.org website, you can also download GnuCash from popular open source repositories such as SourceForge. Wherever you download from, be careful that you are downloading from a genuine site and that the download is free of viruses and malware.

But first, a tip to make your life easier with auto-save

Before we start the main show, here is a quick tip to make your life easier. GnuCash has a friendly feature to auto-save changes every few minutes. Some people find this very useful while entering transactions. However, at the time of going through the tutorial, you don't want this auto-save to kick in. Why? You want to have some breathing time to recover from any errors and correct any mistakes and then save it at your convenience. It is even possible, heaven forbid, that you might want to abandon the changes instead of trying to rectify them. To do this, you might want to exit GnuCash without saving the changes. So, let us politely tell GnuCash, "STOP HELPING ME"!

Launch the GnuCash Preferences dialog from **Edit | Preferences**. Select the **General** tab. As shown in the following image, set the **Auto-save time interval** to **0 minutes**. By setting this to 0, the auto-save feature is turned off. Also, uncheck the **Show auto-save confirmation question**, if it is checked. As we said, users have found that this ability to auto-save is a big life saver. So, don't forget to turn this back on when you are done with the tutorials and start keeping your business books.

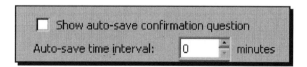

Taking the drudgery out of setting up accounts

Even the smallest of businesses may need as many as a hundred accounts. If your business is somewhat larger, you may need to create a lot more than a hundred accounts. Am I going to make you create that many accounts one by one?

No, I am going to show you how you can create the entire set of accounts needed for a typical small business in under a dozen clicks.

Time for action – creating the default business accounts

We are going to create the account hierarchy for our sample business, **Mid Atlantic Computer Services (MACS)**. This will give you the hands-on feel to create accounts for your business, when you are ready to do that.

1. Select from the menu **File | New | New File**. This will launch the **New Account Hierarchy Setup** assistant.

 GnuCash uses the term assistant to describe what you may have seen in other Windows applications called a wizard. Assistants help you perform tasks that are complex or not frequently performed. Assistants present you with a sequence of dialog boxes that lead you through a series of well-defined steps.

2. Click **Forward** to go to the **Choose Currency** screen.

3. You will find that **US Dollar** is selected by default. You can leave it as it is and click **Forward** to go to the **Choose accounts to create** screen.

4. You will find that **Common Accounts** is checked by default. This option is for users who want to set up personal accounts. We want to set up a business account. So, uncheck this and check **Business Accounts**, as shown in the next screenshot and then click **Forward**:

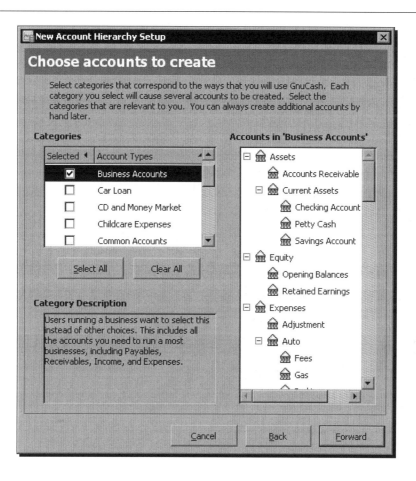

5. In the **Setup selected accounts** screen, click on the **Checking Account** line and it will become highlighted. Click under the **Opening Balance** column in this line, a text box will appear allowing you to enter data. Enter an opening balance of **2000**, as shown in the next screenshot, tab out, and click **Forward**.

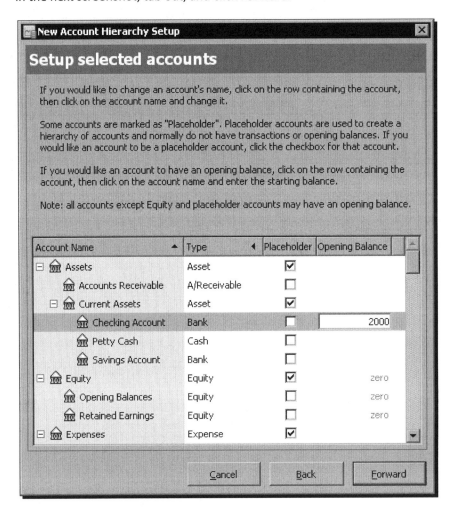

6. In the **Finish Account Setup** screen, click **Apply**.

7. With the previous step, the **New Account Hierarchy Setup** assistant has completed its job. You should now be back in the GnuCash main window showing the freshly minted set of accounts with the title **Unsaved Book - Accounts**.

8. The **Save As** dialog should open. If it doesn't, select **File | Save As...** change the **Save in** folder to your desired folder, put in the filename MACS without any extension, and click **Save As**. If your screen looks like the following screenshot, you have now successfully created the default business account hierarchy for MACS:

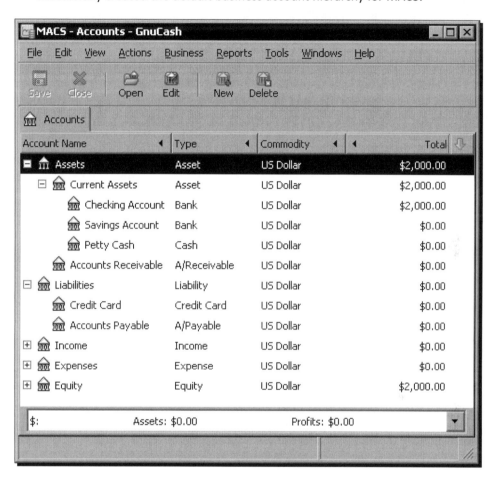

 Most Windows applications require you to save files with a 3 or 4 letter extension. Microsoft Word, for example, requires a .docx or .doc file extension. However, GnuCash uses the longer .gnucash extension. If you fill in the file name, GnuCash will automatically add the .gnucash extension.

What just happened?

There you are. With a small amount of effort, you have not only created a complete set of accounts that would be needed for a typical small business, but you have also learned how to enter opening balances as well. Now that we have that under our belt, let us discuss the key aspects of setting up accounts.

Account hierarchy

As you can see in the previous figure, the account named Assets contains two sub-accounts, Currents Assets, and **Accounts Receivable**. The sub-account Currents Assets in turn contains three sub-accounts, **Checking Account**, **Savings Account**, and **Petty Cash**. Arranging our accounts in this sort of a tree structure is why it is known as the **Account Hierarchy**.

A GnuCash account can contain transactions as well as other sub-accounts. To extend the example of a book that we used earlier, this is similar to how a chapter in a book can contain some introductory text, several sections, and some summary text.

This Account Hierarchy window is the **GnuCash** main window. We will also refer to this as the **Account Tree** window or the **Accounts tab**.

Minimal set of accounts

"What is the minimal set of accounts that I need, if I want to keep my business accounts simple?" If you want to start small or if you want to practice with a set of starter accounts, here is a minimal set of accounts:

- **Assets**: All that your business owns will go under this account
  - Checking Account
  - Cash

- **Liabilities**: All that your business owes will go under this account
  - Credit Card

- **Income**: All your business income, including sales and any other income, will go under this account
  - Sales

- **Expenses**: All your business expenses will be recorded under this account
  - Rent
  - Car
  - Travel
  - Entertainment

- ❏ Meals
- ❏ Office expenses

◆ **Equity**: The money brought in to the business by the owner or partners as equity as well as money taken out of the business by owners or partners as salary, bonus, dividends, and owners' draw will all go under this

- ❏ Opening Balances

Under **Expenses**, feel free to change the accounts to suit the kind of expenses your business has.

Here is one way to visualize your accounting system. Think of transactions as business documents. Accounts are like manila folders. Parent accounts are like hanging folders. The top level accounts are like the drawers. And your accounting system is like a five-drawer filing cabinet. Visualize the five drawers labeled Assets, Liabilities, Income, Expenses, and Equity. Once you have arranged and labeled your hanging folders and manila folders inside the drawers, your task is to then put each document that comes in into the appropriate folder in the filing cabinet.

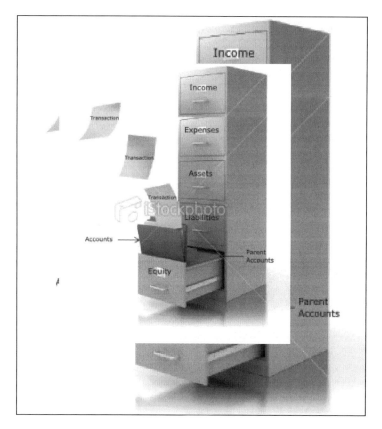

Depending on the size of your business and your need for granular control, you will have to decide how detailed you want your set of accounts to be. You may also want to run it by your accountant and tax consultant to make sure they are comfortable with it. Setting up too few accounts will make it difficult for you to analyze the numbers and take corrective actions. For example, let us say you have travel, entertainment, and office supplies lumped together under a Miscellaneous account. You find that your Miscellaneous expenses for this month are 50 percent higher than last month. What next? You have to spend a lot of time analyzing what caused this unexpected increase in expenditure. On the other hand, setting up too many accounts may overwhelm you, especially if you are a new user.

Can I add and delete accounts as I need them?

Yes, GnuCash lets you do that as and when you want. However, it is not a good idea to keep adding and deleting accounts often. An important aspect of maintaining accounts is to be able to compare expenses, revenue, and so on from month-to-month and from quarter-to-quarter. If the basis has changed, such comparisons with past periods will not be valid.

Pop quiz – understanding accounts

1. Accounts can contain which of the following?

    a. Only transactions

    b. Only sub-accounts

    c. Both transactions and sub-accounts

Have a go hero – creating account hierarchies from multiple templates

Create a new account hierarchy which includes the following three templates:

1. Business Accounts

2. Car Loan

3. Fixed Assets

Two ways of doing this exercise

You can either create a new Account Hierarchy from scratch or add Car Loan and Fixed Assets to the Business Accounts you created in this exercise. To add one or more account hierarchies to the one already created, choose **File | New | New Account Hierarchy**.

Getting your business accounts done just right

Isn't it great that you got a lot done with so little effort? Yes, I know what you are thinking. You did get a whole set of business accounts set up with opening balances as well. But when you scrutinize the list, you find that there are some accounts you don't want and others that you must have but which are not in the default set provided by GnuCash. What now?

We will look at how you can tweak it further, by making selective additions, deletions, and changes.

Time for action – fine tuning business accounts

We will now go through the specific steps needed to create a new account, make changes to an existing account, and delete unwanted accounts.

1. **Creating a new account**: For example, you find that you are spending a lot on auto insurance. However, currently there is no separate account for that. So, we are going to go ahead and create a new account for auto insurance. Select **File | New | New Account...**. The **New Account** dialog will open. Make sure **Expense** is selected as the **Account Type** and **Auto** is selected as the **Parent Account**. Enter **Auto Insurance** in the **Account name** as well as **Description**, as shown in the next screenshot, and click **OK**.

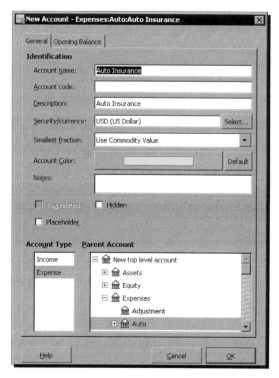

2. **Renaming an account**: You don't care much for the name **Petty Cash** for the cash account. You feel people should take cash more seriously than that. You want to change it to **Cash**. Right-click on the **Petty Cash** account. From the pop-up menu, select **Edit Account**. The **Edit Account** dialog will open. Change the **Account name** and **Description** to **Cash** and click **OK**.

3. **Deleting an account**: You have determined that you don't need an account for Outside Services. So, we are going to go ahead and delete that. Scroll down to the **Outside Services** account, right-click on it, and select **Delete Account...** from the pop-up menu, as shown in the following screenshot. You will get a warning message that "**The account Expenses:Outside Services will be deleted**". Go ahead and click on the **Delete** button to confirm that it is OK to delete it.

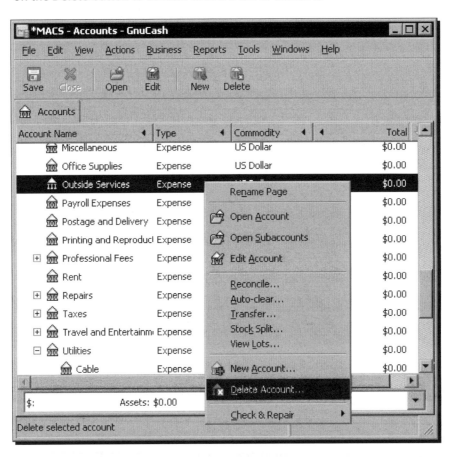

What just happened?

This combination of using a template to create a whole bunch of accounts in one go and then making further tweaks through selective additions, deletions, and changes lets you have the best of both worlds. Without wasting too much time, you now have a set of accounts that are just right for your business and named according to your preference as well.

Account types

GnuCash has the following 11 **account types** and we have listed examples of each account type. Of these, Stock and Mutual Fund account types are mainly used for personal accounts. For a business, when creating new accounts, you will typically select from one of the remaining 9 types:

1. **Bank**: Checking Account, Savings Account

2. **Cash**: Petty Cash or Cash

3. **Asset**: Car, Computer, Office Furniture, Equipment & Machinery, Building

4. **Credit Card**: Credit Card (any type)

5. **Liability**: Loan Principal, Sales Tax (collected and to be paid)

6. **A/Receivable**: Accounts Receivable (on credit sales)

7. **A/Payable**: Accounts Payable (on credit purchases)

8. **Income**: Sales, Interest Income, Reimbursed Expenses

9. **Expense**: Rent, Office Supplies, Car Expenses, Travel, Entertainment, Meals, Loan Interest

When you create a new account, you must pick one of these types. This helps GnuCash to treat the accounts appropriately. For example, while entering transactions, an account of type Bank will display 'Deposit' and 'Withdrawal' columns. An account of type Cash will display 'Receive' and 'Spend' columns.

Parent accounts and top level accounts

The different business accounts that you might want to create for your business can be typically placed into one of these five groups:

1. **Assets**: Things that you own. This can include accounts of type Bank, Cash, A/Receivable, and Asset.

2. **Equity**: The net worth of your business. This can include only accounts of type Equity.

3. **Expenses**: Costs incurred in running your business. This can include only accounts of type Expense.

4. **Income**: Revenue you receive for goods supplied and services rendered by your business. This can include only accounts of type Income.

5. **Liabilities**: Things that you owe to others. This can include accounts of type Credit Card, A/Payable, and Liability.

If you study the account hierarchy that you created from the template, you will find that all accounts are grouped under these five accounts. These five accounts are not only **parent accounts**, they have no parents themselves, thus making them **top level accounts**.

On the other hand, take a look at the account **Auto** under **Expenses**. **Auto** is a parent account with four child accounts:

1. Fees

2. Gas

3. Parking

4. Repairs and maintenance.

But **Auto** itself has a parent account, namely, **Expenses**. Thus it is a parent account but not a top level account.

New account creation tips

As you just saw, when you create a new account, you need to select an account type and a parent account. If you highlight the parent account and then open the **New Account** dialog, the appropriate **Account Type** and **Parent Account** will be selected by default.

In addition to selecting **File | New | New Account...**, there are two other ways of accessing the **New Account** dialog. You can right-click the parent account and choose **New Account** from the pop-up menu. Also, when the Account tab is open, you will see a '**New**' button on the toolbar. This will also open the same dialog.

Sometimes you may want to create a new top level account for things that do not belong in the default five top level accounts created by the template. For example, you may want to create a new top level account for non-operating revenue to keep it separate from operating revenue. Take a look at the **New Account** dialog again. You will see that it has an option to select **New top level account** as the **Parent Account**.

Placeholder account

A GnuCash **placeholder account** is a special type of parent account that can contain only sub-accounts but no transactions. It is convenient for grouping similar accounts under a common account, but it cannot have any transactions itself. For example, you can have a placeholder account Professional Fees with two sub-accounts under that, namely, Accounting Fees and Legal Fees.

Opening balance

If you are just starting your business, life is simple. Well, that didn't come out right. Abandoning the safety and comfort of a regular pay check can feel like leaving on a one-way trip to Mars. But, from the very narrow point of view of figuring opening balances, you are starting with a clean slate. All opening balances are zero. Nothing has happened yet, business-wise.

But if you are switching from another accounting software, a spreadsheet or even a shoebox, you need to decide on a start date. For example, if you are planning to start using GnuCash as of January 1, 2011, your previous system end date is December 31, 2010. For your bank account, for example, enter the ending balance as on December 31, 2010. You will find this on your bank statement.

Take a look at the create New Account dialog once again; you will see a tab marked **Opening Balance**. We didn't need an opening balance for the Auto Insurance account that we created. However, if you find that you need to enter an opening balance for the account that you want to create, you can enter that here at the time of creating a new account.

Pop quiz – understanding account types and hierarchies

1. Which of the following is not a valid account type in GnuCash?

    a. Bank

    b. A/Receivable

    c. Debit Card

    d. Asset

    e. Cash

2. Which of the following are common top level accounts?

    a. Asset, Liability, Equity, Expenses and Income

    b. Asset, Liability, Cash, Expenses and Income

    c. Asset, Liability, Equity, Expenses and Bank

    d. Asset, Credit Card, Equity, Expenses and Income

3. Placeholder accounts can have transactions

    a. Yes

    b. No

    c. Under certain conditions

Have a go hero – tweaking accounts

The Professional Fees account has two child accounts—Accounting and Legal Fees. Change the Professional Fees account into a placeholder account.

How to impress your accountant

Even though we are trying to keep accounting jargon to a minimum, it is a good idea to be on talking terms with your accountant! And, in order to talk to the accountants, you need to speak their lingo, right? Oh no, not all of it, just enough to get across what you want to get done. So, it is good to know that whatever GnuCash calls the 'account hierarchy', the Accountants call the '**Chart of Accounts**'.

If your accountant has GnuCash, you can send a copy of the MACS file that we created earlier. They can open this in their GnuCash application and review.

What if your accountant doesn't have GnuCash?

You can still send it in one of the popular spreadsheet formats such as Microsoft Excel or OpenOffice.org Calc. How will you do that? Go to the **Reports** menu and select **Account Summary**. You should now see the complete hierarchy of accounts that we created in a tabular report format. You can copy and paste this into Microsoft Excel and save it as an Excel file. Alternatively, you can paste this into OpenOffice.org Calc and save it as a Calc ODS file. Accountants are typically very heavy users of spreadsheets and, chances are, your accountant should be able to handle one of these.

Here comes the **MOST IMPORTANT** part. In the e-mail, just say casually, "Here is the draft chart of accounts that I created. When you have a minute, take a quick peek and let me know what you think". That ought to do it.

Strengths and limitations of GnuCash

By now, you know that GnuCash can do business accounting, however, you would like to know how far it can go. For example, you would like to know what type of accounting GnuCash is most suitable for and what kind of accounting it cannot handle.

Business as well as personal accounting

You can use GnuCash for your personal as well as business accounting in the following different ways:

1. Work on only your business accounts.

2. Work on only your personal accounts.

3. Combine your personal accounts and business accounts into one single account. For example, if you have a simple rental type of business, you can keep your rental income and expenses in separate accounts within your personal accounts.

4. Maintain your personal accounts as well as your business accounts in separate files. This is because GnuCash saves one account with all of the related transactions in one file. You can open your personal accounts file, enter transactions, and save it. Then you can open your business accounts file, enter transactions...and so on.

 This is a description of the capabilities of the software. You should check with your accountant and tax consultant regarding the best course of action for your specific financial and tax situation.

However, please note that this book is focused entirely on business accounting. Personal accounting is not within the scope of this book.

Single user

GnuCash is a single user software. Oh, you and your business partner both need access? Your associate will be entering transactions and you must be able to view the reports? You want to know whether there is a way for more than one person to access GnuCash? Yes, there is. As long as you are willing to live with the limitation that only one person can use it at a time.

Sharing a GnuCash accounts file

Here is how two people can share a single GnuCash accounts file. Look for a common folder that both users have access to. This can be a folder on one of the users' PC for which the other user is provided shared access. Or, as shown in the diagram below, it can be a folder on a network file server that both users have access to.

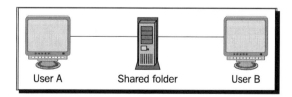

When User A accesses the file, GnuCash will lock that file. If User B tries to open this same file, GnuCash will pop a warning as shown in the following screenshot:

On seeing this message, User B should quit. If User B goes ahead and chooses to **Open Anyway**, then there is risk of data corruption and data loss. However, this message can also appear if the last time you used GnuCash it closed abnormally. This abnormal closing can occur due to a number of reasons including power failure, application, operating system crash, or other such problems. If that is the case, you must select **Open Anyway**. In short, when you see this message:

◆ If you are the only person using it, select **Open Anyway**.

◆ If you are sharing it with others, check whether anyone else is using it first.

Accounting features not supported by GnuCash

GnuCash is suitable for small business accounting. Some small businesses need Payroll, Inventory, or Point of Sale (POS) features. However, GnuCash doesn't have integrated payroll, inventory, or POS modules.

Payroll

Even though GnuCash doesn't have an integrated payroll module, you can create necessary accounts in GnuCash and enter payroll expenses, as needed. In order to work around this limitation, you may choose to use a payroll service provider or a spreadsheet for calculating your payroll.

Business functions other than accounting

Quotations, purchase orders, and other business functions do not result in an accounting transaction. GnuCash is solely devoted to accounting. It doesn't support these other business functions.

Summary

We learned a lot in this chapter about how to set up the accounts needed for a small business.

Specifically, we covered:

◆ **Installing GnuCash on a Windows PC**: We walked through the steps involved in downloading and installing GnuCash on a PC running Windows 7, Vista, or XP.

◆ **Creating a set of accounts**: We learned how to use the built-in template in GnuCash to quickly create a complete set of accounts needed for a typical small business.

◆ **Tweaking the set of accounts**: While the preceding step helped us to make quick progress on setting up accounts, that was not enough. No two businesses are going to be exactly the same. There is always a need to tweak it further. We then looked at how to make account additions, changes, and deletions so that we can get it just right for your special business.

◆ **Entering an opening balance**: We also learned how to enter an opening balance to the accounts, whether created from the template or separately, from scratch. We also reviewed different account types, parent accounts, top level accounts, and placeholder accounts.

◆ **Outputting the set of accounts to a spreadsheet**: We also figured out how to ship the draft 'Chart of Accounts' to your accountants.

◆ **Strengths and limitations of GnuCash**: We quickly reviewed the strengths and limitations of GnuCash as well.

Now that we've created the set of accounts, we have laid the necessary foundation. With that, we are ready to start entering transactions, which is the topic of the next chapter.

2
Transactions – the Lifeblood of a Business

"I don't like keeping books...I just find it boring...But I'll tell you what! I always feel good after completing the book-keeping." – a successful small business owner in his blog.

On the other hand, there are others who look at accounting as a game. If something doesn't balance, they take it on as a fun challenge to track down the problem and find a solution. However, if you are like this small business owner, you may find bookkeeping a boring activity because it is very repetitive. Perhaps, you would rather be out cultivating customers and working on the deals that make your business grow and prosper. However, that is the very reason why we are going to spend some time equipping you with all the tools and tips necessary to get through this bookkeeping part quickly and effectively. With that taken care of, you can be free to devote more time to growing your business.

As a small business, on any given day, you may have several expenses which you might pay by cash, check, or credit card. Also, you might receive sales revenue by check or cash. You might also have other transactions such as repayment of loan, withdrawing cash from the bank, and so on. All of these transactions need to be entered in GnuCash so that you can run reports at the end of the week, month, and quarter. This will help you to see how your business is doing and navigate around potential cash flow hurdles towards your business goals successfully.

So, capturing these transactions quickly and effectively is the heart of establishing a good accounting and financial reporting system which is essential for a successful small business.

In this chapter, we shall cover:

- A quick way to enter simple transactions
- Step-by-step approach to more complex transactions
- Editing and deleting transactions
- Speeding up work by using entry shortcuts
- Minimizing work by reusing transactions

We have done the ground work already by setting up the accounts necessary in the previous chapter. Now we are all set to get started entering transactions.

A quick and easy way to enter simple transactions

GnuCash provides a way by which you can enter simple transactions quickly and easily. It is so simple that on completing it, you will wonder why people are making such a big deal about bookkeeping.

Time for action – entering simple transactions quickly and easily

In this tutorial, we are going to enter a simple transaction of withdrawing $300 cash from the checking account.

1. From the menu, select **Actions | Transfer** to open the **Transfer Funds** window.

2. In the **Basic Information** pane, enter **300** in the **Amount** field, leave today's date unchanged in the **Date** field, enter the check number **2073** in the **Num** field, and enter **Withdraw cash** in **Description**.

3. Scroll down in the **Transfer From** list and select **Checking Account**. You may have to click on the **+** sign to open the tree, if the account is not visible.

4. Scroll down in the **Transfer To** list and select **Cash**. At this point, the window should look like this:

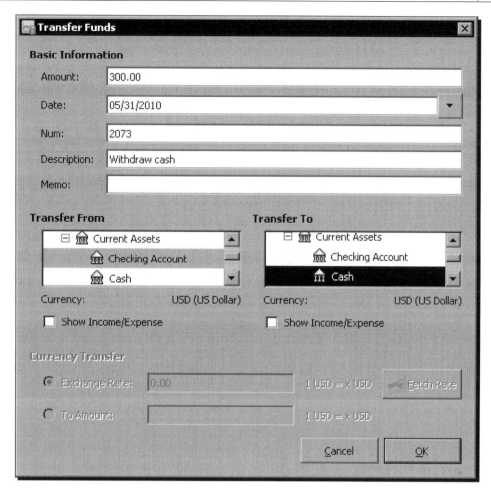

5. Select **OK** to commit the transaction.

6. We will now confirm that the transaction has been entered in the respective accounts correctly. In the **Account** tab, double-click on the **Checking Account**. It will open in a separate **Checking Account** tab. This is known as the **account register** for **Checking Account**. You should now see an entry for the withdrawal of $300 cash and a new balance of $1,700.

7. In the account tree window, double-click on **Cash**. It will open in a separate **Cash** tab. This is the account register for **Cash**. You should now see an entry for the withdrawal of $300 cash and a new balance of $300.

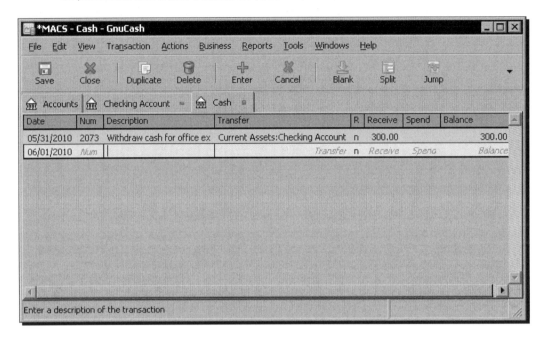

8. When you have double checked all entries and everything looks hunky-dory, make sure you save the changes.

What just happened?

"Hey, I just created my first transaction in GnuCash"? Well, not quite. You already entered your first transaction in GnuCash while setting up accounts. You were having a blast creating a ton of accounts so fast, it didn't seem a good idea to slow you down by pointing out that when you entered an opening balance, you actually created your first transaction.

On the other hand, while opening balances are needed only occasionally, the **Transfer Funds** window gives you a handy tool to enter many business transactions. So, go ahead, celebrate.

Money makes the business world go round

The Merriam-Webster dictionary defines a transaction as an exchange or transfer of goods, services, or funds. As a business owner, you know that every transaction involves funds, directly or indirectly. You also know that the transactions only differ on the source of funds, where the money came from and the use of funds, or where it went. Yeah, I know what you are thinking. Sometimes it feels like that money seems to be going into black holes, never to be seen again. However, hold your hat; GnuCash is here to help you. Oh no, it can't prevent your money from disappearing into black holes. However, you will soon learn how to create reports in GnuCash, showing precisely which black holes it went into!

An example from outside the business world will help us compare business transactions with non-business ones. Non-profits, such as the Salvation Army or your local church, can get a donation without giving something else in return. This is an example of a non-business transaction.

Let us look at some examples of business transactions:

Item	Transaction	Source of funds	Use of funds
1	You pay cash to buy office supplies	Cash	Business expenses
2	You sell products to get paid by check	Sales	Bank balance goes up
3	You buy a part online and charge it to your credit card	Credit card dues go up	Business expenses
4	You invoice a customer for services and allow them 30 days to pay	Service provided	Accounts receivable goes up
5	You withdraw cash from the bank	Bank balance goes down	Cash balance goes up

So, in business terms, we can say that every transaction can be split into its source of funds and use of funds. Thus, a single transaction must always consist of at least two parts, namely, an amount in the "from" account and an amount in the "to" account. Moreover, the two must be equal.

Simple transaction

In the following diagram, the outer box in dotted lines represents the transaction and the inner boxes are splits of the transaction showing the sources and uses of funds:

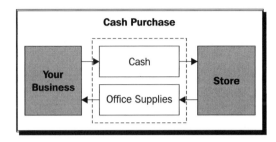

As you can see, it is not very difficult to understand transactions. You just need to answer three basic questions:

1. How much money changed hands? The value of the transaction.

2. Where did the money come from? The source of funds or the "from" account.

3. Where did the money go? The use of funds or the "to" account.

These are examples of simple transactions in which there is one account for each split. These are referred to as simple 2-account transactions in GnuCash.

 We showed a transaction with another party in the preceding diagram. However, there can be transactions without involving another party. Item 5 in the earlier table, withdrawing cash from the bank, is an example of an internal transaction. We moved funds from one account to another. The same rules of transaction apply even for internal transactions. We need a source of funds and a use of funds and the two must be equal.

Checks and balances are good

When accounting was done manually, accountants used to post each side of the transaction separately in the books. This **double entry bookkeeping**, of course, requires twice the amount of work. So, why did they do it? It helped accountants catch arithmetic and data entry errors. As each transaction had to be recorded in two places, the results of additions and subtractions could be double-checked simply by seeing whether the accounts balanced. With computers, arithmetic mistakes are no longer a major issue, although data entry errors still are.

You will be happy to know that in GnuCash, you only need to enter the data once. GnuCash does the double entry bookkeeping for you behind the scenes. You still get all the advantages of double entry bookkeeping, namely, cross checking to see if accounts balance.

But, more importantly, you are now equipped with one more piece of jargon to throw at your accountant. During a lunch conversation, in a matter of fact tone, you can say, "It does double entry bookkeeping. That is another reason why I picked GnuCash."

Pop quiz – understanding transactions

1. In a transaction, how do the source of funds and use of funds compare?

    a. Source of funds is higher

    b. Use of funds is higher

    c. They must be equal to each other

    d. They are unrelated

Have a go hero – entering transactions

Look at the example transactions in the previous table. Enter some transactions using the **Transfer Funds** window based on these examples. Just make up suitable amounts and descriptions, as needed.

Entering a simple transaction in the account register

The account register is the GnuCash window which allows you to view and edit existing transactions or add new transactions to a particular account.

 The account registers were designed by the GnuCash team to resemble a check book register, the log used to keep track of checks issued. This is the reason why they are called registers.

Time for action – entering a simple transaction in the account register

The account register will be the scene of much of your bookkeeping action. Let us get familiar with it first by entering a simple transaction.

1. To open the account register, select the **Expenses:Office Supplies** account in the **Accounts** tab and double-click to open it. Once selected, you can also click the **Open** button in the toolbar or click the right mouse button and select **Open Account**. GnuCash will open the **Expenses:Office Supplies** account register in a separate tab. GnuCash will start a new transaction and put the focus on the date field with today's date as the default one.

2. Let us make sure that your view settings are in line with the steps in the tutorial. Go to the **View** menu and confirm that there is a dot in front of **Basic Ledger** and **Double Line** is not checked, as shown in the following screenshot:

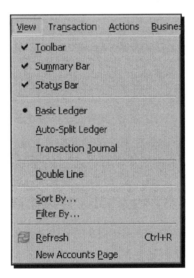

3. Click on the small button on the right of the **Date** field to drop down a date selection calendar. Click on yesterday's date. Click on the small button on the right of the **Date** field once more to close the date selection calendar. Alternatively, you can type in the date.

4. Click on *Tab* to move to the **Num** field. Here you can enter a check, receipt, transaction, or any other number. Enter the receipt number **1019**.

5. Click on *Tab* to move to the **Description** field. This field is used to enter a description for the transaction. Enter the text **Printer ink cartridge set**.

6. Click on *Tab* to move the cursor to the **Transfer** field. Click on the small button on the right side of the **Transfer** field to drop down the list of Accounts. Scroll down, select **Assets:Current Assets:Cash**.

7. Click on *Tab* to move to the **Expense** amount field. Type in the amount **44.95**. Click on the *Enter* key to complete the transaction and move the cursor to the next transaction. You can also select the **Enter** icon, or from the menu, select **Transaction | Enter Transaction**.

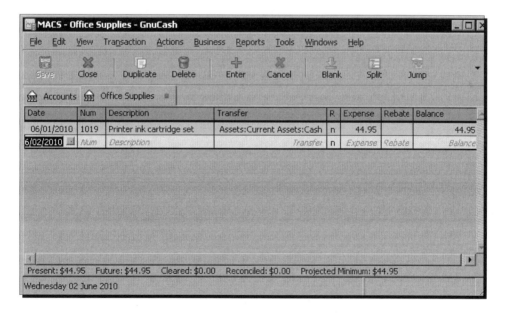

8. Check all entries again and don't forget to **Save** the changes.

What just happened?

As you were going through this tutorial, I am sure, at some point, this thought suddenly popped up in your head, "Hmmm, I could have done this with my eyes closed in the **Transfer Funds** window. Why am I wasting my time with this account register again?"

If you were a disciple in a remote monastery high in the Himalayas, your guru's response would have been, "If you follow my instructions unquestioningly and with utmost faith, at some point when you are ready, you will see the light of knowledge and the true reason will be revealed to you."

However, we are not in the Himalayan monastery. So, let me share the reason with you right away. Yes, you could have done this in the **Transfer Funds** window. However, this is a great way to get familiar with the account register. This will help you to quickly get to the point of entering more complex transactions, which can only be done in the account register. In other words, you can only enter simple 2-account transactions in the **Transfer Funds** window. For anything more complicated than that, you will have to depend on the Account Register.

As we saw earlier, every transaction has two sides – an account that money is transferred from and an account that money is transferred to. GnuCash calls them splits. Thus, a simple 2-account transaction consists of two splits.

Here is a list of the fields in the Checking Account register and how you will use them:

- ◆ **Date**: This field is for the date of the transaction.

- ◆ **Num**: You can enter numbers, or even text, in this field. For example, if this is a deposit, you can enter the check number here. This field is optional.

- ◆ **Description**: Here you should describe briefly what this transaction is all about. Customer or vendor's name, invoice or bill number, and date could all go in here.

- ◆ **Transfer**: We said that every transaction touches two accounts. Now that we are entering the transaction in the Checking Account, we need to select in this field the other account that this transaction touches.

- ◆ **R: R** stands for the **Reconciliation** field. This will default to **n** for 'not reconciled'.

- ◆ **Deposit**: If you are putting money into the Checking Account, you will enter it here.

- ◆ **Withdrawal**: If you are taking money out of the Checking Account, you will enter it here.

- ◆ **Balance**: GnuCash will automatically compute the balance for you.

- ◆ You will notice that the **Deposit** and **Withdrawal** fields change their name depending on the account. In the Cash account, for example, these will be called **Receive** and **Spend** respectively.

Navigating the account registers

In step 1 of the preceding tutorial, we opened the **Office Supplies** account register. You can open as many account registers at a time as needed. When you are done, you can close them by clicking on the **close** button in the toolbar.

Close button on folder tabs

By now, you may have noticed the tiny gray buttons on the folder tabs in my screenshots and wondered what they are. These are close buttons and there are preference settings to have these buttons show up. Go to the **Edit | Preferences | Windows** tab and check the **Show** close button on notebook tabs in the tabs section.

You can rearrange the tab folders to your convenience by dragging the folder tabs. Also, GnuCash will remember which tabs were open when you quit. It will reopen all those tabs when you launch GnuCash next time. So, at the time of closing GnuCash, you can leave any tabs that you need for the next session open.

The **Accounts** tab is the main window of GnuCash and is also the anchor. When the **Accounts** tab is open, you will find the **Close** button disabled. This is the only tab you are not allowed to close.

Jump to account

When you are in a transaction in the account register, you can click the toolbar **Jump** button to jump to the account which has the other split of the transaction. You can also right click and select **Jump** from the context menu or select from the menu **Actions | Jump**. If the other account is already open, it will be brought to the top. If not, it will be opened.

View all sub-accounts of a parent account

Let us say you want to see all of your current assets, different bank accounts and cash, in one place. From the **Account Tree** window, highlight the parent account, **Current Assets**, and select **Accounts | Open Subaccounts** from the menu. You will get a warning **This account register is read-only**. All of the transactions in the sub-accounts will appear in one tab marked **Current Assets+**.

Divide and conquer

Let us take a few common transactions and split them up. Like in a school science project, we will divide up these transactions into the sources and uses of funds. By splitting the transactions up into the two sides, it makes it easier to understand them as well as enter them into GnuCash.

Examples of simple transactions

The business provides a service and receives cash payment of $149.

♦ By providing the service, your sales account should record an income of $149.

♦ Your cash account should show a receipt of cash of $149.

The business receives a cash advance of $300 for building a custom product.

♦ Your Sales Advance account should show that there is an increase of $300 in advances. This is a liability.

♦ Your cash account should show a receipt of cash of $300.

Pop quiz – navigating GnuCash

1. What is the name of the window which allows you to view and edit existing transactions?

   a. **Account Register** window

   b. **Account Tree** window

   c. **Transfer Funds** window

   d. **GnuCash Main** window

2. How do you close the **Accounts** tab?

   a. Using the close button

   b. **Accounts** tab cannot be closed

   c. Using the exit menu

   d. Using control menu close

Have a go hero – entering transactions using the account register

Look at the examples of simple transactions shown previously. Enter some transactions using the accounts register based on these examples. Don't forget to create a Sales Advance liability account before starting to enter the second transaction.

Entering a more complex transaction in the account register

We said earlier that there was an important reason for getting you familiar with the account register. With the simple transaction under your belt, you are now ready to take on bigger things, such as multiple-split transactions. These are often referred to simply as split transactions.

Time for action – entering a split transaction in the account register

Let's say that MACS sold a custom-built PC. In addition to the base price of the PC, MACS is required to collect five percent sales tax and pay it to the state. You can immediately recognize that it is not a simple 2-account transaction. How will we enter this check for $840, consisting of $800 towards sale price, and $40 towards state sales tax, in GnuCash?

1. Preparatory Exercise: Now that you know how to create accounts, go ahead and create a new account **VA Sales Tax** of type **Liability** with **Liabilities** as the parent account. You can refer to *Chapter 1, Getting started with GnuCash* for the specific steps to create a new account.

2. Open the **Checking account register**. GnuCash will start a new transaction and put the focus on the date field with today's date as the default. If not, start a new transaction by selecting **Transaction | Enter Transaction** from the menu. Alternatively, you can click on the **Enter Transaction** button on the toolbar.

3. Click on the small button on the right side of the **Date** field to drop down the calendar and select the previous day's date. Once you have selected the date, click on *Tab* to set that in the **Date** field and move to the **Num** field.

4. In the **Num** field, enter the check number **5096** and click on *Tab* to move to the **Description** field.

5. Enter **Custom built PC** in the **Description** field.
   - Click on the small button on the right side of the **Transfer** field to drop down the list of Accounts. Select **Income:Sales** and click on *Tab* to the **Deposit** field.
   - Enter **840** in the **Deposit** field.

This is the point of departure for a split transaction. If we were entering a simple 2-account transaction, we would have clicked on *Enter* at this point to complete the transaction.

In this case, we received a check for $840, but only $800 is towards sales income. The balance $40 is five percent sales tax payable to the state. How do we show these two different split accounts under sources of funds?

6. Click on the **Split** button on the toolbar or from the menu, select **Actions | Split Transaction**.

7. The display will expand. The first line contains the description and the amount of the transaction. This amount in the transaction line is merely a summary of the transaction's effect on the current account. The partial lines below the transaction line are the split lines. The second line contains the currently opened account name in the **Account** field and the amount of the transaction. The third line contains the transfer account name in the **Account** field. Because the amount is not balanced, GnuCash indicates this by placing gray checkboxes in the amount columns with the unbalanced amount in a blank fourth row, as shown in the following screenshot:

					Tot Depos	Tot Withdr	Balance
Date	**Num**	**Description**					
06/05/2010	5096	Custom built PC			840.00	Withdrawa	
			Assets:Checking Account	n	840.00		
			Income:Sales	n			
						840.00	

(Accounts / Checking Account)

8. When one of the short lines is selected, the column titles will change to indicate that you are now in a split line. The very first and last (**Date** and **Balance**) columns will have blank titles. **Num** will change to **Action**, **Description** to **Memo**, the **Transfer** column will change to **Account**.

9. Skip filling the **Action** and **Memo** columns for now. Move to the missing **Withdrawal** amount field on the third line and fill in the amount **800**. Click on the *Tab* key to move the cursor to the next line. GnuCash will subtract this **800** from the total, re-calculate the remaining amount, and change the **Withdrawal** amount in the next line from **840** to **40**.

10. Click on the small button on the right side of the **Account** column, scroll down, select **Liabilities:VA Sales Tax**, and *Tab* out. *Tab* a couple of more times.

11. The gray checkboxes will disappear and the last blank line will not have an amount, if the transaction is balanced.

12. The disappearance of the gray boxes is your cue to complete this transaction. Go ahead and click on *Enter* to finish up successfully, as shown in the following screenshot:

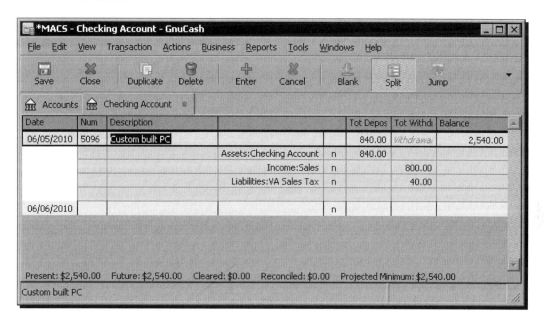

What just happened?

"Hmmm, that was not all that bad. I need to find whoever it was who said that entering split transactions is like going through root canal surgery – messy and painful. And re-educate them."

The need for three or more account transactions occurs when you need to split either the "from" or the "to" account or both in a transaction into multiple accounts.

Balancing the transaction

We said earlier that the left-column amounts must equal the right-column amounts for each transaction. In the example shown previously, the total of the left-column amounts is 840 and the total of the right-column amounts is also 800 + 40 = 840. This is what we mean when we say that the transaction is balanced.

Visualizing split transactions

As a business owner, you know that business is never that simple. Sometimes, multiple accounts may form part of either the source or use side of a transaction. The sales tax example we worked on earlier in the tutorial is one such complex transaction. In Virginia, for example, by the 20th of the following month, you have to file your monthly sales tax return in form ST-9 and pay all the tax collected during that month to the state sales tax department.

Let us try to apply our divide and conquer approach to this example. We can visualize the source of funds being split into Sales and Sales Tax and the use of funds going towards increasing our cash balance, as shown in the following diagram:

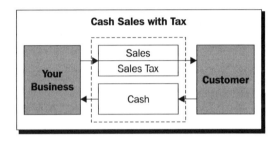

In the preceding diagram, the dashed lines show the entire transaction between your business and the customer. This transaction consists of two equal parts – the source of funds and the use of funds. The source funds on top, in turn, consist of **Sales** and **Sales Tax**. The use of funds, at the bottom, is cash that goes towards increasing your cash balance. In other words, you had sales income, your sales tax liability increased, and you received cash.

Examples of split transactions

Let us look at some more examples of complex or split transactions.

The business delivers a custom product and receives $199 balance payment in cash after adjusting the sales advance of $300 previously received.

- By delivering this product, your sales account should record an income of $499.

- Your cash account should show a receipt of cash of $199.

- What happened to the other $300? Remember our rule that the 'source' side and 'use' must be equal? Your Sales Advance account should now show a decrease of $300.

You write a check for a loan payment of $450 to the bank.

◆ Of this amount, $380 goes to repayment of principal. The $380 principal repayment is not an expense, but it decreases the balance in your Loans Payable liability account.

◆ The balance $70 loan interest is an expense.

◆ Your bank account will show a withdrawal of $450.

Tips for entering split transactions

Some transactions may have many splits. One example is combining the sales tax example that we saw earlier with the adjustment of sales advance example above. However, the humdinger of a split transaction is Employee Payroll. You will have a gross salary or wages and several deductions for federal income tax, state income tax, health insurance, dental, vision, social security, 401(k), and others. You may also have incentive payments, company contribution to 401(k), leave without pay, and other adjustments.

Isn't it comforting to know that all you have to do is create one such payroll transaction for one employee for the first month? After that you can duplicate that and adjust the names and amounts. We will see, later in this chapter, how you can duplicate a transaction. However, it is good to follow these tips, from experienced users of GnuCash, for those very few occasions when you do create these multiple split transactions from scratch:

◆ Use the *Tab* and -> keys to move from field to field and finish the transaction. When you do so, the suggested entry is selected, and you merely have to type over it. If you use the mouse, and type without looking at the screen, it can result in error messages because the figures may contain an odd mixture of commas and periods. Sometimes using the mouse may also end up causing the transaction to either be saved or cancelled prematurely, because you inevitably click somewhere you shouldn't have. Once you are done, use the *Enter* key to complete the transaction.

◆ There should be a "remaining balance" split at the end of the transaction, which is computed as the difference in the balance of the existing right and left column fields.

◆ The main point to keep in mind is that the first split line is the "current account" split. However, you don't have to put a number in right away. What you can do is leave the number empty and then add all the rest of the splits. GnuCash will compute the total on the "blank split" line which, when you're done, you can copy back to the first "current account" split.

◆ When you are entering splits, you never run out of lines. There is always one more blank line until you balance the transaction and click *Enter*.

Pop quiz – understanding transactions

1. For every transaction, the total of the amounts on the right side must be equal to the total of the amounts on the left side.

    a. True

    b. False

    c. Only under certain conditions

    d. Only in special cases

2. Where do we enter a split transaction?

    a. Using the **Transfer Funds** window or from the account register.

    b. Only from the account register.

    c. Only from the **Transfer Funds** window.

    d. Only from the **Account Tree** window

Have a go hero – entering split transactions

Enter a split transaction for the loan repayment example shown previously. Don't forget to create a Loan liability account and an Interest Paid expense account, before starting to enter this transaction.

Anybody can change their mind

That is another way of saying that things went wrong and you want to fix them or start over. That is understandable at any time, but more so while attempting a tutorial. One way of handling that, as we pointed out earlier, is to quit GnuCash without saving. What if you have already saved a transaction and had a thought after that? Yes, GnuCash allows you to change your mind even that late in the game.

Time for action – editing, cancelling, and deleting transactions

We may not be able to get everything right just the first time. So, we need the ability to make changes or even clean up and start over. You can edit a transaction, cancel an edit, or even delete a transaction. Let us see how we can accomplish these:

1. Editing transactions: Remember the $300 cash withdrawal? You suddenly realized that you actually withdrew $350. We are going to edit the transaction to correct this amount. Open the **Cash** account register, click on the amount, then make your changes, and click *Enter*. Check that this change is automatically reflected in both **Cash** and **Checking Account**. By the way, you can make this edit from either one of these accounts.

2. Cancelling edits: In the same transaction, select the **Num** field and change it to **1595** and *Tab* out. Let us say, immediately after tabbing out, you realize that you have edited the wrong field, and horrors! You don't seem to have even a wisp of recollection what the number was that you typed over. Don't panic. You can use the **Cancel** button in the toolbar to revert to the old value. Alternatively, you can right-click and select from the menu **Cancel Transaction**. The GnuCash **Cancel** functions just like **Undo** in other applications.

You can cancel only if you are still in the same transaction. If you had clicked the *Enter* key, clicking on **Cancel** won't accomplish anything. At this point, the only way to rollback the change is to quit GnuCash without saving. However, you will lose any other changes you made since you saved last time.

3. Deleting transactions: Generally if you find a transaction is not right, you can recover from errors by editing it. However, if you have an unwanted transaction or it is easier to start over, you might want to delete a transaction. Make sure the cursor is on the transaction that you wish to delete and click the toolbar button **Delete**. You can also right-click on that transaction and select **Delete Transaction**. You should see a confirmation dialog:

4. Go ahead and click on **Delete Transaction** to confirm the deletion.

5. Don't forget to **Save** to commit all changes.

What just happened?

I can hear you saying, "Boy, that was a big relief. Knowing that I can go back and make changes will let me make those entries more confidently next time." That explains the slow progress in the previous tutorials. Now that GnuCash has provided you the means to overcome the fear of making mistakes, I am sure we are going to fly through the rest of the tutorials!

Beware of the "Don't ask again" booby trap!

As you saw here, when you do a delete, a window will appear to confirm the delete. The window presents two options, **Remember and don't ask again** and **Remember and don't ask again this session**. You are strongly advised NOT TO CHECK any of these options. Too many users have checked one of these options, in a moment of impatience, and have later ended up deleting data unintentionally without any warning.

A similar window called **Save the changed transaction**, with these two options, will appear if you make a change to a transaction and move to another transaction, without saving.

By chance, if you are already caught in this trap, here is how you can get out. You can reset this from **Actions | Reset Warnings**.

Save time by using shortcuts

GnuCash provides several time-saving shortcuts for entering your data.

QuickFill

QuickFill is a feature in GnuCash that tries to guess what you want to enter based on the first few characters you type.

What GnuCash calls QuickFill is more popularly known as auto-complete in several word processing, spreadsheet, and other applications.

◆ **Transaction QuickFill**: When you type the first few characters of a description that you have used before, the QuickFill feature automatically fills in the rest of the entire transaction as you last entered it, and you can then go tweak the values to match.

♦ **Account Name QuickFill**: When you type in the first characters of an account name in either the **Transfer** field of the transaction line or the Account field of the split line, QuickFill will automatically complete the name from your account list. You can follow this with ":" and the cursor will move to the first child account in the list. Then type the first few characters of the child account. For example, to select **Assets:Current Accounts:Checking Account**, you can type in **As:Cu:Ch**.

♦ **Action Field QuickFill**: If you type the first characters of a common action (such as Deposit), GnuCash will fill in the rest.

Data entry shortcuts

Data entry shortcuts allow you to type a single character in place of longer values or multiple steps.

Date field shortcuts: In the Date field, you can type the following shortcuts:

Shortcut	Action
+	to increment the date
–	to decrement the date
]	to increment the month
[	to decrement the month
m	to enter the first date of the month
h	to enter the last date of the month
y	to enter the first date of the year
r	to enter the last date of the year
t	to enter today's date

 In view of the fact that – is used as a shortcut to decrement the date, you cannot type in dates in the format 06-05-2010. Instead, use the format 06/05/2010.

♦ Num field shortcuts: In the **Num** field of the transaction line, you can type + to increment the transaction number from the last one you typed in. Typing – will decrement the number.

♦ Action field shortcuts: The **Num** field shortcuts will also work in the **Action** field of the split line, if you choose to enter split numbers there.

Navigation shortcuts

In the main window:

◆ You can use *Ctrl+Alt+PgUp/PgDn* to switch from one tab to another.

To move around the register, use these keys to save time:

◆ *Tab* to move to the next field, *Shift-Tab* to move to the previous field.

◆ Within a field, you can use *Home* to move the cursor to the beginning of that field and *End* to move the cursor to the end of that field.

◆ *Enter* ↓ to move to the next transaction, ↑ to move to the previous transaction.

◆ *Page Up* to move up one screen, *Page Down* to move down one screen.

◆ If there are lots of transactions in an account register, you can use *Shift-Page Up* to go to the first transaction and *Shift-Page Down* to go to the last transaction.

Computation shortcuts

In the amount field of the account register, you can enter math expressions using +, -, *, and /. GnuCash will do the computation and enter the result in that field. For example, if you paid $89.75 for a meal and left a tip of $17.50, you don't have to add this up separately to figure out how much to enter in the account register. You can enter 89.75 + 17.50 in the amount field and tab out. GnuCash will do the addition and enter the result of 107.25 in the amount field.

Imbalance-USD

While entering the split transactions, if you missed, say, the VA Sales Tax $40 and clicked on *Enter*, what would happen? Remember that GnuCash does double entry bookkeeping behind the scenes. So, it will try to balance the transaction. It will create a new top level account called **Imbalance-USD** and park the out-of-balance $40 there. So, whenever you see this **Imbalance-USD** show up, GnuCash is telling you that you missed out part of a transaction.

How do you fix this? You can open the **Imbalance-USD** account and edit that account by changing the **Transfer** field to VA Sales Tax.

Pop quiz – using shortcuts to speed up bookkeeping

1. What is the Transfer field shortcut for `Expenses:Auto:Repairs` and `Maintenance`?

    a. `Ex:Au:RM`

    b. `Ex:Au:Re`

    c. `Ex,Au,Re`

2. What is the Date field shortcut for entering the first day of the month?

    a. `f`

    b. `m`

    c. `j`

Have a go hero – tweaking transactions

Delete one of the example transactions from the table you entered earlier. Re-enter the same transaction using the accounts register again. Try to use as many shortcuts as possible and yell "Hooray" in proportion to how much it speeds up your bookkeeping work.

A feeling of déjà vu

You had earlier put in a lot of effort to enter a complex transaction. A week later, you are about to enter another transaction and you get a feeling of déjà vu. You feel as if you have been here before.

Time for action – reusing transactions

Wouldn't it be great if you can leverage the effort you had earlier put in to get this type of transaction just right? The good folks developing GnuCash have thought of all that and have just the solution for you – the ability to take an entire transaction and make a duplicate.

1. Place the cursor anywhere in the split transaction we created for sales tax in the earlier tutorial.

2. Go to **Transaction | Duplicate Transaction** or right-click and select **Duplicate Transaction**.

3. A dialog called **Duplicate Transaction** will prompt for a new **Date** and **Number** for the transaction. Select a **Date** and enter **83791** in the **Number** field:

4. Click on **OK** to add the transaction to the register.

5. Edit the transaction so that the new description is **Gaming PC**, the new check amount is **$630**, the new Sales amount is **$600**, and the new sales tax is **$30**.

06/06/2010	83791	Gaming PC			630.00	Withdrawal	3,170.00
			Assets:Checking Account	n	630.00		
			Income:Sales	n		600.00	
			Liabilities:VA Sales Tax	n		30.00	

What just happened?

Note to self. At the next appointment, should ask the dentist whether there is a way to painlessly duplicate the previous root canal surgery – instead of going through the suffering all over again.

Changing the register views

GnuCash has several options to change the way the register looks so that transactions can be seen with more details or in a concise view. The default style is the Basic Ledger. This presents a single line view of transactions to allow the most concise view with all the relevant details.

The default view or style can be changed by going to the View menu. Three submenus will allow you to select the desired option.

- Basic Ledger: The default one line per transaction style. Splits are shown as a summary.

- Auto-split Ledger: This style will automatically expand the splits in any transaction selected.

- Transaction Journal: This style expands all transactions so the complete transaction can be seen.

 When you are in the Basic Ledger view, the Split toolbar button and **Actions | Split Transaction** menu are enabled. However, when you are in any of the other two views, these are superfluous and so will be disabled.

When the window closes, the style will revert to the Basic Ledger style. To make this change permanent, change the style in the **Edit | Preferences | Register Defaults** in the Register display.

- Double Line: Select from the menu **View | Double Line**, and you will see your transaction line expand to two lines. In addition to the **Description** line, you can now see the **Notes** line as well. This helps you enter extra notes, in addition to the brief description of the transaction.

The two other options to change the view of the register are:

- To restrict displayed items with the **View | Filter By ....**

- Changing the sort order **View | Sort By....**

 If you use filtering, don't forget to go back to the **Filter by...** dialog and select **Show all**. I keep hearing about too many people who view a filtered list and later panic thinking that they lost some transactions.

Deleting a transaction in different views

Be careful about which register view you are on while doing a delete. If you're in the **Basic Ledger** view, GnuCash will delete the selected transaction. However, if you're in one of the expanded views, then it depends on which line you're on. On the summary transaction line, it will ask you whether you want to delete this transaction. On a split line, it will ask you whether you want to delete this split. On the anchor split line, it won't allow you to delete. Instead, you will get this warning:

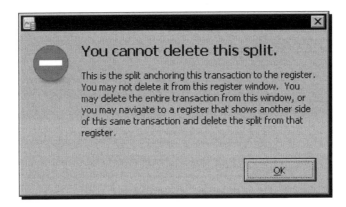

The anchor split line is the line showing the amount associated with the account that is open. For example, in the tutorial on entering a split transaction above, we are seeing a split transaction in the Checking Account register. The first partial line below the transaction line showing a deposit of $840 in the Checking Account is the anchor split line.

Text information in transactions

You might want to record notes and memos with the transaction data to help explain transactions as well as to group and organize information. You might want to keep notes on why a particular expense was incurred. For example, tax consultants advise businesses, when recording business entertainment expenses, to be sure to keep good records on who was present, the dates and times, and the reasons for the entertainment and business discussions that took place. They say this is "must have" information in case you are ever audited by the **US Internal Revenue Service (IRS)**.

These notes are also helpful in other ways. You can search for transactions using text in these fields. You can also sort transactions in the account register by using any of these fields. You can opt to print these fields in reports as well.

There are five places for you to enter such text information; three of those – **Description**, **Notes**, and **Num** – are transaction fields. The other two, **Action** and **Memo**, are associated with each split.

Transaction description

As we saw earlier, the **Description** field is available always in the account register in the same line as the date.

Transaction notes

The **Notes** field is only available when you enable the "double line" mode. Note that this notes field is what gets printed on a check.

Transaction number

You can use the **Num** field for Transaction Number, Check Number, Receipt Number, or another similar purpose. You can enter alpha-numeric text, as needed.

Using the Num field for sorting transactions

You can use the **Num** field to enter a serial number for all transactions in an account within a given date. By default, the account register sorts the transactions by date and, within a given date, by the **Num** filed. This is one possible way of using the **Num** field.

Split action

The **Action** field is only available when you expand the transaction using the "Split" button or in **Auto-split Ledger** and **Transaction Journal** views.

The action field has a drop-down list of suggested entries for different account types. However, you need not be restricted to this list. If the list doesn't meet your needs, go ahead and enter other text as desired.

Example of using Action field

For example, you might want to keep track of **Auto:Gas** expenses marking **Action** as 'Local', 'Richmond', and 'Other'. This will help you filter transactions and create reports for gas expenses incurred on trips to Richmond. If the gas expenses under this category exceed a particular threshold, you intend to consider moving your offices to Richmond.

Split Memo

Similar to the **Action** field, the **Memo** field is only available when you expand the transaction using the "Split" button or in the **Auto-split Ledger** and **Transaction Journal** views.

Pop quiz – viewing the account register

1. What will you do to view or edit notes in a transaction?

    a. View Basic Ledger

    b. View Auto-split Ledger

    c. View Transaction Journal

    d. View Double Line

Have a go hero – saving more data with the transactions

Pick one of the transactions that we entered earlier and fill all optional fields – **Notes**, **Num**, **Action**, and **Memo**.

Summary

We learned a lot in this chapter about the core task in bookkeeping, namely, entering transactions and further tweaking them.

Specifically, we covered:

◆   Simple transactions: If they are simple transactions, we can enter them in the **Transfer Funds** window or in the account register.

◆   More complex transactions: If they are more complex transactions, known as split transactions, we have to use the account register.

◆   Edit, cancel, and delete: Knowing how to edit, cancel, and delete transactions allows us to overcome our fear of making mistakes.

◆   Duplicating transactions: We learned a powerful technique of duplicating transactions, which will help us to save a lot of work in bookkeeping.

◆   Shortcuts: We learned a number of shortcuts to speed up entering transactions.

◆   Navigation: We saw how to open the account registers, close them as well as jump from one account register to the corresponding one which has the other part of the transaction.

◆   Views: We covered the different ways we can view the account register and how it helps us to see the different fields available to enter data.

We also reviewed how to sort and filter the transactions in the account register, so that we can focus on the specific ones we are interested in.

Earlier, we said that the real reason why we are spending all this time and effort to enter the transactions is to be able to see the reports. That will be the topic of our next chapter.

3
Fun and Eye-opening Part - Reports and Charts

"...over the past few years running our online wedding business, I have come to realize that while keeping accurate numbers is boring, analyzing the numbers is actually fun and eye opening!"—from a successful small business owner's web site.

As a small business owner, you may rely on gut feelings to make some important decisions. Some of those decisions can make or break a small business such as yours. It is prudent to challenge and validate those decisions by collecting more facts and figures. It doesn't mean that you should abandon the value provided by the gut feelings and intuition that you bring to your decision-making every day. It simply means that you are going to have to start validating it with more data.

Some of that data on who needs your product or service will come from outside your business in the form of market intelligence and demographic data. However, a more important source of information about the revenue and costs of your business is buried right under your feet in the form of – drum roll please – bookkeeping data. Having come to that realization, aren't you thrilled that you are two steps ahead in that game? We already have a firm grip on setting up the accounts and capturing the bookkeeping information. The reports and charts that we will cover in this chapter provide you the tools necessary to extract this buried treasure and leverage it to operate and grow your business.

So, having survived the bookkeeping part, we are now ready for the fun and eye-opening part. In this chapter we will cover how to:

◆ View standard reports

◆ View the data visually in chart form

◆ Create custom reports and save them for repeated use

◆ Customize style sheets and use with reports

◆ Export reports for use in spreadsheets

So let's get on with it...

Recovering from the unexpected

While you are working in GnuCash, it may happen that Windows shuts down unexpectedly, GnuCash crashes, or there is a power failure. If any of that happens, and later you try to restart GnuCash, you may see a message like, **GnuCash could not obtain the lock for file...That database may be in use by another user...** Don't panic. There is no need to call in a private detective to check who is accessing your accounts behind your back. We saw earlier that whenever you open an accounts file, GnuCash creates a lock to avoid another person opening that file at the same time. When the unexpected shutdown occurred, chances are, GnuCash didn't have time to clean up this lock in an orderly manner.

If you are sharing this GnuCash accounts file with others, check whether someone else is working on it. Once you have made sure no one else is working on it, or if you are the only person who has access to it, you can select **Open Anyway**. Also don't forget to double-check that the transactions you entered just before the crash have been saved.

Viewing standard reports and charts

GnuCash comes with a bunch of standard reports and charts out of the box. It is a good idea to get familiar with what these are and where to find them so that you can view them quickly without a lot of effort.

Time for action – viewing standard reports and charts

You have been using the account registers a lot. You are familiar with different ways to view account registers as well as how to sort and filter the transactions. Once you have got just the precise list of transactions in an account register, you may want to see a report of those transactions and print them.

1. Viewing a report: From the **Accounts Tree** window, double-click **Checking Accounts** to open its account register.

2. From the **View | Filter By...** menu launch the filter dialog. In the **Date** tab, choose **Select Range** and enter a **Start** and an **End** date.

3. From the menu select **Reports | Account Report**. A report of just the transactions in that account register will open in a new tab marked **Register** as shown in the following screenshot:

Assets:Current Assets:Checking Account - Register Report

Date	Num	Description Memo		Transfer	Deposit	Withdrawal	Balance
05/23/2010		Opening Balance	Equity:Opening Balances	$2,000.00			$2,000.00
05/31/2010	2073	Withdraw cash for office expenses	Assets:Current Assets:Cash			$350.00	$1,650.00
06/05/2010	5096	Custom built PC	-- Split Transaction --	$840.00			$2,490.00
06/06/2010	83791	Gaming PC	-- Split Transaction --	$630.00			$3,120.00
06/15/2010		Loan repayment	-- Split Transaction --			$450.00	$2,670.00

Total Debits	$3,470.00	
Total Credits		$800.00
Net Change	$2,670.00	

4. Viewing a chart: From the menu select **Reports | Income & Expense | Income & Expense Chart** to view the following chart:

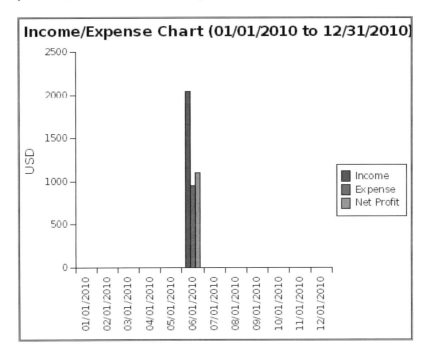

What just happened?

GnuCash has a ton of built-in reports and charts that will meet the needs of most businesses readily. It is not required that you become familiar with all of these. The trick is to be aware of what is available as well as to know where to go and look when you need a specific report or chart.

Reports specific to the account register

Whenever you are in an account register, you will notice that you have two extra menu items under the **Reports** menu, below a separator line, named **Account Report** and **Account Transaction Report**. The **Account Report** lets you view and print the account register that is currently open. The **Account Transaction Report** lets you view and print a single transaction in the account register that is currently open. When you move to another window, such as the **Accounts Tree** window or a report, you won't see these because these two reports are specific to the currently open account register.

Reports and charts

Other than the two reports that are specific to the account register, GnuCash has several other reports and charts that are available from any screen. The **Profit & Loss** Report, also known as the **Income Statement**, as well as the **Balance Sheet**, are the two most popular financial terms that you will hear from accountants, bankers and investors.

Income Statement (Profit and Loss Statement)

The Income Statement summarizes your business income and expenses during a specific period of time. It is also known as the **Profit and Loss Statement** or simply **P&L**. The difference between income and expenses for a period is your profit or loss. To generate the report, from the menu select **Reports | Income & Expense | Profit & Loss**. Alternatively, you can select **Income Statement**. After opening the report, you can open the **Report Options** dialog by clicking on the **Options** toolbar button or from the menu **Edit | Report Options**. You can set the **Start Date**, **End Date**, and several other report options here.

Balance Sheet

The **Balance Sheet** is simply a snapshot of the financial condition of your business. The Balance Sheet summarizes your assets, liabilities, and net worth as it is at a particular point in time.

> The important thing to remember about an Income Statement is that it represents a period of time such as the last month, quarter, or year. This contrasts with the Balance Sheet, which represents a single point in time, such as the last day of the quarter or the last day of the year.

A chart is worth a thousand numbers

If a picture is worth a thousand words, then a chart is worth a thousand numbers. Charts help you to quickly and easily recognize patterns in the data. Scanning data in tables takes more time and you may overlook important data buried in tables.

GnuCash provides you with a bunch of charts on expenses, income, assets, and liabilities.

> **Refreshing chart and report data**
> If you made some changes to the data after opening a chart or report, use the **Reload** button to refresh the chart or report. You can also use the menu **View | Refresh**.

Other reports

Like we said, the financial statements such as the P&L and the Balance Sheet are of interest to accountants, bankers, and investors. However, you get to meet them only once in a while. In the meantime, you have a business to run and decisions to make on a day-to-day basis. You know that making those decisions requires reports based on operations data.

Here is a list of other reports available in GnuCash along with a brief description of the reports. We will be covering **Custom Reports** and reports under the **Sample & Custom** menu later in this chapter. The reports listed under the menu **Reports | Business** will be covered in a subsequent chapter. The tax reports will be covered in the chapter on taxes. The **Budget Reports** will be covered in the chapter on budgets. The reports that are specific to personal accounts are out of the scope of this book.

Report name	Report description
Account Report	As you saw in the preceding example, the **Account Report** lets you view and print an account register. If you want to change the date range or the set of transactions printed in the report, then you need to go back to the account register, make adjustments to it, and then re-run this report.
Account Transaction Report	The **Account Transaction Report** lets you view and print a single transaction.
Account Summary Report	The **Account Summary Report** provides a listing of accounts and balances as it is on a particular date.
Transaction Report	Lists transactions from all the accounts that occur within a date range. The transactions are grouped by accounts. This report is the same as the **General Ledger Report**.

Assets & Liabilities Reports:

Report name	Report description
Asset Barchart	Shows a stacked bar chart summarizing the value of your assets over a period of time. Current assets, such as cash and bank, as well as fixed assets, such as building and equipment, will be shown.
Asset Piechart	Shows a pie chart summarizing the value and allocation of your assets as on a given date, such as the end of the financial year.
Balance Sheet using eguile-gnc	This report is under development. Not for business use.
General Journal	Simply shows a date-wise list of all transactions.
General Ledger	Lists transactions from all the accounts that occur within a date range. This report is the same as the **Transaction Report**.
Liability Barchart	Shows a stacked bar chart summarizing the value of your liabilities, such as loans and accounts payable, over a period of time.

Report name	Report description
Liability Piechart	Shows a pie chart summarizing the value of your liabilities as on a given date, such as the end of the financial year.
Net Worth Barchart	This report shows a bar chart summarizing your assets, liabilities and net worth every month over the financial year. Net worth is the difference between your assets and liabilities.

General Journal Report

If you get an error while opening the **General Journal** report, try closing all the account registers first and then opening the report.

Income & Expense Reports:

Report name	Report description
Cash Flow	Shows all the cash inflow into the selected set of accounts as well as the entire cash outflow over a given period. It also shows the difference between the two.
Equity Statement	Shows the initial investment or the opening balance equity for the financial year, any new investments that came in, as well as any owner's draw. This will also show any net earnings that will go towards boosting this equity or any net loss that will erode the equity.
Expense Barchart	A stacked bar chart of different expenses by month through the financial year.
Expense Piechart	A pie chart showing a breakdown of different expenses during the financial year.
Expenses vs. Day of Week	A pie chart showing expenses by day of the week. Very useful for day-of-the-week sensitive businesses such as restaurants.
Income & Expense Chart	A bar chart showing income and expenses by month through the financial year. We covered this in the tutorial above.
Income Barchart	A stacked bar chart of different types of income by month through the financial year.
Income Piechart	A pie chart showing a breakdown of different types of income during the financial year.
Income vs. Day of Week	A pie chart showing income by day of the week. Very useful for day-of-the-week sensitive businesses such as restaurants.
Trial Balance	This simply shows the balance in every account as on a given date.

Reports that your accountant may ask for

The Trial Balance and the **General Ledger** will be of interest to your accountants. Accountants view the **Trial Balance** as the index page and the **General Ledger** as a drill-down list of individual transactions that make up each account on the **Trial Balance**. So, it is good to be familiar with these so that if they ask for it you will know what they are and how to get them.

All these reports can be broadly grouped into the following:

◆ Reports that are of interest to your investors and bankers: The Balance Sheet and Profit & Loss Statement (also known as the Income Statement) belong here. Also, the Asset, Liability, and Net Worth charts belong here. Of course, your accountant will help finalize these and so these will be of interest to your accountant too. You will be interested in these too, when you are wearing your investor's hat.

◆ Reports that are of interest to your accountant or tax consultant: The Trial Balance and the General Ledger are the starting point for your accountant or tax consultant. To drill down further they may ask for Transaction Reports, Account Reports, and Account Summaries.

◆ Reports that are of interest to you to control the operations of the business: The income, expense, cash flow reports, and charts will be of interest to you when you are wearing the Chief Operating Officer (COO) hat, which is probably only for about 75 hours per week.

As you can see, GnuCash has far more reports than any one business will ever use. You will have to pick and choose which one you want based on the problem you are trying to solve. If, for example, you find the need for keeping a tighter control on your expenses, then you can try out the Expense Barchart, Expense Piechart, Expenses vs. Day of week, and Income & Expense Chart, and determine which one is closest to what you need. You can either use that report as it is or customize it further, as you will soon see in the next section.

Pop quiz – viewing standard reports

1. Which are the two reports that are only available when an account register is open?

    a. Balance Sheet and Trial Balance

    b. Account Report and Account Transaction Report

    c. Income Statement and Profit & Loss

    d. Balance Sheet and Profit & Loss

Have a go hero – viewing standard charts

Find and view the Expense Barchart and the Expense Piechart.

Creating a custom report and saving it

Standard reports and charts are good to quickly view data. However, you will have your own preferences about what data you want to see and how you want to see it. This is why the ability to customize a report is very important.

Time for action – creating a custom report and saving it

Let's say that you want to create an Account Summary:

1. From the menu select **Reports** | **Account Summary**. The Account Summary report will open in a new tab. You notice that it is for the period ending on the last day of this financial year. Also, you find that the few relevant numbers are buried in a sea of zeroes.

2. Click on the toolbar button **Options**. You can also select **Edit** | **Report** from the menu **Options**.

3. The checkbox **Include accounts with zero total balances** in the **Display** tab will be checked by default. Uncheck it. The checkbox **Omit zero balance figures** in the same tab will be unchecked by default. Check it.

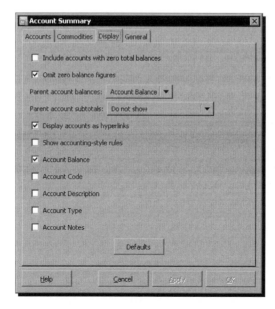

4. In the **General** tab, type **MACS** in the **Company name** field.

5. Click on the **Stylesheet** drop-down list and select **Technicolor** and then click **on OK** to see the following screenshot of the report:

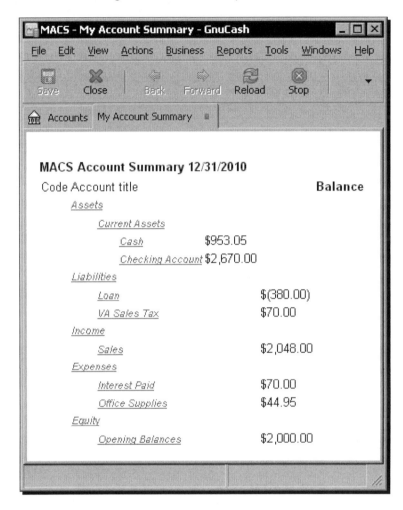

6. Now that you have jumped through enough hoops, you want to make sure this report is saved and saved for good. You may have earlier noticed the **Add Report** button on the toolbar but you may have also noticed that it has remained stubbornly disabled. Go back to the **Report Options** dialog by clicking on the **Options** toolbar button. In the **General** tab, change the name of the report to **My Account Summary**. Click on the **OK** button to see the name of the report change to **My Account Summary**. Once you have changed the name of the report, the magic happens and the **Add Report** button becomes enabled.

7. Go ahead and click **Add Report**. You can also select **File | Add Report** from the menu.

8. You will get a confirmation message, **Your report "My Account Summary" has been saved into the configuration file "C:\Documents and Settings\<username>\.gnucash\saved-reports-2.4"**. Click on **Close**.

9. At this point if you select **Reports | Custom Reports**, from the menu you should see a dialog box with your saved report, **My Account Summary**, as shown in the following screenshot:

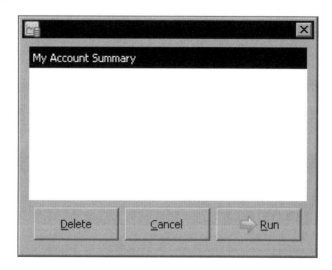

What just happened?

As we said earlier, GnuCash ships with a rich set of standard reports. However, the ability to customize them and save them for repeated use gives you a powerful tool to get precisely the data you want and formatted to your specific preference.

Tips for customizing reports

Here are a few tips that you may find useful while customizing reports:

♦ Exclude columns: You can exclude unwanted columns by deselecting them. You will find this useful if you don't want long notes and memos crowding out your data.

♦ Avoid zero balances: If you have a lot of zero balances, you can deselect them.

◆ Display as hyperlinks: You can choose to display some fields, such as accounts, as hyperlinks. This is helpful for drill down purposes. For example, when you are looking at a report you may want to go to that account and look at the details to see how a number was arrived at.

◆ Show subtotals: You can choose whether to show subtotals or not.

Shortcut for saving a customized report

Simply leave the customized report open when you quit GnuCash. As you may have already noticed, GnuCash makes a note of all the open tabs when you quit. It recreates all of them when you restart it.

Tips for customizing charts

Here are a few tips that you may find useful while customizing charts:

◆ **Show Table**: Earlier we said that charts help you to quickly recognize patterns in the data. However, you should also exercise care with charts to avoid misinterpretations. Experts say that this is especially important if you are working under time pressure or if high risk is involved. Which small business is not under time pressure and with high risk? One way to avoid misinterpreting charts is to have the numbers alongside the chart. For this reason, many of the GnuCash charts have a **Show Table** option in the **Display** tab of the **Report Options** dialog.

◆ **Step Size**: This option is available on bar charts to select the interval that each bar represents. Typical values are **Day**, **Week**, **Month**, **Quarter**, and **Year**.

◆ **Plot Width** and **Plot Height**: There are width and height options for most graphs, which specify the displayed dimensions in pixels.

◆ **Bar charts** – stacked or side by side: There is a **Use Stacked Bars** option for bar charts which specifies whether to stack the bars or show them side by side.

◆ **Bar charts** – limit the number of bars: The bar charts have a **Maximum Bars** option to limit the number of bars in crowded charts.

Sample & Custom Reports

These reports are accessed from the **Reports | Sample & Custom** menu:

Report name	Report description
Welcome Sample Report	This report is under development. Not for business use.
Custom Multicolumn Report	This report is used to place multiple reports into a single report window in dashboard style.
Sample Report with Examples	This report is under development. Not for business use.

When you open the Custom Multicolumn Report, you will see a totally blank report. This is a test of persistence. The intention is to separate the wheat from the chaff – those who persist from those who give up too soon. You are made of sterner stuff. Hang in there. Click on the **Options** button. Go to the **Contents** tab, select the reports from the **Available Reports**, and add them to the **Selected Reports**. Increase the **Number of columns** in the **General** tab. Click on **Apply** or **OK** to see the Multicolumn Report.

Custom Multicolumn Report

Though this report is meant for multiple reports, try and limit it to two reports or a report and a chart. Also, don't go for more than two columns.

Pop quiz – customizing a report

1. Which one of the following is not an essential step for saving a custom report?

    a. Change the name of the report.

    b. Click on the **Reload** button.

    c. Click on the **Add Report** button or select **File | Add Report**.

Have a go hero – further customizing a report

Select one of the charts, customize it, and save it for future use.

Working with stylesheets

Style, they say, is a distinctive manner of expression and it is intensely personal. No wonder you were not happy with the stylesheet options for the reports. Whichever one you selected, you were left with the vague feeling that it needs to be tweaked further.

GnuCash gives you the ability to create your own stylesheet and save it for future use. For example, when dealing with customers, banks and investors, you can deliver documents in a distinctive and uniform style that makes your business stand out among the noisy crowd of competitors out there.

Time for action – working with stylesheets

We are going to take one of the stylesheets and customize it to suit our needs.

1. Select **Edit | Style Sheets** from the menu, and the **Select HTML Style Sheet** window will open. You should see the **Default** and other stylesheets that ship with GnuCash.

2. Click on the **New** button. This will open the **New Style Sheet** window.

3. Select a **Template** from the drop-down and type **MACS** in the **Name** box and click on **OK**. The **HTML Style Sheet Properties** dialog will open as shown in the following screenshot:

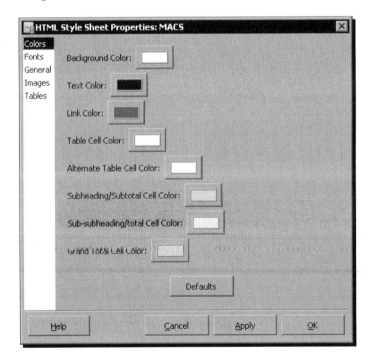

4. Select the **Fonts** tab. Change the **Number cell** and **Text cell** fonts to **Verdana**.

5. This is an optional step. In the **Images** tab, if you have a suitable image file, select it for **Heading Banner**.

6. Click **OK** to save and close this dialog. Also close the **Select HTML Style Sheet** window. So far you have created a custom stylesheet. Next we will apply it to our report.

7. If you have the **Account Summary** tab still open, you can use that. If not, go ahead and select from the menu **Reports | Account Summary**. Click on the **Options** toolbar button.

8. In the **Display** tab don't forget to uncheck **Include accounts with zero total balances** and check **Omit zero balance figures**, if you have not already done so.

9. Change the **Parent account subtotals** to **Show subtotals**.

10. In the **General** tab, change the **Stylesheet** to **MACS** and click on **OK**. You should now see the **Account Summary** report with all of your selections, and the newly created stylesheet applied, like the following screenshot:

What just happened?

This ability to create a custom stylesheet and assign it to reports and charts will let you have a uniform look and feel for all the reports of your business.

 When you make changes to a stylesheet, which you are already using with a report, you will have to **Reload** the report to see the changes take effect.

Pop quiz – creating stylesheets

1. To create a new stylesheet, where will you start?

    a. With the report open, click on the **Options** button. Alternatively, from the menu, select **Edit | Report Options**.

    b. From the menu select **Edit | Style Sheets**.

    c. From the menu select **Reports | Edit Style Sheets**.

Have a go hero – creating a custom stylesheet hands on

Create a new custom stylesheet for your business.

Exporting reports

You tried to customize the report by setting the options. Then you tried applying a stylesheet. After that you created a custom stylesheet of your own. However, at the end of it all, you found that you were not getting the report exactly the way you wanted it. What next?

If you are up against the limitations of GnuCash, then it is time to take the data and look for another application that will let you format it the way you want it. Accounting data is typically in tabular format and the presentation might need charting capability as well. A spreadsheet application such as Calc from OpenOffice.org or Microsoft Excel is well-suited to formatting tabular data as well as creating charts.

Fortunately, GnuCash lets you export report data readily in a convenient format so that it can be opened in popular spreadsheets and other applications.

Time for action – exporting reports

Let us see how we can export reports and charts in HTML format and open them in popular spreadsheet applications:

1. As the first step, create or open the report that you want to export.

2. From the menu select **File | Export | Export Report**. The **Save HTML To File** dialog will open.

3. Select the folder where you want to save this exported report. Give it a file name with the extension `.html` and click **Export**:

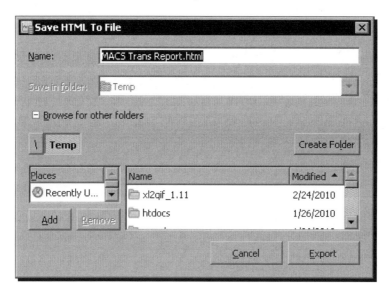

4. OpenOffice.org Calc spreadsheet: Click on the **A1** cell in the top-left hand corner of the spreadsheet. From the menu, select **Insert | Link to External Data**. Click on the ellipsis next to the URL of the external data source field and select the HTML file from the folder where you saved it. In the **Available tables/ranges**, select **HTML_all** and click on **OK**. The report will appear in the spreadsheet.

5. Microsoft Excel: Select **File | Open** and select the HTML file from the folder where you saved it. This is the same **Transaction Report** that you will see in GnuCash. It lists transactions from all the accounts that occur within a date range. The transactions are grouped by accounts. However, it is now formatted making use of the spreadsheet features, as shown in the following screenshot:

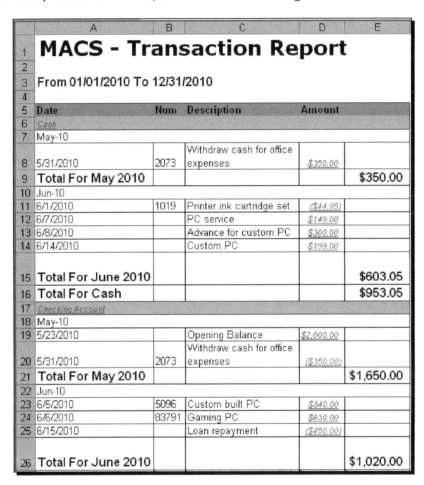

What just happened?

HTML is an open standard used for creating web pages. The ability to export the data in a standard format such as HTML allows you to use external applications for further formatting and for printing that report.

Shortcut for exporting a report to OpenOffice.org Calc

With the report open in GnuCash, you can click and drag the mouse to select all text. Simply paste it into Calc. The **Text Import** dialog will open. Click on **OK** and the report data will be imported into Calc.

If you export a chart to an HTML file format, it cannot be opened in spreadsheets. This is because it is an image file, not tabular data. However, it can be opened in a browser such as Firefox or Microsoft Internet Explorer. If you do want the tabular data, try the **Show Report** option in the charts. That can be opened in the spreadsheets.

Pop quiz – saving exported reports

1. What is the file name extension for saving exported reports?

    a.   `.html`

    b.   `.lck`

    c.   `.gnu`

    d.   `.rep`

Have a go hero – exporting charts in HTML format

Export one of the charts to an HTML file format. Then open it in your favorite browser such as Firefox or Microsoft Internet Explorer.

Summary

We learned a lot in this chapter about GnuCash reports and charts.

Specifically, we covered:

◆ Standard charts and reports: We saw how to quickly view and print reports and charts that come built-in with GnuCash.

◆ Customizing reports: We also stepped through how to customize these reports by using report option settings.

◆ Save the customized reports: We learned how to save the customized reports for future use.

- ◆ Custom style sheets: We also learned how to create custom style sheets.
- ◆ Export reports: We also went through the steps to export reports in standard formats that can be used by popular spreadsheet applications for further formatting and printing.

Now that you have seen how to use the transaction data to create reports and charts for business decision making, you may have come to the sudden realization that it is important to make sure those transactions are accurate. In the next chapter we will look at one important process for cross-checking and validating those transactions.

4

How not to Get Lost in the Transactions Jungle

"Bank account reconciliation need not be a chore. With a little preparation, some forethought, and a meticulous mind set, balancing a check book can be quick and easy. The result? Financial peace of mind." – from a web article about how to start a home-based business.

Let us first look at what experienced outdoors people do to avoid getting lost while hiking in the wilderness. From this let us see what tips we can glean that can help us avoid getting lost in the transactions jungle.

How not to get lost while hiking in the wilderness

If you are a hiker, you may have encountered a situation like the following:
You're hiking north to south. Your map shows a campsite further down south and to the west of your destination. According to the map, two trails will be turning off to the west. You want to take the second of these two trails.

On the other hand, some trails shown on a map have been known to vanish without a trace. In order to protect against such a contingency, you can use your compass to draw a line from a landmark in the map towards the trail and see where it intersects the trail. Charting your location on a map using known landmarks that appear on the map is a proven way to avoid getting lost when hiking in the wilderness. In the same way, reconciling your accounts with that of your bank and your credit card company is the proven way to validate your bookkeeping. If you are on a long hike, it is prudent to check your position often, so that you can make corrections before you stray too far off from your intended path and end up getting lost.

In this chapter we shall cover:

- Manual **bank reconciliation** using a printed monthly statement
- Why you should avoid editing or deleting a reconciled transaction
- Electronic bank reconciliation using a downloaded statement
- **Credit Card reconciliation**
- Why you should exercise care in selecting the account while importing transactions for the first time.
- How to recover if you pointed at the wrong account.

So let's get on with it....

Manual reconciliation

Did you ever wish that someone would double-check your entries? If you did, your wish has been granted. There is someone keeping track of all your transactions. I can see that you are taken aback, "What? Someone is watching me over my shoulder?" No, this is not George Orwell's 1984 and Big Brother is not watching you. Relax. It is just your bank and your credit card company who are watching your transactions, as they should, and sending out detailed statements every month, again, as they should.

The double entry bookkeeping system of GnuCash does make sure that if you enter one part of a transaction, you enter the other matching part too. For example, if you enter a cash withdrawal of $300 from your bank and your bank balance is now less by $300 and you forget to enter an increase of cash balance of $300 in hand, the double entry system will make sure that you enter that too. However, if you forget to enter the entire transaction, the double entry system cannot help you. This is where reconciliation comes in.

Time for action – reconciling with a printed monthly statement

Let's say that you just received your monthly bank statement in the mail. We are going to use the transactions listed by the bank and the closing balance shown by them to verify that we didn't overlook any transactions while making our entries. In this tutorial, we will reconcile the closing balance shown in the printed bank statement. We will verify whether the checks that appear in the bank statement are indeed in your books and make a note of a check that you wrote towards the end of the month that has not yet cleared.

1. Open the account register of the account you want to reconcile, in this case, **Assets:Current Assets:Checking Account**.

2. Click on the toolbar button, **Reconcile**. You can also select **Actions | Reconcile...** from the menu. The **Reconcile Information** dialog will open.

3. The **Interest Payment** dialog may pop up automatically. Click on **Cancel**.

4. In the **Reconcile Information** dialog, change the **Statement Date** field to the date of the bank statement that you are reconciling with as seen in the following screenshot:

4. Make a note of the ending balance shown in the bank statement and type that value over the **Ending Balance** field and click OK. The Reconcile window opens.

5. The two panes called **Funds In** and **Funds Out** list all the unreconciled transactions. The **R** columns show whether the transactions have cleared or not. Those that have cleared will show a green check mark.

6. Your bank statement shows the initial deposit of $2000. If that row is already selected, click the space bar to check it. If not, click on that row and it will be checked.

7. Your bank statement also shows the cash withdrawal of $350. Check that as well.

8. You wrote a check on 05/29 for an amount of $95. However, that has not yet shown up in the month end bank statement. Don't check that.

The Space bar will let you quickly run through a long list

If you have a long list of transactions and want to mark them quickly as reconciled, the *space bar* is your friend. A single press of the *space bar* will mark a transaction as cleared and move the focus to the next line. Thus, if you keep the *space bar* down, you can mark several transactions in quick succession.

9. With those items checked, your **Reconciled Balance** in the bottom-right pane will be equal to the **Ending Balance** and the **Difference** will become **$0.00**. This is when the magic happens and the **Finish** button gets enabled as you can see in the following screenshot:

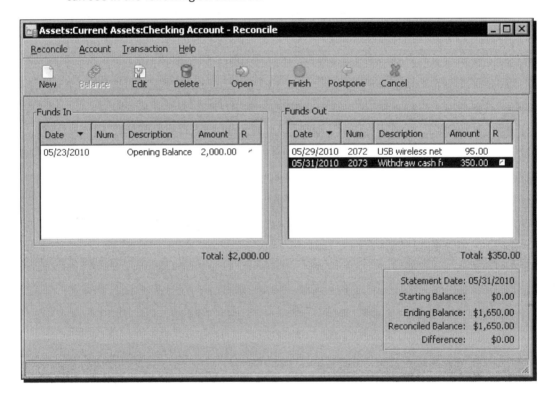

10. Now that the reconciliation has been successfully completed, go ahead and click **Finish** to seal the deal.

What just happened?

For bank accounts and credit card accounts you will receive regular monthly account statements from the financial institution that provides that service. It is prudent, of course, to check these statements to ensure that the bank or credit card company has not made any errors recording your transactions. At the same time, you can check that you, yourself, have not made any errors recording these transactions in GnuCash.

Postpone

You are partly through the reconciliation process and suddenly realize that you have to take care of something else first. Do you have to cancel and redo everything all over again? The **Postpone** button is there just for that very reason. Clicking the **Postpone** button will, in effect, pause the reconciliation process. It will not mark the transactions that you checked off so far as **y** for reconciled. However, it will mark them as **c** for cleared. You can come back at any time and re-run the reconciliation from where you left off.

Thus, reconciliation is nothing but comparing the closing balance shown on the monthly bank statement with the closing balance reported in the GnuCash Checking Account. At first glance, you might think you could just check that the account balance on the statement matches the account balance in GnuCash. Sometimes that will work, but the balances can often differ for a variety of reasons:

- You may have written checks that have not yet been presented to the bank. Typically, this will happen to checks written by you at the end of the month. You will have recorded these transactions in GnuCash, but they may not yet show up on your bank statement.

- The bank statement may include transactions that you have not yet recorded in GnuCash. Common examples include bank fees and interest.

- The bank may have made an error-recording transactions on their system.

- You may have made an error recording your transactions in GnuCash.

The process of reconciling the difference between the two balances is called account reconciliation. You can perform an account reconciliation using a pencil and paper, but GnuCash includes a handy feature to make reconciling your accounts relatively painless.

Reconciliation is useful not only to double-check your records against those of your bank, but also to get a better idea of outstanding transactions, for example, uncashed checks.

Once you have reconciled against your bank statement, you are very unlikely to change that transaction - whilst you may re-assign the expense account side as often as you like.

Points to note about reconciling

 The "starting balance" is what GnuCash remembers as your previous reconciled balance. When you reconcile for the first time, this will be 0.

The **R** column shows the status of each transaction split as follows:

◆ **n**: new

◆ **c**: cleared

◆ **y**: reconciled

You can change the status of individual transaction splits from **n** to **c** or back from **c** to **n** simply by clicking on them in the **R** column in the account register. For example, if you discovered that a particular check cleared the bank, you can mark it **c**. When you get the next bank statement and start the reconciliation process, this entry will appear with a check mark and save you further work. However, you can't mark transactions y one-by-one to indicate they are reconciled. This can only be done by the reconciliation process and it happens only at the time you click on **Finish**.

 Reconcile window keyboard shortcuts

Tab moves to the next pane and *Shift + Tab* moves to the previous pane.

Space bar marks that transaction as checked and moves to the next row.

↑ and ↓ navigates through the entries within the current pane.

Can I edit or delete reconciled transactions?

The short answer is NO. Why? This is because, you marked those transactions as cleared only when you saw the entries show up in the bank statement and the amount matched. Based on all those entries that you marked as cleared, the closing balance of the bank matched the closing balance in GnuCash. After doing all that painstaking work, if you go back and make changes to the reconciled transactions, it tends to upset the apple cart.

Mark split as unreconciled?

If you accidentally or otherwise click on the **R** column in an account register that has it marked as **y**, meaning reconciled, you will see a warning from GnuCash as shown in the next screenshot:

Change reconciled split?

If you are trying to edit an amount that has been previously reconciled, GnuCash will pop a warning as shown in the following screenshot:

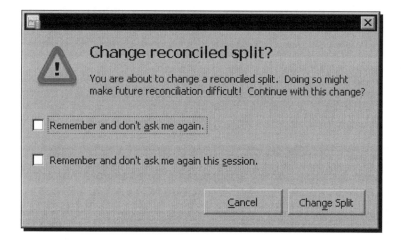

Delete a transaction with reconciled splits?

If you are trying to delete a transaction that has been previously reconciled, GnuCash will pop a warning as shown in the following screenshot:

When you see any of the above warnings, as we said earlier, it is better to back off and click **Cancel**. However, on rare occasions, if you have compelling reasons to do so, make a note of what changes you made and make sure to follow up and complete any related cleanup work that is needed.

If you do make changes to reconciled transactions, be prepared for any unreconciled transaction to show up in the reconciliation window or for deleted transactions to hold up the completion of the reconciliation successfully, and click **Finish**.

Pop quiz – reconciling with a bank statement

1. In the **Reconcile Information** window, what is the ending balance you will enter?

   a. Ending balance from GnuCash

   b. Ending balance from my bank statement

   c. Ending balance calculated by me

   d. Accept the default offered by GnuCash

2. In the **Reconcile** window which transactions will you check?

   a. The correct transactions.

   b. The transactions that appear in GnuCash.

   c. The transactions that appear on the bank statement.

   d. The transactions that seem to be missing.

Have a go hero – postponing a reconciliation

Practice postponing reconciliation and later coming back and finishing it.

Electronic reconciliation

Walking through every step of the manual reconciliation process, I could hear your protest, "I stopped getting paper statements in the mail a long time ago". This is why:

- The paper statement takes too long to reach me by snail mail.
- I get enough junk mail anyway.
- I don't want to kill more trees, if I can help it.
- If I get a paper statement, I will have to shred it when I am done, so that it doesn't fall in the hands of the dumpster divers and I end up being a victim of identity theft.

OK, OK, OK, I get the message. That section on manual reconciliation was written for those unfortunate people who are still living in the ancient paper age. Have pity on the poor souls. We are now ready to address the needs of the digital generation, like you.

If your bank provides a service to allow you to log in and download your monthly statement in OFX/QFX format, you are in luck. GnuCash has a feature that lets you import that statement and do the reconciliation electronically.

Time for action – reconciling with a downloaded electronic statement

Let's say that you have downloaded the OFX file from your bank and saved it in a folder of your choice. The file should have a file name extension of .ofx. We will now walk you through the steps for doing the reconciliation in GnuCash using this downloaded statement:

1. In GnuCash, select from the menu **File | Import | Import OFX/QFX**. The **Select an OFX/QFX file to process** dialog will open. Find the folder, select the OFX file that you want to import and click **Import**. The **Select Account** dialog will open as shown in the following screenshot:

 The first time you import a new downloaded OFX file, GnuCash asks you to select the account associated with that download. From then on, it remembers.

2. Under **Assets**, expand **Current Accounts**, select **Checking Account**, and click on **OK**. The **Generic import transaction matcher** window will open as shown in the following screenshot:

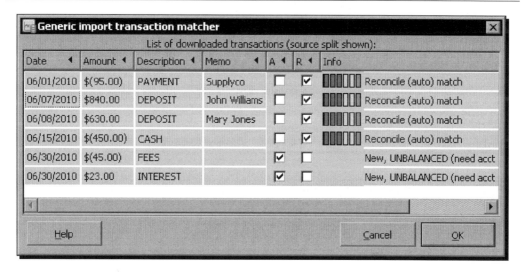

3. Click on the **Help** button and the context-specific **Transaction List Help** will open as shown in the following screenshot:

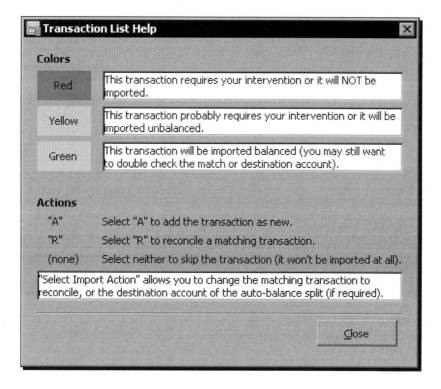

4. Familiarize yourself with what the colors mean and what actions are available.

5. Close the **Transaction List Help** window.

6. Back in the **Generic import transaction matcher**, the first four lines are green, indicating that GnuCash found the closest matching entries in the **Checking Account**. As you can see the check dated 05/29, which didn't clear in the month of May has now cleared and shows up in the June statement.

7. However, we have two yellow lines that require our intervention. Double click on the INTEREST line. The **Select Account** dialog, which we saw earlier, will appear. Open the **Income** account tree, select the **Interest Income** account and click **OK**. That line will turn green.

Please note that double clicking on the yellow line, as described previously, is the only way to launch the **Select Account** dialog for reconciliation. There is no right mouse menu or other way to get there.

8. Double click on the FEES line and open the **Select Account** dialog again. We earlier created an account to charge bank fees. Now you can select **Bank Fees** in the **Select Account** dialog and click **OK** to see that line also turn green, as shown in the following screenshot:

> New, transfer $45.00 to (manual) "Expenses:Bank fees"
>
> New, transfer $(23.00) to (auto) "Income:Interest Income"

9. Now that we have green signals all the way, let us grab this opportunity to drive right through. Click on **OK** to complete the import.

What just happened?

As you can see, electronic reconciliation makes your life easier, especially as your business grows and the number of transactions grows with it. GnuCash does most of the matching automatically, leaving only very few that need your manual intervention. Also, GnuCash does the color coding of transactions so that you can quickly browse through the green ones just to make sure nothing is amiss, and then focus on resolving the yellow ones. Finally, you can decide what to do with the red ones, if any.

OFX (**Open Financial eXchange**) is a data format standard for exchanging and downloading financial information into financial and accounting packages. It was originally created by Intuit, Checkfree, and Microsoft in 1997. According to Wikipedia, 39 different financial and accounting software packages support OFX.

QFX (**Quicken Financial eXchange**) is Intuit's proprietary version of the standard OFX financial exchange file format.

Use OFX if you can get it, because it is non-proprietary. However, if all you can get from your bank is QFX, GnuCash can use that too.

Reconciliation FAQ

Here is a list of frequently asked questions about the reconciliation process and our answers:

Q: I find myself having to go through and manually tick every single transaction. Doesn't GnuCash have a **Check all** or similar button to tick all the transactions?

> ❑ A: No, there is no **Check all** button. However, as we said earlier, you can use the space bar to check items. That has the additional effect of also moving the selection to the next line. So, for example, you can just hold the space bar down until all the entries in a column are checked.

Q: What if I don't have an account and have to create a new one for charging an amount to?

> ❑ Thankfully, GnuCash has provided a **New Account** button in the **Select Account** dialog just for such occasions. You can click that button to create a new account, which you can then select in the **Select Account** window.

Q: I am not able to complete the reconciliation. The **Finish** button is grayed out. How do I enable it?

> ❑ A: The **Finish** button is grayed out because the ending balance you entered in the **Reconcile Information** window doesn't match the total of the transactions that you checked off individually. In the bottom right pane of the **Reconcile** window you will see the **Ending Balance**, **Reconciled Balance** and **Difference**. As you keep checking off items, the **Reconciled Balance** and the **Difference** will keep changing. As soon as the **Reconciled Balance** is the same as the **Ending Balance** or, in other words, the **Difference** is zero, the **Finish** button will become enabled. Take a look at step 10 in the Manual Reconciliation tutorial above.

Q: Every time I launch the **Reconcile** window, the **Interest Payment** window keeps popping up automatically. My account doesn't pay interest. How do I switch this off?

    ❑   A: The **Interest Payment** window has a long button at the bottom called **No Auto Interest Payments for this Account**. If you click this, the **Interest Payment** window won't bother you again.

Q: In my **Reconcile Information** window the **Starting Balance** is incorrect. GnuCash doesn't provide a place for me to enter the correct **Starting Balance**. How do I fix this? How does GnuCash compute this number, anyway?

    ❑   A: The **Starting Balance** comes from your previous reconciliation. You may find that this is incorrect, either because you skipped reconciling for one or more months or you changed or deleted a reconciled transaction. Here is how you can handle this situation. Simply ignore the **Starting Balance** and try to reconcile to the **Ending Balance**. Of course, you may have to go back and fix any errors you made, such as editing or deleting a reconciled transaction, perhaps inadvertently.

Q: I need to charge an expense to multiple accounts. How do I do that?

    ❑   A: The **Select Account** dialog will allow you to select only one account to charge into. It doesn't have a feature to handle multiple splits. If you don't select an account and leave the **A** column checked, GnuCash will automatically charge the amount to **Imbalance-USD**. After the reconciliation is complete, you can open the **Imbalance-USD** and change it to the correct multiple split transaction.

Q: I accidentally marked a reconciled transaction from **y** to **n**. Now I am able to mark it **c**, but not able to change it back to **y**. How do I do that?

    ❑   A: You can mark individual transactions **c** for cleared in the account register. However, you can't mark individual transactions **y** for reconciled in the account register. Marking them **y** for reconciled is done by the reconciliation process. The unreconciled transaction will show up in the **Reconcile** window and you can run the reconcile process as often as needed.

Q: My bank does provide electronic statements, but OFX/QFX is not one of the options. What now?

  □ A: Even though GnuCash supports the import of QIF, CSV (Comma Separated Values) as well as fixed width formats, these are not suitable for reconciliation. As we saw earlier, 39 different financial and accounting software packages support OFX. As a result, most banks do provide support for this format. If your bank does not, you might first try asking your bank for this. If there is sufficient interest among its customers, your bank may be able to add support for this option. If not, then you may have to resort to manual reconciliation.

Q: My friend says that he doesn't have to enter transactions by hand. Instead, he imports them using the electronic statements from his bank, thus saving a lot of time and effort. Can I not do the same?

  □ A: If you just take what the bank statement shows on blind faith then you'll never notice if they mistakenly charge you due to any oversight. The very purpose of reconciliation is to use your accounts to make sure the bank doesn't overcharge you by mistake, as well as to use the bank statement to make sure you didn't miss out on some transactions. If you simply import the bank statement, it will defeat this very purpose of double checking. Also, the imported description may not be to your liking. It may be very brief and ambiguous and in all caps.

Income and expense accounts

Income and expense accounts are not directly reconciled, because there is no statement to check them against. However, to the extent your income and expenses go through your bank or credit card, they are being checked indirectly when you do the bank and credit card reconciliation.

Balancing your cash account

With a cash account, though, you might want to adjust the balance every once in a while, so that your actual cash on hand matches the balance in your cash account. In parallel you might want to investigate why it didn't balance. If you are the one handling the cash, perhaps you are failing to enter some of the transactions. If someone else is doing it, you might want to implement some checks and balances to prevent a recurrence.

The way some people rectify this discrepancy is to enter a transaction in the cash account with the destination account as one of the expense accounts, and enter the withdrawal. This way the current cash on hand matches the GnuCash account balance.

Credit card reconciliation

Credit card reconciliation is very much like bank reconciliation:

◆ If you get a paper statement from your credit card company, you can follow the manual reconciliation process that we walked through earlier.

◆ If, on the other hand, your credit card company allows you to download the statement in OFX/QFX format, you are in luck. You can go through the electronic reconciliation process that we walked through previously. Just make sure you select the right credit card account to import into when you do the reconciliation for the first time.

Unlike in a bank statement, you will find that there are different types of items on a credit card statement to deal with:

◆ Service charge: Just like you created a separate account under Expenses for Bank Fees, you may want to create a Credit Card Service Charge account under Expenses.

◆ Interest charged: Banks pay you interest, if you maintain a positive balance. On the other hand, credit card companies will charge you interest on the balance you owe them. You may want to create a Credit Card Interest Charge account under Expenses.

◆ Reversed transactions for returned items: If you bought an item and returned it back to the store, the store may simply reverse the transaction on the same card. If this happens soon enough, you may not even see the transaction on your statement, saving you the trouble of reconciling. However, if you returned it later, it may show up on your statement as a reversed entry with a negative charge.

While doing the reconciliation, if you find any discrepancies, this is the time to call the credit card company and have the discrepancy resolved.

Vital point to remember when importing an OFX file

The first time you import an OFX file, whether from your bank or your credit card company, as we saw earlier, GnuCash will ask you to select an account to import it into. Once you select an account, GnuCash will remember that and won't bother you again and again asking you to select an account to import into. I can hear you say, "Great! That is what I like in my software. Remember what I said and don't bug me over and over." Unfortunately, there is a flip side to such unfailing memory. If you made a mistake on the first attempt and want to go back and change the account to import into, GnuCash doesn't provide you a way to do this over. So, do it carefully the first time. Make sure you are clear in your mind about which account you want to import your OFX file into, before you start the task so that you are not guessing or accidentally stumbling into the wrong account.

Pop quiz – reconciling with an electronic statement

1. What are the formats that are not supported for electronic reconciliation?
    a. OFX
    b. CSV
    c. QFX
    d. QIF
    e. Fixed width

2. Checking A in the Generic import transaction matcher will do what?
    a. Mark the transaction as reconciled.
    b. Mark the transaction as cleared.
    c. Add the transaction as new.
    d. Mark the transaction as accepted.

Have a go hero – reconciling a credit card account

Do a reconciliation of your credit card account.

Recovering from wrong selection of account

As we said earlier, GnuCash doesn't provide a way to change the account to import an OFX file into, once you have made a selection. However, in spite of all of our warnings, if you have got yourself into this mess, here is how to get out. This is the GnuCash equivalent of what is known in the football world as a "Hail Mary pass". I am referring to the very long forward pass in American football, made in desperation, especially one thrown at or near the end of a half. Use this with caution.

Time for action – changing the account to import into

Let us say that the first time you imported your bank statement you selected **Savings Account** by mistake instead of **Checking Account**. We are going to walk you through the steps to recover from the selection of this wrong account. Though this is a risky process, this is the only way of starting over:

1. Make a backup of your accounts file.

2. Create a new account and call it **Temp Savings Account**.

3. Select the account that you are erroneously directing your OFX data to, namely **Savings Account**. Right click and select **Delete Account....**

4. GnuCash will pop the **Delete Account** confirmation dialog, as shown in the following screenshot, and will give you the option of moving all transactions into another account. Check **Move to** and select **Temp Savings Account** from the drop-down list:

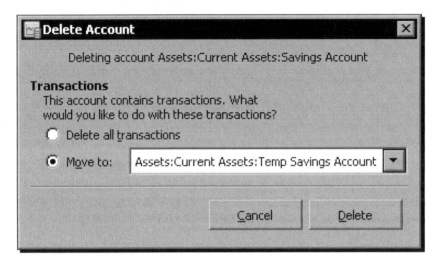

5. Next click **Delete**. Verify that **Savings Account** has been deleted and all transactions that were earlier in that account have been transferred to **Temp Savings Account**.

6. Rename **Temp Savings Account** back to **Savings Account**.

What just happened?

Of course, as the proverb goes ""Prevention is better than cure". It is better to try to keep a bad thing from happening than it is to fix the bad thing once it has happened. However, there are times, especially while learning something new, when you may get yourself into a bad situation like this. If that happens, it is good to know that there is a way out, although a somewhat risky one.

 However, please note that if you do use this work around, any saved report that referred to the original **Savings Account** will error out. You may have to recreate those reports.

Pop quiz – changing the account to import into

1. To change the account to import into, which account should you delete?

    a. The account that you want to import into.

    b. The account that you previously selected as the account to import into by mistake.

    c. The Imbalance-USD account.

    d. The temporary account.

Have a go hero – recovering using the backup file

Assume that the deletion process went wrong and you ended up losing transactions. Reopen the backup file that you created to recover all the transactions.

Summary

We learned a lot in this chapter about how to reconcile with your bank and credit card company every month.

Specifically, we covered:

- Manual reconciliation: You learned how to do the reconciliation, if you get printed monthly statements in the mail from your bank or your credit card company.

- Electronic reconciliation: On the other hand, if your bank or credit card company allows you to download electronic statements, we saw how to take advantage of that to further automate the reconciliation process.

- Changing or deleting reconciled transactions: We also saw why it is important not to change or delete reconciled transactions.

- Select the right account to import into: We stressed why it is important in GnuCash to make sure that you select the right account to import into the first time you import into an account.

- Recovering from the wrong selection of an account: If you pointed to the wrong account, we showed how you can recover from such a mistake.

Reconciliation won't help you with any other type of errors such as booking expenses to the wrong accounts. However, it will make sure that none of the transactions that go through your bank or your credit card account are overlooked. In this day and age, when there are hardly any cash transactions, this is huge for peace of mind for small business owners like you.

Now that we've learned about how to avoid getting lost in the transaction jungle, we are ready to learn how to automate repetitive transactions – which is the topic of the next chapter.

5

Repetitive Work? Let GnuCash do it

"You're a business owner, not a "numbers" person – but you still need a basic understanding of accounting and finance if you're going to stay in the black." – from the editorial review of a book on finance and accounting for entrepreneurs.

According to professional dog trainers, training your dog to fetch the daily newspaper is not really difficult, as long as your dog is big enough to carry a newspaper in its mouth. Some dogs are natural fetchers and carriers, and some will never want to do this. If your dog likes playing fetch, you can teach the dog to bring in the paper with the help of some incentives, such as dog biscuits. Having taught your dog, you can check one recurring task neatly taken care of.

As a small business you will have a number of transactions that repeat monthly. In some types of businesses, you might have transactions that repeat semi-monthly, weekly, or even daily as well. Examples are expenses such as rent, utility bills and mortgage payments, subscriptions such as newspapers, magazines, professional memberships, and services such as web hosting, janitorial, paper shredding and others. Every month you keep getting a bill and you find that you are repeating the same or a similar transaction over and over again. Computers are supposed to save us from the drudgery of having to do such repetitive work. Right? Right, but the software we use must be capable of enabling such automation to happen.

Welcome to GnuCash. Say a quick "Thank you" to the development team who thought of all this and built these user-friendly features in GnuCash.

In this chapter let us look at how we can set up GnuCash to help us through such repetitive transactions:

- Creating scheduled transactions from the account register
- Timely reminders provided by GnuCash
- Using the Scheduled Transaction Editor to set them up in bulk

So let's get on with it...

Let GnuCash worry about recurring transactions

When it comes to learning, GnuCash is what some people call "quick on the uptake". All you have to do is show it how to do it one time, and GnuCash will be able to do the subsequent transactions repeatedly in a timely manner.

Time for action – creating a recurring transaction from the register

Let us say that you signed up for a business internet connection last month and paid the first month's subscription by credit card. One way of entering each month's transaction is to wait for the bill to arrive, make the payment, and then enter into GnuCash by hand. However, there is a better way. This will not only save you a lot of time but GnuCash will also pop up a timely reminder, in case there are penalties for late payment.

1. Open the **Expenses:Internet** account register and create the $99.50 payment for the first month manually. Use **Liabilities:Credit Card** as the **Transfer** account. Use a date of a month ago plus a couple of days. For example, if today's date is 07/19/10, use 06/17/10 as the transaction date. (Why? This is because, we don't want to wait for another month to see how GnuCash reminds us for the second month's payment.)

2. Once the preceding transaction has been created and saved, right click on that transaction, and select **Schedule...** from the context menu. You can also click the **Schedule** toolbar button or select **Actions | Schedule...** from the menu. Don't forget to make sure the cursor is on that transaction when you do so. The **Make Scheduled Transaction** window will appear as shown in the following screenshot:

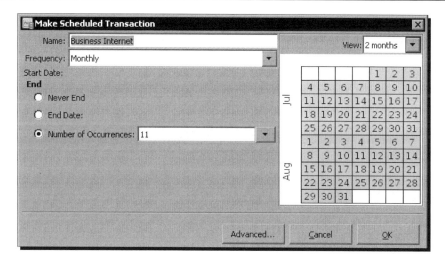

3. Select **Monthly** in the **Frequency** list. You should see the same date marked with a yellow dot in each month in the calendar on the right.

4. Enter **11** in **Number of Occurrences**. (We have entered the first month manually and we want 11 more to be scheduled to match our commitment of 12 months.)

5. Click on **Advanced...** to open the **Edit Scheduled Transaction** dialog as shown in the following screenshot:

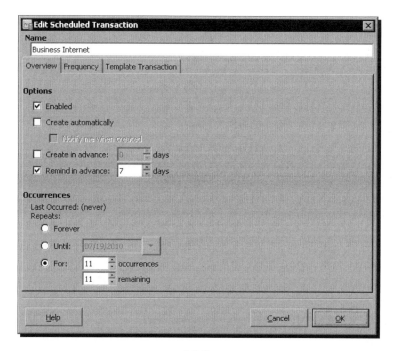

6. In the **Overview** tab, **Enabled** in the **Options** pane will be already checked. Check **Remind in advance** and type **7** in the box for **days**. Alternatively, you can click on the up arrow until you get **7**.

7. In the **Occurrences** pane, **For 11 occurrences** and **11 remaining** will be already filled.

8. Take a look at the **Frequency** tab and **Template Transaction** tab to become familiar with the contents. Don't change any of the values.

9. Click **OK** to complete the **Scheduled Transaction** set up.

What just happened?

You took one transaction that you created and not only made it repetitive, but also set it on a timeline so that it comes up at the appropriate time. By setting up this scheduled transaction in GnuCash, you dropped two mangoes with one stone (we prefer this metaphor to the more popular, but less animal-friendly one. Feel free to swap the mango with another fruit depending on the type of tree you used to throw stones at in your childhood):

◆ You have saved yourself the effort required to make 11 more transactions.

◆ You have entrusted the task of keeping track of the bills to GnuCash. As you have probably experienced sometimes, bills go missing. Bills by snail mail get misdelivered or thrown out inadvertently along with the pile of junk mail. Electronic bills may be missed due to system glitches. If you don't pay the bills on time, you are probably looking at penalties at best and disruption of service at worst.

SX is an abbreviation for **Scheduled Transaction**. You may see this abbreviation used in some GnuCash documentation and messages.

As you have seen, it is pretty easy to take any existing transaction and make it into a scheduled transaction. If you know the number of transactions, then you can set the number of occurrences. If, on the other hand, you know the date when a transaction will end, you can set the end date instead.

Start and end dates

In the **Make Scheduled Transaction** dialog, even though there are fields marked **Start Date** and **End Date**, you can't enter any value there. If you would like to enter any of these dates, click on the **Advanced...** button and open the **Edit Scheduled Transaction** window. You can enter **Start Date** in the **Frequency** tab and **Repeats Until** in the **Occurrences** pane in the **Overview** tab.

Setting up a scheduled transaction is the first step of the process. You have asked GnuCash to remind you seven days in advance about the next payment. GnuCash will remind you when you start GnuCash when that seventh day reminder period comes up. In the next tutorial, we will see what your options are when that reminder appears on the screen.

Pop quiz – creating a recurring transaction

1. You need to make a payment twice a month. What selections will you make in the **Frequency** tab?

    a. Select **Frequency Daily** and **Every 15 days**.

    b. Select **Frequency Semi-Monthly**.

    c. Select **Frequency Weekly** and **Every 2 weeks**.

    d. Select **Frequency Twice-a-month**.

Have a go hero – creating a recurring split transaction

Take a split transaction, such as a loan repayment that includes repayment of principal and interest charges, and create a scheduled transaction for it.

A stitch in time saves nine

As a small business owner, you wear many hats. Each of those hats seems to come with its own sets of tasks for you to accomplish. It is no wonder that you are always trying to stretch the number of hours in the day and the number of days in the week. In all this whirl of activity, who can remember when the next transaction has to be entered? Well, GnuCash can and it does so with robotic precision. Let us see how the reminders show up.

Time for action – triggering scheduled transactions

Whenever you launch GnuCash the **Since Last Run** process will run automatically and look for any transactions to be created or reminded about since the last time you started GnuCash. The **Since Last Run** dialog will pop up showing them. If, by chance, you cancelled it at that time because you were in a rush to get to something else, you can also launch it manually whenever you want it.

1. Run the **Since Last Run** process using the **Actions | Scheduled Transactions | Since Last Run…**menu.

2. The **Since Last Run...** window will pop up showing any scheduled transactions that are to be created or reminded about, as shown in the following screenshot:

 If there are no scheduled transactions in the system to be created or reminded about, all you will see is a message saying, **There are no Scheduled Transactions to be entered at this time**. If that happens, you may have to go back and do the previous tutorial to set up at least one scheduled transaction.

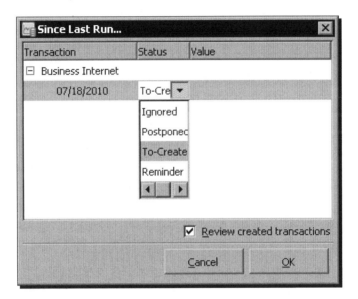

3. Click on the transaction selecting that row. Click on the text under the **Status** column and it will become a drop-down list as shown in the preceding screenshot.

 Postponed as well as **Reminder** will postpone the transaction until you start GnuCash the next time. **Ignored** will cancel this occurrence of the transaction for good.

4. Select **To-Create**, tab out or click somewhere else on the window so that the focus shifts away from that field, check the **Review created transactions** checkbox, and click **OK**.

Please note that, after making a selection in the drop-down list, tabbing out, or clicking somewhere else on the window, so that the focus shifts away from that field, is essential. Without that your selection will not take effect.

5. You will be back in GnuCash with the freshly created transaction showing in a **Created Transactions** tab as shown in the following screenshot:

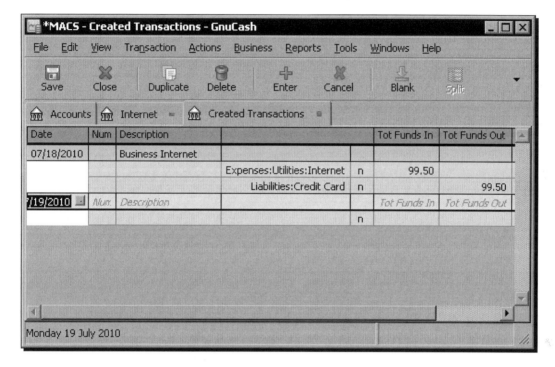

6. Check and make sure that the **Description**, **Transfer** accounts and amounts are OK.

7. Don't forget to save your work.

What just happened?

Thus GnuCash is like an eager valet ready to remind you about the transactions due, the first chance it gets, namely when it starts. However, you can deal with these transactions at that time or at a later time depending on your preference.

Is it Easter already?

Some of you may recall the Easter Eggs. Oh, I am not talking about the decorated chocolate eggs or plastic eggs filled with jelly beans hidden by the Easter Bunny, for children to find on Easter morning. I am talking about the games hidden by the not-so-bunny developers in some of the early software applications. The magic sequence for launching the flight simulator game in Excel 97 went somewhat like this, "Create a new worksheet. Click on *F5*. In the **Go To** window, type **X97:L97** and click on *Enter*. Click on the *Tab* key. Hold the *Ctrl* and *Shift* keys while clicking the **Chart Wizard** toolbar button."

GnuCash has such a neat Easter Egg hidden in it with rewards far better than just a pastime like the flight simulator game. I am referring to the **Status** field of the **Since Last Run** dialog. Too many people have struggled with it because it is neither intuitive nor easy to find. However, now that you are familiar with where it is and how to use it, you are well armed with the power tools needed to get the most out of GnuCash.

Three different scenarios

After you have set up the Scheduled Transactions, there is no mystery about which ones got created when and which ones didn't. The **Since Last Run...** dialog is the only way Scheduled Transactions get created. If, as we recommended, you checked the **Review created transactions**, you will see the created transactions as well. However, you need to be aware of three different scenarios that can happen:

 ◆ No Scheduled Transactions to create at all: You will see an information dialog as shown in the following screenshot:

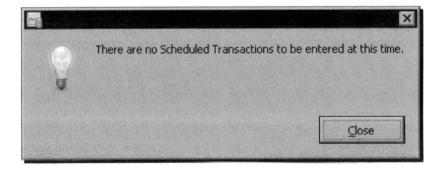

 ◆ Only **Create Automatically** Scheduled Transactions: The **Since Last Run...** dialog will appear as shown in the following screenshot showing the **Status** as **Created** for the **Create Automatically** transactions.

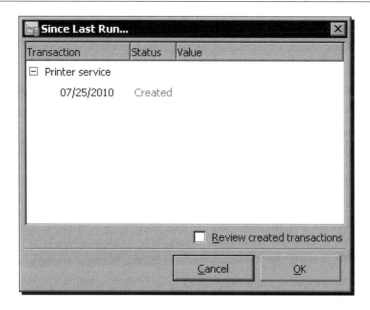

- ◆ Both automatic and normal Scheduled Transactions: **The Since Last Run...** dialog will show both automatic and normal scheduled transactions. The **Create Automatically** transactions will be created and the status marked as **Created**. The normal transactions will be presented for you to review and take action.

 Create Automatically is an option that means, "Don't bother waiting for my approval, just go ahead and create this scheduled transaction." Of course, the transaction will get created only when you launch GnuCash at the time when the **Since Last Run** process runs.

Be cautious like an accountant

Accountants are cautious types. There is a reason for that. They know, perhaps from personal experience, the kind of glitches one can get into otherwise and, more importantly, what it takes to get out of it. When in Rome, do as the Romans do. When doing accounting do as the accountants do, namely exercise caution.

We recommend that you don't check **Create Automatically** for the time being. Also, make sure you always check **Review created transactions** every time. This way you will be able to control what the Scheduled Transactions module does and also watch the resulting transactions. Once you have become comfortable with the results, namely either the module does what you expect it to do or you have gotten used to its quirks, you can selectively check **Create Automatically**.

Pop quiz – triggering scheduled transactions

1. You want GnuCash to display the scheduled transactions created by it so that you can make sure they are OK, before saving them. What will you do?

    a. In the **Overview** tab of **Edit Scheduled Transaction** window, check **Notify me when created**.

    b. In the **Frequency** tab of **Edit Scheduled Transaction** window, check **Notify me when created**.

    c. In the **Since Last Run...** window change the status to **Review**.

    d. In the **Since Last Run...** window check **Review created transactions**.

Have a go hero – triggering scheduled transactions

Create a scheduled transaction from one of your existing transactions and set it to **Remind in advance 7 days**. Let us say that after creating the transaction, you received a notification from the bank that you won the lucky draw and that your first payment is waived. When you get the first reminder, change the **Status** to **Ignore** and **OK** it.

Tool to create many recurring transactions

If you have a small and patient family, you can perhaps get away with a small griddle that can only make one pancake at a time. However, if you are running a popular restaurant feeding freshly made hot cakes to the hungry masses who have places to go to and things to do, you need large capacity commercial restaurant griddles. Similarly, if you want to set up scheduled transactions once in a while, you can do it from the account register. However, if you want to set up a large number of recurring transactions in one go, GnuCash has more robust professional grade equipment for that.

In GnuCash, there are two ways of creating scheduled transactions, from the account register or from the scheduled transactions editor. The **Scheduled Transactions Editor** may be faster if we have several scheduled transactions to create at once.

Time for action – creating scheduled transactions in bulk

As we said earlier, another way of entering a scheduled transaction is from the **Scheduled Transactions Editor**. Let us look at an example:

1. From the menu select **Actions | Scheduled Transactions | Scheduled Transaction Editor**. The **Scheduled Transactions** window opens. It already has the one scheduled transaction for Business Internet that we set up from the account register previously.

2. Click **New** to create another scheduled transaction. The **Edit Scheduled Transaction** window opens.

3. Enter **Monthly phone bill** in the **Name** field at the top.

4. In the **Overview** tab **Enabled** will be already checked in the **Options** pane. Check **Remind in advance** and enter **7 days**.

5. In the Occurrences pane check **For** and enter **12 occurrences** and **12 remaining**.

6. Switch to the **Frequency** tab. Select **Monthly** in the **Frequency** field. In the **Start Date** field enter a date of over a month ago from the current date. For example, if today's date is 07/16/2010, enter 06/15/2010. This will save you from waiting for a month to check whether your scheduled transaction works. Make sure **Every 1 months** is set. Set **On the 15th except on weekends: Use previous weekday**. Verify that the appropriate dates are highlighted with a yellow dot in the calendar as shown in the following screenshot:

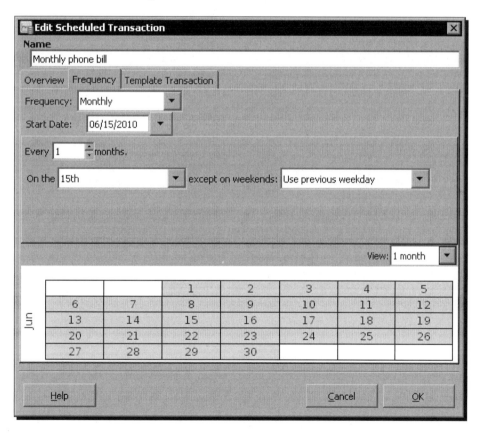

7. In the **Template Transaction** tab, enter **Phone** in the **Description** field. Skip the **Notes** field and select **Assets:Current Assets:Checking Account** in the **Transfer** field. In the **Tot Funds Out** field enter **billamt**. In the next line, select **Expenses:Utilities:Phone** in the **Transfer** field and enter **billamt** in the **Tot Funds In** field. The screen at this point will look as shown in the following screenshot:

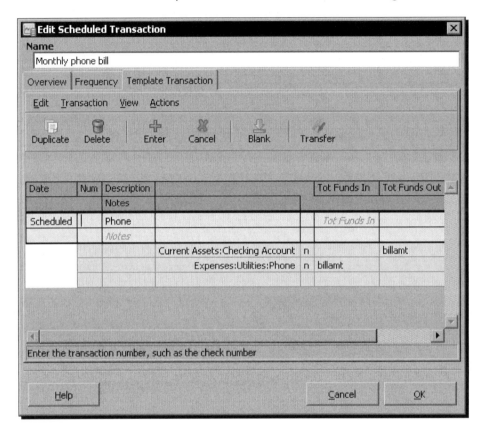

8. Go ahead and click **OK**.

9. You will see a confirmation message; **The current template transaction has been changed. Would you like to record the changes?** Go ahead and click **Yes** to complete the set up of this scheduled transaction as shown in the following screenshot:

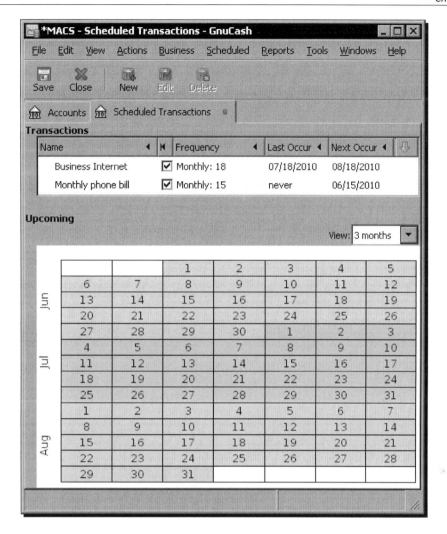

10. Don't forget to click **Save** to save your work so far. Close GnuCash using the **File | Quit** menu and then restart it again.

11. You will find that the **Since Last Run...** dialog opens automatically at the time of launching GnuCash as shown in the following screenshot. This is because there are scheduled transactions with prior dates, in this case one which is over a month ago and another which is a day ago:

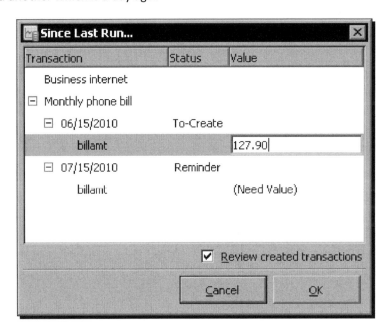

12. For the **06/15/2010** date, select the **billamt** line and click on the **(Need Value)** field. It will become a textbox. Enter the amount **127.90** and tab out.

13. For the **07/15/2010** date, select the **billamt** line and click on **To-create**. If you remember our Easter Egg you will know that it will become a drop-down list. Select **Reminder** from this list and tab out.

14. Check **Review created transactions** and click **OK**.

15. GnuCash will show the freshly created transaction in the tab marked **Search Results**. Verify whether the transaction is correct.

What just happened?

As we saw previously, we can set up a number of scheduled transactions to make our bookkeeping tasks lighter. The little that is left can be done with a timely nudge from GnuCash.

Schedule a transaction without knowing the amount

Do you have any doubt at all that you will get a phone bill next month? None whatsoever. Do you know how much your phone bill will be? Not unless you have a flat fee plan. GnuCash will remind you about the phone bill in advance (the number of days can be specified by you).

Sometimes the bill arrives a few days earlier or a few days later and the amount varies depending on usage and other factors. Therefore, you don't want GnuCash to keep entering the same amount on the same day of the month. That would be counter productive. You want to have the flexibility to make these changes, as needed, before entering the transaction.

In short you want to have the cake and eat it too. However, I have news for you, good news, that is. GnuCash will allow you to do just that. It will remind you on time that a transaction needs to be entered, it will present a pre-filled transaction to you, wait on you to change the date, amount and whatever else you wish to change, and then let you create it.

You can put in a placeholder name instead of an amount in the template transaction. You will be prompted to enter an amount at the time the scheduled transaction is to be created. However, for this placeholder there are some restrictions on what names are acceptable and what names are not:

1. You cannot have a space in the placeholder name, such as "Bill amount".

2. The placeholder name cannot start with a number, such as "1stamount".

3. The good part is you are not expected to know what an acceptable name is and what is not. If you give the placeholder an unacceptable name, such as "Bill amount", GnuCash will pop an error message when you tab out of the field, as shown in the following screenshot:

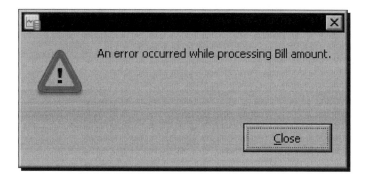

Go ahead and change the name until the error goes away.

When using placeholders, don't check **Create automatically**. You will get an error message, **Scheduled Transactions with variables cannot be automatically created** (**variable** is GnuCash's name for a placeholder). Understandably, automatic transactions can only be created when you have provided all of the data needed to create them. All this message is saying is that you can't select the **Create automatically** checkbox for the scheduled transaction. **Create automatically** means "don't bother asking for my approval to create this scheduled transaction, just go ahead and do it." Scheduled transactions with placeholders require a dialog to ask for the values for the placeholders. **Create automatically** and placeholders are thus not compatible.

Thus placeholder names give you a way to deal with amounts that might vary from bill to bill, without losing the advantages of setting up scheduled transactions.

Estimated value

Instead of putting a placeholder, some people prefer putting in an estimated value. You could create the scheduled transaction with "Est." in the **Num** field. Once you have received the bill you can update the transfer amounts, delete the **Est** in the **Num** field, and save it.

Scheduled Transactions FAQ

Here is a list of frequently asked questions about the Scheduled Transactions process and our answers:

- Q: When does the **Since Last Run** process run?
    - A: The **Since Last Run** process runs every time you start GnuCash. You can also run it manually from the **Actions | Scheduled Transactions | Since Last Run...** menu.

- Q: I have a number of scheduled transactions that occur every four weeks. The dialog for setting up Scheduled Transactions does not have an option to set a four-weekly cycle. How can I do that?
    - A: Select **Weekly** in **Frequency** and then set **Every 4 Weeks**. Verify that the dates that are highlighted with yellow dots are what you are looking for.

◆ Q: How do I delete a Scheduled Transaction?

  ❑ A: Open the **Scheduled Transactions** window. You can do this from the **Actions | Scheduled Transactions | Scheduled Transaction Editor** menu. Select the Scheduled Transaction that you want to delete. The **Delete** button in the toolbar will become enabled. Click on the **Delete** button. The confirmation message **Do you really want to delete this transaction?** will appear. Click **Yes**.

◆ Q: What transactions will appear in the **Since Last Run...** dialog on a given day?

  ❑ A: The **Since Last Run...** dialog will show all transactions from the last time **Since Last Run...** was run till today. It will also include any transactions that you set up to create in advance as well as those that you set up to remind in advance.

◆ Q: What does the **Ignored** option in the **Status** column do? How do I use it?

  ❑ A: If you want to skip one occurrence completely, you can mark it **Ignored**. For example, let us say your internet company has given you a special offer in which, if you pay for 11 months, the 12th month is free. On the 12th month, instead of a bill you get a letter thanking you for your patronage and reminding you to extend your contract by another 12 months. In that case, you can simply change the **Status** to **Ignored** and the transaction will go away.

◆ Q: Can I create a scheduled transaction with a start date well in the past?

  ❑ A: If needed, you can create a scheduled transaction which has a start date well in the past. When you run the Since Last Run process, all of the remaining transactions till today's date will come up in the list of transactions to be created. You can then choose to create all of them in one go.

◆ Q: Is there some way I can see all the scheduled transactions that I have set up in a calendar? I can see the dates highlighted with yellow spots. However, I don't know what the transactions are.

  ❑ A: Click on any date on the calendar, in any of the scheduled transaction windows that display a calendar. A small window, following your mouse, will show you what is planned for that day including date, name, and frequency. As you move the mouse to different dates on the calendar, the transactions planned for that date will be shown. To make the small window disappear, just click on the calendar one more time.

Create post dated transactions

There is one option at the time of creating a scheduled transaction that we didn't discuss in detail, **Create in advance**. This will create the transaction before the transaction date. In other words, it will create a post dated transaction. For example, if you set a transaction due on 15th of the month to **Create in advance 7 days**, the transaction will be created on the 8th with the transaction date set to the 15th.

> Some people find it useful to create transactions for recurring expenses in advance, so that they can see the funds requirement in advance and have time to arrange the funds.

To make it abundantly clear that you have some transactions that are dated in the future, GnuCash will show the future-dated transactions separately in the account register below a thick blue line as shown in the following screenshot:

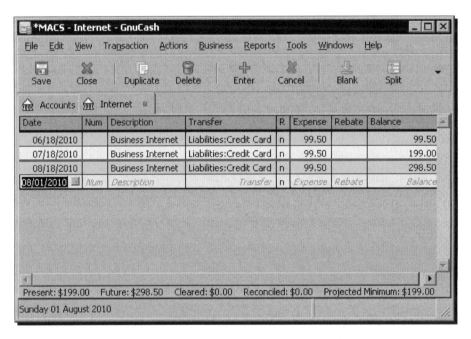

What was that question again? No, you shouldn't pour syrup over the stack of scheduled transactions that you freshly created. Why? This is because your accountant prefers your transactions and your explanations to be crisp.

Pop quiz – using the Scheduled Transaction Editor

1. How will you set the start date of a scheduled transaction?

   a. Set the **Start Date** in the **Frequency** tab of the **Edit Scheduled Transaction** window.

   b. Set the **Start Date** in the **Overview** tab of the **Edit Scheduled Transaction** window.

   c. Set the **Start Date** in the **Template Transaction** tab of the **Edit Scheduled Transaction** window.

   d. Create the scheduled transaction on the start date.

2. Which of the following are valid placeholder names?

   a. Internet bill amount

   b. 2010 bill amount

   c. phonebill

   d. 2010phonebill

Have a go hero – using the Scheduled Transaction Editor

You created a scheduled transaction for the phone bill successfully. Now when you look at it in the **Scheduled Transactions** window, you realize that you left the **Last Occurrence** as **never** by oversight. Edit that transaction and change it to 24 occurrences to cover the period of the 2-year contract that you signed.

Summary

As you saw, the Scheduled Transactions module is full of not so obvious, hidden, and undocumented features. However, once you know where to find them and how to use them, you will find that they are very powerful.

Specifically, we covered:

◆ Creating a scheduled transaction from the account register: You put in a lot of effort and created a transaction in the account register. Now you can ask GnuCash to repeat it several times in the future by making it a scheduled transaction.

◆ Triggering a scheduled transaction: You have already set up one or more scheduled transactions. We learned how to trigger them and what options you have.

◆ Setting up several scheduled transactions in one go: We learned how to use more powerful tools in GnuCash that make it easy to set up a bunch of scheduled transactions.

- Editing and deleting scheduled transactions: We also learned how to tweak scheduled transactions to suit our needs and delete unwanted ones.

If you have set up a lot of repetitive expense transactions to be created automatically in GnuCash, you may get the feeling that it is a great way to spend money without your intervention. There is an antidote for that feeling. Go ahead and look for ways to set up recurring revenue and income transactions. You will feel better once you have some of those up and running. Thus, the ability to set up scheduled transactions is a powerful tool in GnuCash. You can train GnuCash to take care of much of your repetitive bookkeeping work, and you don't need to buy any dog biscuits either.

Now that we've covered the basic bookkeeping aspects, we are ready to get started with business beyond basic transactions.

6

Business Mantra: Buy Now, Pay Later

"Even if you can afford to buy your paperclips with cash—don't." – web article offering financial advice to start-up businesses.

Probably one of the most highly practiced forms of cash on delivery today in the US is pizza delivery. With about 65,000 pizza restaurants in the US we can guesstimate that the number of pizza deliveries per day will easily run into millions. Some people do pay over the phone in advance, before their pizza is delivered, but most still present the delivery person with cash or check and, hopefully, a suitable tip. Therefore, if you are in the pizza delivery business, you don't have to worry about credit sales.

Credit is the lubricant for the wheels of business

On the other hand, if you are selling to a business, they will expect you to provide trade credit. Net 30 is standard in many businesses, with a discount offered for earlier payment. An example **credit term** is 2/10 Net 30. This is shorthand for 2% cash discount if paid within 10 days, otherwise due in 30 days. You will be able to negotiate those terms, but it is unlikely that you can get your business customers to pay cash on delivery. Unless, of course, you are selling something that is hard to get or in short supply or you are providing an exclusive service.

In order to offset this cash flow problem, at least partially, it makes smart business sense to negotiate favorable credit terms with all your vendors. Many suppliers may require you to pay for initial orders by cash, check or credit card until your business has been deemed credit worthy. Once you have established that you can pay your bills on time, it is possible to negotiate trade credit terms with your suppliers. This is the rationale for the above advice about even buying paper clips on credit. The ready availability of free and flexible trade credit is one source of funding for most businesses in the US. **Trade credit** is easy to get because, if one vendor doesn't provide credit, you can always find another one that will. It is free because interest is not charged. It is flexible because, even with contracted payment terms, some businesses don't seem to pay promptly as committed.

Of course, there is a downside to not paying on time. If you do not pay on time, some vendors may withdraw credit terms offered to you. That will be counter-productive. Also, many vendors report payment data to business credit rating services. Your business credit rating will get dinged, making it difficult for you to get credit terms with quality vendors.

You are going to have a ton of transactions that you need to keep track of as well as follow up and take action in a timely manner. In order to play this game of selling on credit and buying on credit well, you need systems that can keep track of both payments due to you as well as payments owed by you and remind you so that you can take the necessary actions in a timely manner. In short, you need GnuCash.

In this chapter we shall learn about:

- Accounts Receivable: How to create invoices for credit sales, create reports of payments due.
- How to set the starting Invoice Number.
- Processing payments when we receive them.
- Accounts Payable: How to keep track of bills for credit purchases, get reminders for bills due, and make payments.

So let's get more familiar with how to make this cash flow a savvy part of running a business on the right track.

Billing terms and customers

Prior to creating invoices and posting credit sales in Accounts Receivable, there are a couple of prerequisite steps – setting up billing terms and adding customers. Out of these, adding customers is a required step. You cannot create an invoice unless that customer is in the system already. However, setting up billing terms is optional, but recommended.

Time for action – setting up billing terms and adding customers

Let us say that you are about to make your first sale on credit. You will soon be creating an invoice and sending it to your customer. Prior to that, we are going to do two preparatory steps. First, we are going to set up a billing term of 2/10 Net 30. Next we are going to add the name and other details of Acme Inc, the customer, from whom you are about to win a contract:

1. Prerequisites: Make sure you have an **Accounts Receivable** account in your account hierarchy. Typically, you will find this under **Assets | Current Assets**. If you do not have one, go ahead and create a new **Accounts Receivable** account. This should be of type **A/Receivable** and, preferably, have **Current Assets** as the parent.

2. Register Your Company: After you have built your account structure, you will want to register the GnuCash file as belonging to your company. This information is required for creating the invoice. Click on **File | Properties**. In the **Business** tab, type your **Company Name** and **Company Address**. In **Company ID** add your GST number: **GST: 1234-5678RT**. Click on **OK**.

3. Create Billing Term: Before entering a new customer and creating an invoice, it is preferable to enter your billing terms. Select from the menu **Business | Billing Terms Editor**. The **Terms** window will open. Click on **New** and the **New Billing Term** window will open.

As we said earlier, if you can persuade your customer to pay cash on delivery, it will help your cash flow. Even better, of course, will be if you can get an advance payment. If you can't get either of those terms, try to keep the credit period as low as possible. Also, offer an incentive for your customers to pay earlier by offering an attractive discount.

4. Enter **Std** for **Name**, **Standard** for **Description**, and **Days** for **Type**. Enter **30** in **Due Days**, **10** in **Discount Days** and **2.00** in **Discount %** as shown in the following screenshot.

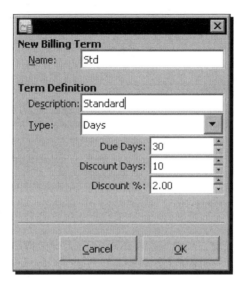

5. Click on **OK**. You have now created a billing term that you can use while creating the invoice. Also create another **Extended** billing term as shown in the following screenshot:

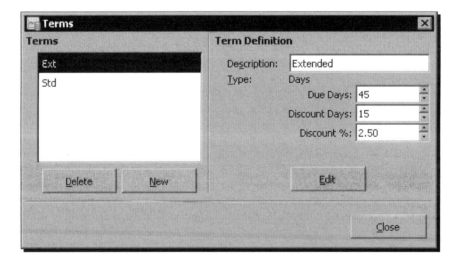

6. You are now all set to add your first customer to the system. From the menu, select **Business | Customer | New Customer....** In the **Identification** pane of the **Customer** tab, leave **Customer Number** blank. GnuCash will generate numbers sequentially. Fill in **Acme Inc** in the **Company Name** and enter a **Billing Address**. Leave the **Active** checkbox checked; otherwise this invoice won't appear in searches.

7. In the **Billing Information** tab select **Std** from the dropdown list. Enter **20** in **Discount** and enter **20000.00** in **Credit Limit**. Leave the two tax fields untouched for now as shown in the following screenshot:

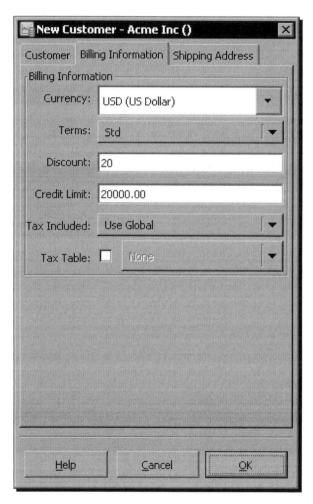

8. Leave the **Shipping Address** tab blank for now. Click on **OK**. You have now created your first customer.

What just happened?

You may have standard payment terms that you may want to quote as a matter of routine. However, if there is a special opportunity either by way of a large contract or if there is a potential for an ongoing business opportunity you may relax that and be willing to offer special terms. For the benefit of your team as well as for your own clarity, you might want to codify these options in advance and define what the standard terms are and what could be special terms.

Invoices and Accounts Receivable

When you make a cash sale, you will enter the fact that you made a sale into your sales account and, depending on whether you received cash or a check, you will make an entry into one of those accounts as well. In a credit sale, the entry in the sales account remains the same. However, you need to show that a customer owes you money in a different type of account. Say "Hello" to **Accounts Receivable**. Accountants often refer to this simply as **A/R**. A/R keeps track of products or services provided by your business to customers on credit for which payment has not yet been received. This is an asset, because the expectation is that you will receive payment soon. Accounts receivables are shown under current assets in your Balance Sheet because they are typically due within one year.

Time for action – keeping track of credit sales

You have completed the contract for Acme Inc. successfully. Congratulations! You are now ready to invoice. We will take you through the steps for creating the invoice, posting it, formatting it and printing it ready for mailing.

1. From the menu, select **Business | Customer | New Invoice...**.

2. In the **Invoice Information** pane, leave **Invoice ID** blank. GnuCash will generate numbers sequentially. Enter a date of over a month ago in the **Date Opened** field. This will help you to process the payment right away (for the purposes of this tutorial), without having to wait for a month for the invoice to become due.

 GnuCash automatically generates Invoice IDs starting with 000001. This cannot be changed from the user interface. However, if you have to change this, we will show you a workaround later in this chapter.

3. In the **Billing Information** pane, for **Customer** click **Select...**. The **Find Customer** dialog will open.

4. In the **Search Criteria** pane change **contains** to **matches regex**. Enter a **.** (dot) in the next text box as shown in the following screenshot.

 regex is an abbreviation for a regular expression. This is a geek formula for efficiently matching and finding names and other text. Until you have hundreds of customers, all you need to do is use the dot, get a full list of customers, scroll down, and pick the one you want. When you do have a large number of customers, you can select the **contains** option, type in a partial name and get a match.

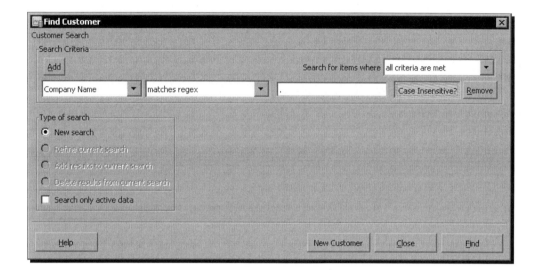

5. Click **Find**. You should now see the full list of customers. Select **Acme Inc** and click **Select**.

6. Enter Acme **PO# 7398 dt 07/01/10** in **Billing ID**. This is the reference to the Purchase Order that you received from your customer Acme Inc.

7. **Terms** will change to **Std** automatically. This is based on the selection that you made at the time of creating this customer. You have the option of changing it for each invoice, if that invoice has special terms. However, leave it as **Std** for this invoice as shown in the following screenshot:

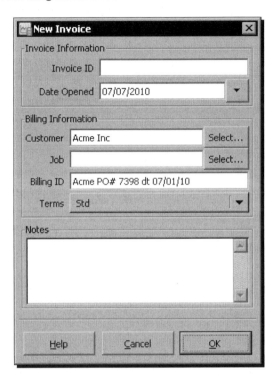

8. Click **OK** to launch the **Edit Invoice** window.

9. The top part of the **Edit Invoice** window will be populated with all the information that you provided so far. The **Invoice ID** should now have an auto-generated ID of **000001**.

9. Under **Invoice Entries,** tab to the **Description** field and enter **Firewall set-up**. Tab to the **Income Account** field and select **Income:Sales** from the drop-down list. Enter **1.00** under **Quantity**, **395.00** under **Unit Price**, and leave the **Discount** as **20.00**. GnuCash will calculate the **Subtotal** for you by multiplying the **Quantity** by **Unit Price** and applying the **Discount** % to the total as shown in the following screenshot:

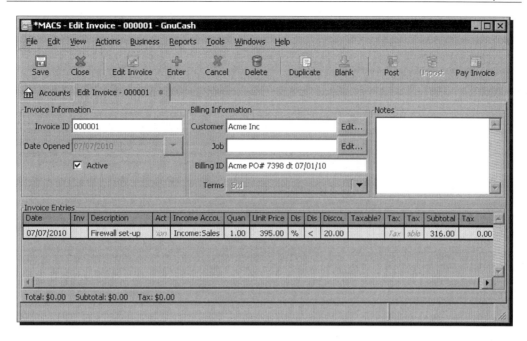

10. Once you have completed all that and verified that everything is in order, you can **Save** the invoice and come back and **Post** it later. However, we are ready to **Post** the invoice right away. Go ahead and click the **Post** toolbar button. A confirmation dialog will pop up asking you, **Do you really want to post the invoice?** The transaction gets recorded in the accounts only when you post it. Even though you can unpost an invoice, you may have to deal with tax and other complications. Therefore, you should take a moment to review the invoice before posting as shown in the following screenshot:

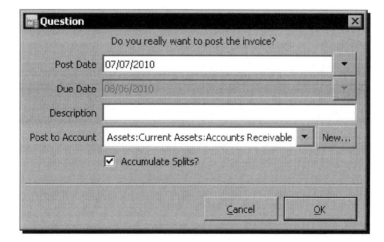

11. Click **OK** to post the invoice. You will find that the **Edit Invoice** tab changes to **View Invoice**.

12. Now open your **Sales** account and confirm that a $316.00 revenue transaction from Acme shows up. Most importantly, open your **Accounts Receivable** and confirm that an entry of $316.00 shows up under the name of Acme with a due date 30 days from the date of invoice.

13. Next we are going to format and print the invoice. Preparatory Exercise: Create a new style sheet and name it MACS Invoice. Please refer to *Chapter 3, Fun and Eye-opening part - Reports and charts* for a tutorial that shows how to create a custom stylesheet.

14. From the menu select **Reports | Business | Printable Invoice**.

15. You will have a blank report because you have not selected an invoice yet. Click the **Options** toolbar button to open the **Report Options** window.

16. In the **General** tab in **Style sheet**, select MACS Invoice. In **Invoice Number** click **Select...** and find the invoice.

17. In the **Display Columns** tab uncheck **Action**.

18. In the **Display** tab uncheck **Billing Terms** and change the **Extra Notes** to **Thank you for your business**. Click **OK** to close the **Options** window.

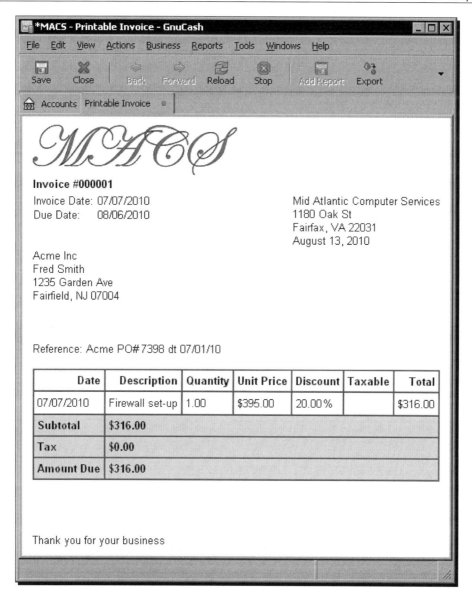

19. Go ahead and print the invoice shown in the previous screenshot by using the menu **File | Print Invoice**.

What just happened?

Your ability to find good credit-worthy customers with a growing demand for your goods and services and negotiate favorable trade credit terms is where your business skills can shine. However, the not so glamorous bookkeeping plays an important part too. Unless you have the systems in place to keep track of who owes you payment, what the terms are and when they become due, you won't be able to follow them up and collect it in a timely manner. At best this will impact your cash flow because you didn't follow up in a timely manner on payments due. At worst, some of these will become bad debts and either expensive to collect or they will have to be written off as uncollectible.

GnuCash has four modules that form part of the Accounts Receivable system. The credit sales transactions will be tracked in the Accounts Receivable account. However, you do not directly make entries in this account from the account register, as in the case of other accounts. Instead, as you saw in the preceding tutorial, you will be working with the four GnuCash A/R modules, available from the **Business | Customers** menu. These four modules are – Customers, Invoices, Jobs, and Process Payments. **Jobs** is an optional module. This feature is useful when you are executing multiple contracts for the same customer, and would like to view all the invoices related to a single contract separately. We will cover the Jobs module in a later chapter.

Invoice printing

The Printable Invoice without any stylesheet is very plain because it is designed to be printed on your letterhead. However, you can create a stylesheet of your choice and apply that style, as we saw in this tutorial so that you can print on plain paper as well.

You can print an invoice from the **View Invoice** window as well. When View Invoice is open, you can select from the **File | Print Invoice** menu.

Most of the things on the invoice can be changed using the **Report Options** dialog.

Some people prefer not to show a **Due Date**. Instead they prefer to show something indirect, like Net30, being the shorthand for 30 days credit that we discussed earlier. However, there is no easy way to make that change in GnuCash.

If you want to make the above change, or create a PDF of the invoice so that you can send it attached to an e-mail, or create a style beyond what GnuCash allows you to do, then you know that you are pushing the limits of what GnuCash can do. Please see the **Exporting Reports** section in the Reports chapter to see how to take your data out so that you can use it in your favorite word processing or spreadsheet program to edit and format it to your very specific preferences.

Receivable Aging report

Depending on the number of credit transactions you have, you will want to run a report every day or every week to see which payments are due and overdue. To see a Receivable Aging report, select from the **Reports | Business | Receivable Aging** menu.

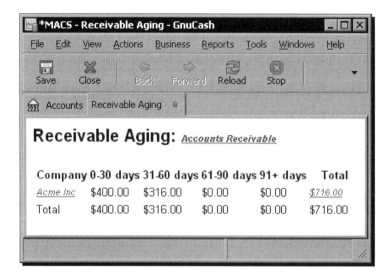

You can use the report shown in the preceding screenshot to come up with an action list of which payments to follow up and how.

 Please note that the **Receivable Aging** report shows how old each invoice is, not when the payment is due.

List of unpaid invoices

Your other option is to create a list of unpaid invoices from the **Find Invoice** dialog. From the menu, select **Business | Customer | Find Invoice**. In the **Search Criteria**, in the drop-down list on the left, select **Is Paid?** In the middle drop-down list, select **Is not**, and then leave the **set true** button pushed down as shown in the following screenshot:

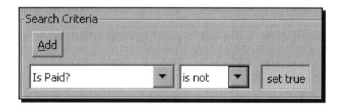

With that all set, click **Find**. You should now see a list of all unpaid invoices as shown in the following screenshot:

You can click on the **Due** column header to sort the list of invoices by due date. However, this list does not show the due amount nor is there any easy way to print this. You will have to print the screen using either a graphic tool such as GIMP or Paint or a word-processing program.

Unpost

If you created an invoice and after posting it realized that you made a mistake, then GnuCash provides you a way to undo this. Find the particular invoice and open it in the **View Invoice** window. You will see a toolbar button **Unpost**. You can click this button to undo the transactions done that you posted earlier. You will see a confirmation dialog as shown in the following screenshot:

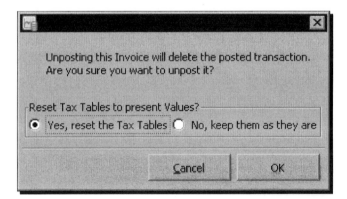

Click on **OK** and the invoice posting will be unposted.

As we saw earlier, GnuCash generates sequential invoice numbers. If I unpost an invoice, will it not break my chain of invoice numbers? It sure will. Accountants, auditors and the IRS all seem to take an undue interest in such missing invoice numbers. Here is a tip to avoid such unwanted attention. For the next invoice that you need to create, instead of creating a new invoice, edit this unposted invoice and use it. As an added bonus, in this age of green, you can feel good that you have done your bit for the day by recycling an invoice number successfully.

Pop quiz – adding customers and creating invoices

1. In the **Find Customer** dialog, what **Search Criteria** will you enter to get a list of all the customers?

    a. Company Name contains *.

    b. Company Name does not contain *.

    c. Company Name matches `regex` .(dot).

    d. Company Name does not match `regex` .(dot).

Have a go hero – finding invoices

Often you will be looking for an invoice starting from the customer. See if you can find a customer, get a listing of all their invoices and find one of the invoices from that list.

Setting the starting invoice number

Are you ready for brain surgery? We are referring to GnuCash's brain. As we saw earlier, GnuCash starts invoice numbering at 000001 and keeps incrementing it. What if you want to start the next invoice at 002501? Unfortunately GnuCash doesn't provide a User Interface for setting the starting invoice number. However, we are not the types to give up so easily. So, we are going to get it done by opening the GnuCash accounts file and directly editing the last invoice number stored there.

Time for action – setting the starting invoice number

We want the next invoice to start with the number 2501. We are going to directly edit the file where GnuCash saves all the accounts data in order to achieve this objective:

1. From the menu select **Edit | Preferences | General**.

2. In the **Files** pane, you will see the **Compress files** checkbox. Uncheck it as shown in the following screenshot:

3. Exit GnuCash using the **File | Quit** menu.

4. Most important step: Make a backup of your accounts file.

5. Use a plain text editor such as Notepad and open the GnuCash accounts file.

 Word processing programs such as OpenOffice Writer or MS Word are not suitable for this work. They store formatting data, in addition to the text. This messes up the GnuCash data file.

6. Search for the text **gncInvoice**. You should find it near the top of the file. You will see the corresponding **value** in the very next line. Change the number to **2500** as shown in the following screenshot:

```
 MACS - Notepad                                    _ □ ×
File  Edit  Format  View  Help
</slot>
<slot>
  <slot:key>counters</slot:key>
  <slot:value type="frame">
    <slot>
      <slot:key>gncCustomer</slot:key>
      <slot:value type="integer">1</slot:value>
    </slot>
    <slot>
      <slot:key>gncInvoice</slot:key>
      <slot:value type="integer">2500</slot:value>
    </slot>
    <slot>
      <slot:key>gncVendor</slot:key>
      <slot:value type="integer">1</slot:value>
    </slot>
  </slot:value>
</slot>
</book:slots>
```

7. Save and close the text editor.

8. Start GnuCash again and confirm that there are no errors at the time of starting and that all your data seems to be intact. If it is, heave a big sigh of relief. If not, verify that your back up file is intact. Heave the other big sigh of relief. The one that says, "Thank goodness. I had sense enough to take a backup." Start at step 1. Rinse and repeat until you get it right.

What just happened?

Operation successful. Patient survived, though we had to use the backup of the GnuCash brain a couple of times. However, we won't tell anyone about that little secret of ours. Especially not to our medical doctor friends.

 Please note that the number stored is that of the last invoice created. In this case, we set that as 2500. The next invoice will be created with the serial number 002501. As you can see, GnuCash will add the leading zeroes automatically.

Pop quiz – setting the starting invoice number

1. Which of the following are allowed for creating the next invoice with the next number?

   a. MACS1000.

   b. 2011-1000.

   c. 2011.1000.

   d. 1000.

Processing payment

You negotiated favorable credit terms, you invoiced promptly, you had good reports showing when the payments became due and you followed up timely and diplomatically. All of that diligence and persistence paid off. Literally. You now have the check on hand. Congratulations! Now, you are ready to go ahead and enter the transaction in the account register, right? Not really!

Time for action – when the check is on hand

As we said earlier, the **Accounts Receivable** account is special. You didn't enter the invoice amount in A/R. You simply posted the invoice and the amount magically showed up in A/R. In the same manner, we won't enter the receipt of payment in the A/R directly from the account register either.

1. When you are in the **View Invoice** tab, you will see an extra menu item under **Business** called **Pay Invoice**. You will also see the **Pay Invoice** toolbar button show up. Go ahead and click that. The **Process Payment** window will open as shown in the following screenshot:

2. Pretty much everything on the left pane is pre-filled conveniently for you. You can change the **Date**, if needed.

3. On the right hand side, you need to select a **Transfer Account**. In this case, you received a check. Go ahead and select **Checking Account** under **Current Assets**. Click on **OK**.

4. Confirm that the appropriate entries have been made in **Accounts Receivable** and the **Checking Account**.

5. Go to **Find Invoice** and find this invoice. You should see a small green check mark under the **Paid** column for this invoice.

What just happened?

Payments received by you against delivery to customers can be entered in the account register directly. However, payments received against invoices are special and GnuCash requires you to treat them with special care. This is because the matching invoices have to be marked as paid. For this reason GnuCash provides a special module called **Process Payment** for this very purpose. The three modules, namely **Customer**, **Invoice**, and **Payment Process** work in a coordinated manner to make sure that all the transactions are entered and tracked properly.

If you receive payment against an invoice, you must record it through **Payment Process**. In addition to making the register entries, this takes care of marking the invoice as paid. Do not directly enter it in the account register.

Partial payment

If you receive partial payment against an invoice, you can go ahead and process that partial payment against your invoice. For example, if your invoice is for $3000 and you receive $2000, you can enter $2000 in the **Process Payment** dialog for that invoice. GnuCash will reduce the Accounts Receivable by $2000 and keep track of the remaining balance of $1000 from that customer on that invoice.

Pop quiz – choosing an account

1. You have received a check payment from a customer against an invoice that you sent to them earlier. What are your options for entering that payment in GnuCash?

   a. Checking account register.

   b. Process payment.

   c. Process payment or checking account register.

   d. Process payment and checking account register.

Have a go hero – processing a partial payment

Process receipt of a partial payment against one of the outstanding invoices and check what happens to the A/R account and the balance amount in the invoice.

Bills and accounts payable

Accounts Payable, or **A/P** in accountants' parlance, refers to products or services purchased by your business on credit from vendors for which payment has not yet been made. This is a liability, because your business owes money to others and you will have to pay it sooner or later.

Fortunately, the A/P system follows the A/R system like a clone. There are a few differences that we will highlight. However, for the most part, you can follow processes similar to that of A/R.

Time for action – keeping track of credit purchases

We will now go through the steps of adding a vendor to our database, entering a bill and making a payment against that bill when it becomes due:

1. Prerequisites: Make sure you have an **Accounts Payable** account in your account hierarchy. Please see *Chapter 1, Getting started with GnuCash* for a tutorial on how to create an account. Typically, you will find this under **Liabilities** or under **Current Liabilities**. If you do not have one, go ahead and create a new **Accounts Payable** account. This should be of type **A/Payable** with **Liabilities** as the parent.

2. You will find all of the modules for this tutorial under the menu **Business | Vendor**. Create a New Vendor.

3. Create a new Bill and make the date of the bill of over a month ago with the payment due in 30 days. This will help you to process the payment right away (for the purposes of this tutorial), without having to wait for a month for the bill to become due. In the **Edit Bill** window, you can use the following values: **06/23/10, PC Kits, Expenses:PC Kits, 1, $349.50, $349.50**.

4. When you click **Post** you will get the confirmation dialog, **Do you really want to post the invoice?** Click on **OK**.

5. Close GnuCash and restart it. Now that we have posted a bill from a month ago, and it is due in 30 days, the **Due Bills Reminder** dialog will pop-up when GnuCash restarts. You can also launch this from the menu **Business | Due Bills Reminder** as shown in the next screenshot:

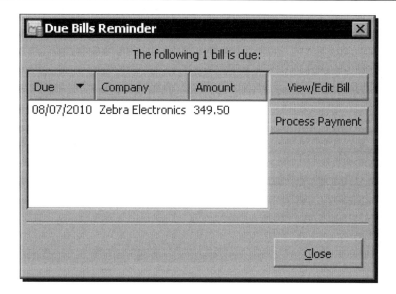

What just happened?

As we saw earlier, if you are selling to business customers, they will expect you to provide trade credit. That requires a large cash outlay to keep your business running with adequate working capital. It is possible that you have what is popularly known as "deep pockets", which is another way of saying that you are the heir to a large fortune or you are the winner of the mega millions lottery. If you are none of the above, your very survival as a start-up business depends on your ability to negotiate good trade credit terms with your vendors. If you are one of the above, why are you messing with a start-up business anyway, instead of lounging around on a Caribbean beach?

 GnuCash refers to Customer Invoice and Vendor Bill. To keep them in sync and avoid confusion, we are following the same terminology. However, both are invoices. The term 'Invoice' is commonly used in business-to-business (B2B) transactions while 'Bill' is used in consumer transactions.

As we said earlier, your ability to find reliable, quality vendors, and negotiate good trade credit terms is where your business skills can shine. However, the not-so-glamorous bookkeeping plays an important part too. Unless you have the systems in place to keep track of to whom you owe payment, what the terms are, and when they become due, you won't be able to follow them up and pay in a timely manner. At best some of your vendors will withdraw any credit terms that they gave you. At worst, your business credit rating will take a hit. Any time a vendor runs a credit check, which they always do, and you should do too, all of that bad payment history will show up and severely impact your credit terms and cash flow.

When you make payments against delivery to a vendor, it can be entered in the account register directly. However, payments made against invoices are special and GnuCash requires you to treat them with special care. This is because the matching bills have to be marked as paid. For this reason GnuCash provides a special module called **Process Payment** for this very purpose.

For quick reference, let us summarize the few ways in which the GnuCash A/P system differs from the A/R system:

1. You don't have to create **Billing Terms**. This time we will let your vendor worry about that.

2. The **Due Bills Reminder** is unique to the A/P system. We will see more about the due bills reminder in the next section.

Due bills reminder

The due bills reminder will only show you bills that are due within the "days in advance" setting in preferences. You can change this from the menu **Edit | Preferences** and select the **Business** tab. So if your setting is set to seven days, as shown in the next screenshot, it will only show bills due within seven days. A bill due within eight days will not show. If you have no bills due within that time then the dialog will not even appear as shown in the following screenshot:

 When a bill passes its reminder date, the **Due Bills Reminder** will pop up automatically as soon as you start GnuCash. As we saw in the chapter on scheduled transactions, the **Since Last Run** process will also pop up, when you start GnuCash, if there are any scheduled transactions that have to be brought to your attention. You can attend to them, one by one, or cancel or close them and get to them through the appropriate menu items at your convenience.

Pop quiz – keeping track of credit purchases

1. You entered a bill and posted it by mistake. How will you rectify this error?

    a. Unpost

    b. Unpay

    c. Unbill

    d. Undo

Have a go hero – keeping track of credit purchases

Make a payment well in advance before the due date to take advantage of the discount offered by the vendor. However, please note that the system will not calculate the discount automatically.

Summary

We learned a lot in this chapter about keeping track of payments when we sell to our customers on credit as well as when we make purchases on credit.

Specifically, we covered:

- Creating customers and invoices: We learned how to add new customers to our business database, how to create invoices, how to keep track of payments due, as well as how to process payments when we receive them.

- Creating vendors and entering bills: We saw how to add vendors to our database as well as how to enter bills as and when we receive them.

- Reports of invoices and bills: We also saw how to create reports that will help us to follow up on payments due to us as well as payments we owe.

- Setting the starting invoice number: Even though GnuCash doesn't provide a means for us to set the starting invoice number, we saw how that can be done by editing the GnuCash accounts file directly.

We also discussed how to recover from entries made in error or incorrectly.

Now that we've learned about handling credit sales and credit purchases, which are the two foundations of business accounting, we're ready to go into planning to reach your business goals with the help of a budget – which is the topic of the next chapter.

7

Budget: Trip Planner for your Business

"Most owners seem to feel that learning how to budget is more frustrating than just hoping the numbers will all work out, if only they sell enough widgets." – extracted from a web article offering tips for small business owners.

You were telling me about this great Trip Planning website, which lets you select the following options for a road trip once you select the origin and destination anywhere in US or Canada:

- ◆ Select your route preferences
  - ❑ Avoid tolls
  - ❑ Favor scenic roads
- ◆ Select facilities
  - ❑ Lodging quality
  - ❑ Camping
  - ❑ National parks
  - ❑ Travel stops: gas, food, restrooms

Once you have made the selections, they produce a personal trip itinerary for you. They mark out roads with steep grades and roads with HOV restrictions. They calculate distance in miles and budgeted time for each leg. As an added bonus, they throw in tips on how to keep your pet happy, safe, and comfortable on the trip. That was for a trip involving a week of your time, costing a couple of thousand dollars. The worst consequence of exceeding your budgeted time on the scenic road? Less time at the lake. And you swore that you were never going to turn the key in the ignition again without such a Trip Planner.

Now you are telling me that you don't have a **budget** for your business, with revenue in six figures that could make or break your career and change your life? Yes, you told me that every time you made an attempt to get a budget going, the steps were so confusing and in accountant's jargon that you just couldn't get yourself to begin to touch that with a ten foot pole. We are here to change that. We understand the accountants' language. We even talk to them in their language.

In this chapter we shall cover the following:

◆ Budget: Tutorial on creating budgets and reporting budget vs. actual.

◆ Employees and payroll: GnuCash doesn't have a payroll module. However, we will show how to enter payroll data for employees. We will also cover employee expense voucher processing.

◆ Depreciation: We will recommend ways of setting up accounts for depreciation and making entries.

◆ Paying yourself (also known as owner's draw): We will walk through the steps involved in cash withdrawals by the owner.

So let's get on with it...

Budget

There are two main reasons why you may want to create budgets. As you so readily agreed with us earlier, you want a trip planner for your business. You will use this on a day-to-day basis to run your business and make decisions. The second reason is if you are seeking outside finance for your business from a bank, investor, or other lender. They will require you to submit your business plan along with projected financials.

Time for action – creating a budget for your business

You are going to create a budget for the next three months to serve as a guide for your operations. Typically, investors, banks and other lenders will need financial projections for a longer period. As a minimum they will need one year projections which may go up to 3 to 5 years in many cases.

1. From the menu select **Actions | Budget | New Budget**. A new budget screen will open.

2. Click on the **Options** toolbar button. The **Budget Options** dialog will open. For this tutorial, we are going to select a beginning date of three months back. This is only for the purposes of this tutorial and will allow us to quickly run Budget vs. Actual reports.

3. In the **Budget Period** pane, change the **beginning on** date to a date three months ago. Change the **Number of Periods** to **3**. Type in the **Budget Name MACS Jun-Aug Budget** as shown in the following screenshot and click on **OK**.

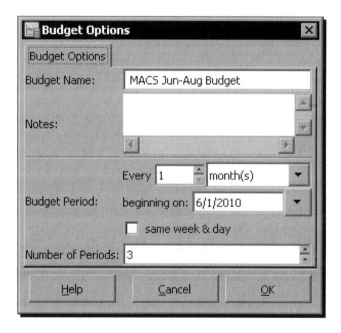

4. The budget screen will show a list of accounts with a column for each month. The date shown in the title of each column is the beginning of that budget period.

5. Now enter the budget values by simply clicking on the cell and entering the amount as shown in the following screenshot.

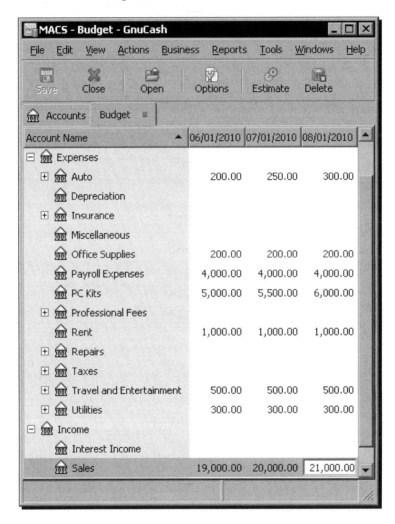

Using the Tab key while entering budget amounts

Don't use the *Tab* key. The value entered in the previous field seems to vanish into thin air if you use the *Tab* key. Instead use the *Enter* key and the mouse.

6. When you are done entering all the values, don't forget to save changes.

7. Now that the budget has been created, you are ready to run the reports. From the menu select **Reports | Budget | Budget Report**.

8. In the **Options** dialog select all the **Income** and **Expenses** accounts in the **Accounts** tab. Check **Show Difference** in the **Display** tab and click **OK** to see the report as shown in the following screenshot:

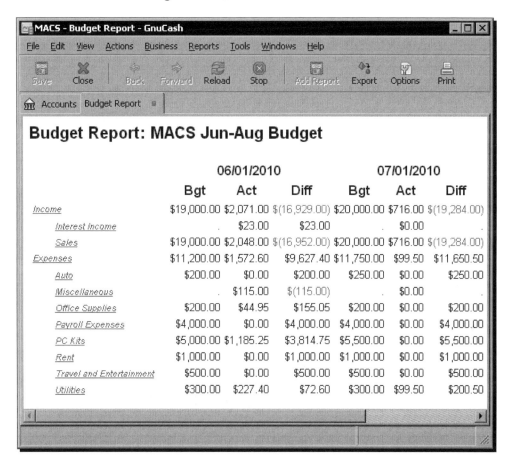

We are going to create the Cash Flow Budget in a spreadsheet. Go ahead and copy the data from the preceding report to the spreadsheet of your choice, following the steps we outlined in *Chapter 3, Fun and Eye-opening part - Reports and charts* in the *Exporting Reports* section. Put in additional rows and formulas along the lines shown below. We are showing the cashflow for a six month period in the following screenshot to make it easier for you to see some of the trends and business challenges more clearly:

	A	B	C	D	E	F	G
1	Cash Flow Budget: MACS Mar-Aug 2010						
2		Mar	Apr	May	Jun	Jul	Aug
3	Sales	$17,500	$18,000	$18,500	$19,000	$20,000	$21,000
4							
5	Checking A/C Opening Bal.	$9,000	$7,950	$7,450	$7,200	$7,200	$7,950
6	Interest Income	$200	$200	$200	$200	$200	$200
7	Sales collection	$17,000	$17,500	$18,000	$18,500	$19,000	$20,000
8	Total Income	$17,200	$18,000	$18,500	$19,000	$20,000	$21,000
9	Auto	$200	$225	$250	$275	$300	$325
10	Depreciation	$500	$500	$500	$500	$500	$500
11	Insurance	$300	$300	$300	$300	$300	$300
12	Interest Paid	$650	$625	$600	$575	$550	$525
13	Miscellaneous	$500	$500	$500	$500	$500	$500
14	Office Supplies	$200	$200	$200	$200	$200	$200
15	Payroll Expenses	$4,000	$4,000	$4,000	$4,000	$4,000	$4,000
16	PC Kits	$4,750	$5,000	$5,250	$5,500	$5,750	$6,000
17	Rent	$1,000	$1,000	$1,000	$1,000	$1,000	$1,000
18	Repairs	$200	$200	$200	$200	$200	$200
19	Taxes	$500	$500	$500	$500	$500	$500
20	Travel and Entertainment	$500	$475	$450	$425	$400	$375
21	Utilities	$300	$300	$300	$300	$300	$300
22	TotalExpenses	$13,600	$13,825	$14,050	$14,275	$14,500	$14,725
23	Loan Repayment	$150	$175	$200	$225	$250	$275
24	Owner's Draw	$5,000	$5,000	$5,000	$5,000	$5,000	$5,000
25	Checking A/C Closing Bal.	$7,950	$7,450	$7,200	$7,200	$7,950	$9,450
26							
27	Accounts Receivable	$30,000	$30,000	$30,000	$30,000	$30,000	$30,000
28	Accounts Payable	$10,000	$10,500	$11,000	$11,500	$12,000	$12,500
29	Bank Loan	$19,850	$19,675	$19,475	$19,250	$19,000	$18,725

What just happened?

What if you had tomorrow's news... TODAY? His name is Gary Hobson. He gets tomorrow's newspaper today. He doesn't know how. He doesn't know why. All he knows is when the early edition hits his doorstep, he has twenty-four hours to set things right. You may recall that in the TV series early edition, Kyle Chandler who plays the role of Gary Hobson uses this knowledge to prevent terrible events each day.

What if we told you that you can get tomorrow's news for your business today? You can prevent terrible events from happening to your business. You can get tomorrow's sales, expenses, and cash flow in the form of a budget. Mistakes are far less costly when made on paper than with actual dollars.

 Sometimes budgets are referred to as projections. For example, banks, investors, and lenders will ask for a business plan with profit and loss, balance sheet, and cash flow projections. Other times, these are called forecasts, especially when referring to sales forecasts. Regardless of whether we call them budgets, projections or forecasts, we are referring to the future. Unlike the rest of bookkeeping, which is concerned with the past, budgeting is one area, which tries to look in the crystal ball, and attempts to see what the future might look like, or what you are committing to make it look like.

If you are running a business without a budget, I am sure there are times when the thought flashes through your mind, "I wish I had known that earlier." Your budget is the crystal ball that enables you to see the future, and do something about it. Generally, when you complete a budget, you will have a number of revelations. For example, you might find that your cash flow is going into negative territory in the third month. The budget allows you to perceive problems before they occur and alter your plans to prevent those problems.

Start with just three budgets

While there are many different budgets you can create, we recommend just three to serve as your Trip Planner – a sales forecast, an expense budget, and a cash flow projection that are detailed in the following sections. Of these, you can do your sales forecast and expense budget in GnuCash. However, for the cash flow projection, you will start in GnuCash but export it to a spreadsheet and refine it there.

Sales forecast

Sales are the cornerstone of a budget. It is crucial to estimate anticipated sales as accurately as possible. Base estimates on actual past sales figures. Once you target sales, you can calculate the related expenses necessary to achieve your goals.

Look at what sales you achieved last year, and extrapolate from that. You can add to that based on additional lead generation and sales campaigns that you might have identified. New business owners without this kind of history may try to determine how much business their competitors seem to be able to do, and use that as a guide. Try to make the forecast realistic. If you shoot for an unrealistic target, you can easily spend excessive amounts in promotional expenses and the sales may not materialize.

Expense budget

When you used to pay cash for expenses, life was simple. Perhaps you never did and perhaps you don't agree with me. Put that aside for a moment and stay with me here. It was easy to know when you were running out of money to spend. The wad of currency in your wallet got thin and eventually it ran out altogether. This is the age of plastic. With automatic debits, recurring payments, and electronic bill pay, you could easily be spending money you don't have. That seemed to ring a bell? Great! Now that I have your undivided attention, let us go ahead and review the **expense budget** that we created earlier.

Don't forget to add the cost of lead generation and the sales campaign costs that were assumed while creating the sales forecast. Also, you might want to provide for an estimated percentage overall inflation rate for the year.

Cash flow projection

With the same **sales forecast** and the same expense budget, you can go from a comfortable cash position at one end of the spectrum to going bankrupt at the other end of the spectrum. Let us say, for example, that your sales team is able to exceed their quota by extending 90 days credit. However, you are not able to get more than 15 days credit from your key vendors. This means you will have to find enough cash to cover about 75 days worth of A/R. This is the reason why the author of the web article we quoted earlier was skeptical of the fact that selling enough widgets is a substitute for a budget.

In the preceding example, the cash situation is so obvious that you don't need a **cash flow** projection to know that you are going to fall short. However, in other situations it may not be so obvious that you are going to fall short. For example, if you are offering a variety of credit terms to different customers and different products. Also, in addition to sales and expenses you will have to take into account other cash flow items such as loan repayments, owner's draw, and so on. Even more importantly, it may not be obvious what actions need to be taken to improve the cash flow. In short, you need a cash flow projection.

We recommend that you create the sales forecast and expenses budgets in GnuCash, create a report, and paste it into a spreadsheet such as OpenOffice Calc or MS Excel for creating your cash flow projection. There are several advantages to doing this in a spreadsheet:

1. You can rearrange the rows, to your convenience, like we did in the tutorial earlier.
2. You can put in formulas.
3. You can do what-If analysis or simulation by making copies of this spreadsheet.

You might ask, "Why at all create my budgets in GnuCash, if I am going to export it into a spreadsheet anyway." The main advantages to creating the budget in GnuCash are the ability to estimate based on past period actuals and the ability to create the budget vs. actual reports. The Diff column in the report helps you to focus on the few accounts requiring your attention, when you have a large number of accounts.

You can take cash flow management steps to ensure that the gaps are closed, or at least narrowed, when they are predicted early. These steps might include lowering your investment in accounts receivable or inventory, or looking to outside sources of cash, such as a short-term loan, to fill the cash flow gaps.

Estimating based on previous period actuals

If you have past transactions recorded in GnuCash, the easy way to create your first draft is to let GnuCash estimate the budget values by looking at those transactions. First, open a budget or create a new one. Select one of the accounts for which you want GnuCash to estimate. Then click on the **Estimate** toolbar button. In the **Estimate Budget Values** dialog, select the **Start Date**. GnuCash will start at that date and look forward for the duration of your budget. For example, if you are making an annual budget, and you select Jan. 1, 2010 as the Start Date, GnuCash will look at all the transactions in that account from Jan. 1, 2010 through Dec. 31, 2010. Here is a screenshot:

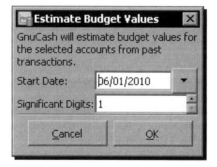

 There is no specific way to select multiple accounts for doing this estimation. You have to select one account at a time and create the estimates.

Financial projections for investors and lenders

As part of a business plan, a budget can help convince a loan officer that you know your business and have anticipated its needs.

In addition to the three budgets that you created for your own internal control needs, investors and lenders might ask for two more budgets, namely the Balance Sheet and the Income Statement (also known as the Profit & Loss statement or P&L). GnuCash has built-in reports for these two. Therefore, you can generate these two reports from an existing budget.

How to create a business plan?

Once you have created your budgets, you have the data required to create a Business Plan. You can consider free business plan templates with instructions available from **SCORE** (www.score.org). SCORE is a resource partner with the U.S. Small Business Administration (SBA).

Budget balance sheet

The first one is the projected balance sheet:

1. From the menu select **Reports | Budget | Budget Balance Sheet**.

2. Click on the **Options** toolbar button.

3. In the **Display** tab, uncheck **Include accounts with zero total balances** and check **Omit zero balance figures**. This will make sure that zero balance accounts and figures are suppressed so that you won't be distracted by those.

4. In the **General** tab uncheck **Single Column Balance Sheet**. This will create the balance sheet in the traditional two column format with Assets in one column and Liabilities in another column.

5. In the same **General** tab make sure the budget you earlier created is shown selected in the **Budget** dropdown list. If not, select it. Click on **OK**.

You should see a two-column balance sheet with the **Total Assets** on the left-hand side and the **Total Liabilities & Equity** on the right-hand side, nicely balanced.

Budget income statement

The other report that investors, banks, and other lenders ask for is a projected income statement also known as the **Profit & Loss (P&L)** Statement.

1. From the menu select, **Reports | Budget | Budget Income Statement**.

2. Click on the **Options** toolbar button.

3. In the **Display** tab, uncheck **Include accounts with zero total balances** and check **Omit zero balance figures**.

4. In the **General** tab make sure the budget you earlier created is shown selected in the **Budget** dropdown list. If not, select it. Click on **OK**.

You should see the projected income statement with **Total Revenue** on top, **Total Expenses** at the bottom, and the net income for the selected period below that. The **Budget Profit & Loss** report creates the same report.

Budget revision

Remember that a budget is a living document. Market conditions may change, you might land some unexpected new customers, or you may develop a new product or service that becomes a hit. Don't abandon your budget and start shooting from the hip. Revise your budget, and stick to the new budget you've developed. It is not prudent (that word again!) to keep revising your budget for every little change. Typically, you need to consider a budget revision, under the following conditions:

◆ There has been a drastic change in the direction of the business as a result of any of the reasons that we outlined previously.

◆ In the case of an annual budget, if there have been a number of small changes, many business people find it convenient to make a mid-year budget revision.

Pop quiz – creating a new budget

1. Which menu allows you to create a new budget?

    a. **Business | New | New Budget**

    b. **Reports | Budget | New Budget**

    c. **File | New | New Budget**

    d. **Actions | Budget | New Budget**

2. What selections will you make in the **Budget Options** dialog to create a quarterly budget?

    a. Select **year(s)** and **4 times**

    b. Select **Every 3 month(s)**

    c. Select **Every 13 week(s)**

    d. Select **Every 91 day(s)**

Have a go hero – understanding cash flow budgets

In A Study in Scarlet, Sherlock Holmes says, "From a drop of water a logician could infer the possibility of an Atlantic or a Niagara without having seen or heard of one or the other." I give you more than a drop of water. I give you an entire cash flow budget in the tutorial above in a spreadsheet. Study that spreadsheet carefully. Let us see whether you are able to identify the business challenges the owner of MACS has taken on during the 6-month period. Go ahead and hide the following list and jot down your thoughts on a piece of paper or a digital device. You can then compare it with our list:

- Increase sales from 17K per month to 21K per month
- Maintain the average A/R at 30K, even while increasing sales
- Acknowledging that more sales will mean more auto expenses
- Make an effort to reduce Travel & Entertainment expenses even while trying to increase sales
- Commit to keep the loan repayment up even under tight cash flow conditions

Employees and payroll

Payroll is a financial record of salary and benefits provided to an employee. This is one of the more complex transactions in terms of accounting, simply because there are many different deductions and matching payments to be made to various tax authorities and health insurance and other vendors.

Payroll is an expense. Deductions may have to be stored in a short term liability account. This is useful for things such as taxes, which may be paid to the government at a different time from paying employee salaries.

Time for action – making payroll entries in GnuCash

We are going to enter the payroll accounting entries for one employee with appropriate deductions for federal and state income tax and FICA tax:

1. We have created a spreadsheet of the calculations that we are going to use in making the payroll entries. Take a moment to study the following screenshot:

	A	B
1	MACS Payroll Calculation	
2	Gross pay	$4,000.00
3	Add: FICA Tax Company Contribution	$306.00
4	Total Cost of Employee	$4,306.00
5		
6	Less: Federal Income Tax	$480.00
7	Less: State Income Tax	$200.00
8	Less: FICA Tax Employee Contribution	$306.00
9	Total deductions	$986.00
10	Net pay = Gross pay – Deductions	$3,014.00

2. Create the expense accounts: You need two expense accounts – one **Payroll Expenses** for gross pay and another **Employer FICA Tax** for the company contribution to FICA tax.

3. Create the liability accounts: The tax amounts deducted from the employee's gross pay are owed to the appropriate government agencies. We need to create liability accounts to hold these amounts until they are due. Go ahead and create three accounts, **Federal Income Tax**, **VA Income Tax**, and **FICA Tax** of **Account Type Liability** with **Liabilities** as the **Parent Account** as shown in the following screenshot:

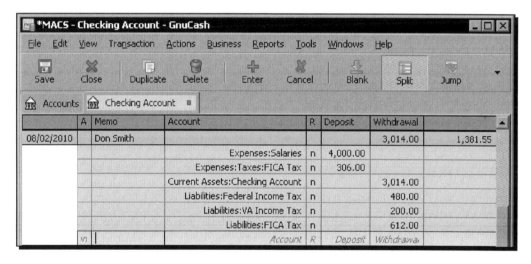

What just happened?

Monthly salaried employees are typically hired with a gross pay. However, when it comes to making payment, there will be several deductions. When you record payroll in GnuCash, it is done with a single split transaction. This split transaction will populate the appropriate expense and liability accounts. If you want to look up any of the payroll details for a particular employee, at any time, you can simply open and view the split transaction.

Net pay

For example, most employees in the US will typically have the following deductions:

- Federal income tax
- State income tax
- FICA tax

There will be other deductions such as county or local taxes, separate deductions for health, dental, and vision insurance, 401(k) or other retirement plan contributions and so on. The net pay thus calculated becomes payable to the employee and it becomes an expense to the business.

Liability accounts

The business owes these deducted amounts to the respective tax authorities. In addition, the bookkeeping system must keep track of company contribution to social security tax, Medicare tax, health insurance, 401(k), and so on. These are also employee-related expenses to the business. However, these payments are not made at the same time as the payroll. So, these amounts must be accumulated in respective liability accounts so that the correct amounts can be paid, when they become due.

Calculation spreadsheet

As we said, GnuCash doesn't have an integrated payroll module. Any calculation of deductions and company contributions must be made outside of GnuCash. This is the reason why we used a payroll calculation spreadsheet in the above tutorial. The spreadsheet can have all the formulas and lookup tables set up so that you can enter the gross salary in one cell and get all the computed values ready to be posted into GnuCash.

Split transaction map

The following split transaction map covers just the three taxes listed previously, of which the federal and state income taxes are entirely payable by the employee, while the FICA tax has an employee contribution and an equal company contribution.

Account	Increase	Decrease
CurrentAssets:Checking		Net Salary
Expenses:Salaries	Gross Salary	
Liabilities:Federal Income Tax		Federal Income Tax
Liabilities:VA Income Tax		VA Income Tax
Liabilities:FICA Tax		Employee FICA Tax
Expenses:FICA Tax	Company FICA Tax	
Liabilities:FICA Tax		Company FICA Tax

Payroll FAQ

Here is a list of frequently asked questions about the payroll process and our answers:

- Q: If I use a single Payroll account for all employees, how will I see per employee information?
    - A: Use reports to view information for each employee.
- Q: I have a number of employees. Creating this complex payroll entry seems to be a lot of work.
    - A: If you are thinking, "Oh boy, am I going to be doing all of that for each payroll period for each employee?" Relax. If you recall, we covered the **Duplicate Transaction** feature in the section *A feeling of déjà vu* in *Chapter 2, Transactions – the Lifeblood of a Business*. Each time you need to create a new transaction, you can take the payroll transaction you created and duplicate it. Then you can change the description and amounts and save it.
- Q: How do I print payroll checks?
    - A: When making the Payroll entry, enter only the employee name in the **Description** field. If you decide to use GnuCash's check printing capabilities, the check will automatically be made out to the employee name correctly. If you want to record other information in the transaction besides the employee name, use the **Notes** field. You can view this **Notes** field in the account register in double-line mode as explained in *Chapter 2, Transactions – the Lifeblood of a Business*; in the *Changing the register views* section.

Employee and expense voucher

When employees spend their own money on behalf of the business, or they draw a cash advance from the business and need to account for expenses incurred, or they use a company card for business expenses, they need to submit an **expense voucher** to account for the amounts.

Under the **Business** menu you will find the **Employee** menu item with the **Employee**, **Expense Voucher**, and **Process Payment** modules.

You will find that these modules follow the same process as we covered in detail under Customer Invoices and Vendor Bills. You can follow the same process for Expense Vouchers as we followed for Invoices in the *Invoices and Accounts Receivable* section of *Chapter 6, Business Mantra: Buy Now, Pay Later.*

Pop quiz – calculating payroll

1. At the time of paying an employee, the amount deducted from gross pay towards employee's contribution to FICA Tax will be accounted as:

    a. An expense

    b. A liability of the business to be paid to the government later

    c. An asset of the company

    d. A liability of the employee to be paid to the government later

2. The Federal Income Tax account to hold the amount deducted from employees' salary will be of what Account Type and with what Parent Account:

    a. Account Type "Asset" and Parent Account "Assets".

    b. Account Type "Liability" and Parent Account "Liabilities".

    c. Account Type "Expense" and Parent Account "Expenses".

    d. Account Type "Income" and Parent Account "Income".

Have a go hero – adding more deductions to payroll

Create a payroll transaction showing a deduction for health insurance premium as well.

Depreciation

When you buy capital assets such as computers, office equipment, cars, office furniture, and appliances, the tax laws may not allow you to write off all of the cost as business expense right away against business income. However, you are allowed to write them off over a period of time. This monthly expense write-off is known as **depreciation**.

Time for action – making depreciation entries for assets

You bought a computer with a high speed processor, extra memory, and disk space, for $3000, to serve as your small business server. Let us walk through how you will account for the purchase of the capital asset initially and how you will account for the depreciation expense each month:

1. Create a new account called **Office Equipment** with **Account Type** as **Asset** and **Parent Account** as **Assets**.

2. On the date of purchase make an entry showing an **Increase** of $3000 in the **Office Equipment** account and select the **Checking Account** in the **Transfer** column.

3. We are going to apply a straight-line method of $50 depreciation per month over the 60 month period. This is just an example. More details follow in this section about what depreciation rates are allowed by tax laws. On the last day of the month, create a transaction in the **Expenses:Depreciation** account showing an expense of $50 and select the **Office Equipment** account as the **Transfer** account as shown in the following screenshot:

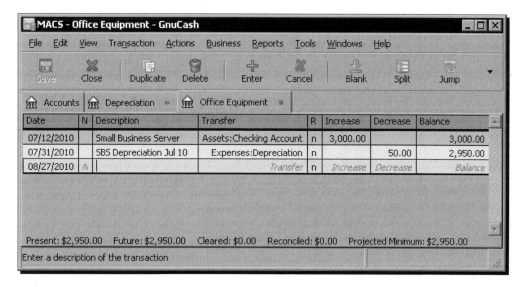

What just happened?

By charging 1/60 of the capital cost each month as depreciation, at the end of the 60 month period, you would have written off the entire value of the capital asset.

Handling repetitive transactions easily

You may find it convenient to set up a scheduled transaction for creating a monthly depreciation entry for each asset.

Typically the **Internal Revenue Service (IRS)** in US allows you to write off capital assets over the following period:

- Some manufacturing tools: 3 years.

- Computers, office equipment, cars, and construction equipment: 5 years.

- Office furniture and appliances: 7 years.

- Commercial buildings: 39 years.

The above are just broad indications for you to get the overall picture. IRS also allows you to choose either a straight line or a declining balance method of depreciation. In the straight-line method the cost of the asset is depreciated over the life of the asset in equal amounts per year as shown in the following screenshot:

Cost of the asset: $4000		Life of the asset: 4 Years	
Year	Book value = Prev. Yr Book value - Depreciation	Depreciation = Cost value * 0.25	Cumulative Depreciation
1	$4,000	$1,000	$1,000
2	$3,000	$1,000	$2,000
3	$2,000	$1,000	$3,000
4	$1,000	$1,000	$4,000

Straight Line Depreciation Method

Depreciation = Cost value * 0.25

In the declining value method, the depreciation is a fixed percentage of the book value. The book value starts as the cost of the asset in the first year. In subsequent years, the book value is the previous year's book value less depreciation for that year. The following screenshot shows the same asset seen in the earlier example, if we apply the declining value method of depreciation:

Cost of the asset: $4000		Life of the asset: 4 Years	
Year	Book value = Prev. Yr Book value - Depreciation	Depreciation = Book value * 0.5	Cumulative Depreciation
1	$4,000	$2,000	$2,000
2	$2,000	$1,000	$3,000
3	$1,000	$500	$3,500
4	$500	$250	$3,750

Declining Balance Depreciation Method

■ Depreciation = Book value * 0.5

Under certain conditions IRS allows you to deduct the entire cost of an asset in the year you acquire the asset and start using it for business. There are also accelerated depreciation methods that allow more depreciation in the initial years and progressively less later. For new assets put into use in 2009, the US Congress has approved special 50% bonus depreciation. Therefore, you should consult an accountant or a tax consultant to find out what are the best options for your specific situation.

Land, though a capital asset, is typically not allowed to be depreciated.

> **You can capitalize all the associated costs**
>
> In addition to the purchase of the asset itself, any costs associated with getting the asset into a condition so that you can use it should be capitalized. For example, if you buy a piece of equipment, its shipping costs, installation costs, and training of your staff to operate the machine, all these costs can be included in the cost of the equipment.

Pop quiz – charging depreciation on capital assets

1. What type of account is a depreciation account?

    a. An asset account.

    b. A liability account.

    c. An expense account.

Have a go hero – applying a different depreciation method

The declining balance method is another form of depreciation allowed, instead of the straight-line method. Create a schedule of depreciation to be applied, to the same asset in our earlier example, using the declining balance method.

Owner's drawing

The Owner's **Drawing Account** is sometimes known as either the Personal Account, the Withdrawal Account, the Directors Account, or the Partners Account. This type of an account is nothing but a convenient way to distribute business profits to the owner or partners. US tax laws tend to collect income tax from small business owners based on the profits made before accounting for the owner's salary. Any salary drawn by the owner cannot be treated as an expense to the business for the purposes of calculating taxable profits. Therefore, owner's draw is a popular form of paying the owner or partners without causing tax complications.

If, instead you choose to pay the owner or partners a salary, you will have the following disadvantages:

* You have to exclude this from other employee's salaries, when calculating tax-deductible business expenses.

* You will not have the flexibility of varying the owner's drawing from month-to-month depending on the profitability of the business.

Whether to pay salary or owner's draw as well as the tax treatment depends on what type of corporation your business is and other factors. What we are showing here is an example. You should seek the advice of an accountant or a tax consultant regarding your specific situation.

Time for action – entering owner's draw in your books

We are going to look at one example where the owner has decided to have an owner's draw of $10,000.

1. Make sure you have a **Drawing Account**. If not, create one. This should be of type **Equity** and have Equity as the **Parent Account**.

2. On the last date of the month, write a check from the business account to your personal account and create an entry in the **Drawing Account**, as shown in the following screenshot, with the **Transfer** account being the **Checking Account** and the amount being **$10,000**.

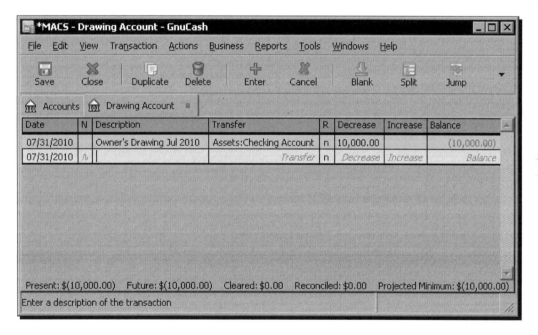

What just happened?

One prudent approach to paying the owner is a monthly fixed sum as owner's draw to cover the owner's personal expenses. At the end of the year, depending on how well the business has done and the cash position, the owner can draw an annual bonus. This also helps you to visualize the benefits of running your business. How? If you make a monthly withdrawal that is roughly equivalent to what you can earn as a salaried employee, then you can readily see what is the extra benefit that you get by way of an annual bonus by putting in all those 80 hour weeks, running your own business.

If you don't follow the system outlined by us above, there are a few ways in which draws can happen:

- ◆ You write a check to "cash" with no memo
- ◆ You use your business debit card for personal use
- ◆ You use your business ATM card to withdraw funds from the bank for personal use
- ◆ You initiate bank cash transfers from your business to your personal account.
- ◆ You write a check from your business to pay a personal expense.

If you draw cash through any of these means, make sure you enter them in the accounts with a matching increase in the Drawing account.

Talking about a prudent approach, you will owe at least two large chunks of taxes from the owner's draw. There may be others. You need to set aside 15.3% self employment tax every time you draw some amount from the business. This self employment tax is nothing but the 7.65% FICA tax that we saw earlier in the payroll section. Except that now you are paying the employee contribution as well as the company contribution and so it has got doubled. You will also owe estimated income tax that is payable each quarter. So, you will do well to keep these amounts aside before planning to spend the money.

Pop quiz – setting up a Drawing account

1. What type of account is a Drawing account?
   a. Expense account
   b. Income account
   c. Liability account
   d. Asset account
   e. Equity account

Have a go hero – setting up Drawing accounts for a partnership

Let us say that you have a partnership account with two partners. Set up two Drawing accounts to show the withdrawal of the two partners separately. Please follow the same method as we outlined for creating a drawing account for a sole owner, except create two of those. Also, use each of the partner's names in the account name to clearly identify them. This way each partner's drawing can be tracked separately.

Summary

We covered budgets and several business-specific bookkeeping topics in this chapter.

Specifically, we covered:

- ◆ Budgets: We noted that budgets are called forecasts or projections at times. We looked at why budgets are needed, how to create them, and how to create reports showing budget vs. actual comparison.

- ◆ Employees and Payroll: Payroll accounting is complex because of the many deductions and the company's contributions. We saw how to make it easier to create them and how to use the Duplicate Transaction capability to reuse them.

- ◆ Depreciation: Tax law allows capital purchases such as office machines and furniture to be written off over a period of time. We saw how to account for the allowed monthly depreciation.

- ◆ Owner's draw: US tax law doesn't allow owners to draw a salary as a business expense. So, the way for the owners to pay themselves is through owner's draw. We showed how to account for that and to make sure that self employment tax is provided for as well.

Now that we've covered budgets and other business topics it is time to take a look at how to account for tax, which is the topic of the next chapter.

8
Making Tax Times Less Stressful

"In 1862, in order to support the Civil War effort, Congress enacted the nation's first income tax law. It was a forerunner of our modern income tax in that it was based on the principles of graduated or progressive taxation and of withholding income at the source." – history of the income tax in the United States.

You may not jump for joy but, at least, it may make you feel somewhat better to know that taxes on income and sales are not of recent origin and there is plenty of evidence to show that they existed in some form or the other even in ancient times.

According to the literature of the Sangam period (circa 200 BC to 200 AD), the kings of southern India had an eight member council to administer the kingdom that included an accountant and a treasurer. The revenue of the state was from sources like customs, tolls, and land tax. For special projects, such as the raising of the banks of the river Cauvery by the Chola kings, farmers had the option of sending one man per joint family to work on the project.

In ancient times, small business owners went by different names. They were called traders and artisans. They maintained their accounts in dried palm leaf manuscripts. They did the math either mentally or using an abacus. Now that we have got somewhat better equipment, let us see how we can make tax times less stressful:

- ◆ First we are going to see how to map GnuCash accounts to income tax schedules.
- ◆ Next we will see how to create reports that will align with the way the **Internal Revenue Service (IRS)** wants you to report income and expenses. Also, you will learn how to generate a data file that you can import into many tax filing applications.
- ◆ Then we will move on to setting up sales tax rate tables.

- Finally we will see how to apply the appropriate sales tax rates to your invoices and generate a report to show the amount of sales tax owed.

So let's see how we can better prepare for tax time.

GnuCash currently supports only US business types for income tax

The GnuCash income tax module that we will see in this chapter covers only the following US business types:

- Individuals who file US Internal Revenue Service (IRS) Form 1040 for Profit and Loss from Business
- Partnerships who file US IRS Form 1065
- Corporations who file US IRS Form 1120
- S Corporations who file US IRS Form 1120S

From these, we will be using the example of individuals who file Form 1040. This form will typically be used by self-employed persons as well as sole proprietors of businesses. Within this Form 1040, the specific section that we will cover in more detail is Schedule C. Schedule C covers the income of the business for the tax year and deductible expenses as well as the resulting net profit or loss of the business.

At present, only US business types are supported in GnuCash. For other countries, you can export the numbers to a spreadsheet and aggregate the numbers to match the tax categories and line items, as needed.

Setting up income tax related accounts

Employed people may not want to acknowledge it, but they are certainly having a cushy time- at tax time. For them, the employer deducts tax at the source every month and gives the IRS the form named W-2 at tax time. Once a year they file their tax return, attach this form W-2, and claim any refund or pay the small amount of tax that may be due, as the case may be.

As a small business owner, on the other hand, you have to worry about tax matters that weren't your problem when you worked for someone else. For starters, you are responsible for twice as much FICA taxes as you paid when you were employed. You need to make tax payments to the government quarterly. So you need to keep track throughout the year of how much you have earned and what you have paid to the government. In short, you need a good bookkeeping system, such as GnuCash.

Time for action – mapping GnuCash accounts to tax schedules

You set up the account hierarchy for your business based on how you want to manage and control your business on a day-to-day basis. However, when it is the time to make tax payments, which is now every quarter, you need to regroup your accounts in the way IRS wants them reported. We are going to look at how to do that using the tax features of GnuCash.

1. From the menu select **Edit | Tax Report Options**. The **Income Tax Identity** window will pop up. Enter the name of your business and in the **Type** field, select the business entity type with the matching US tax form that you file as shown in the following screenshot:

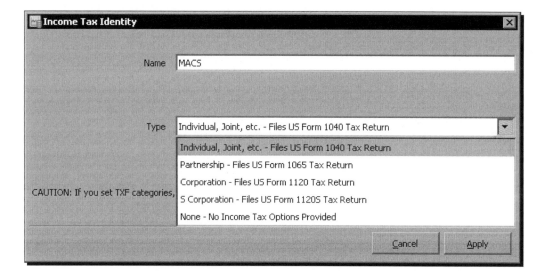

2. Once you click **Apply**, you should be in the **Income Tax Information** window. In the **Accounts** pane, **Expenses** will be selected by default.

3. Open the **Expenses** account tree to see the individual accounts. Select **Professional Fees** and then click on the **Select Subaccounts** button. All of its subaccounts will be selected. The **Tax Related** checkbox should be already checked by default. If not, check it.

4. The **TXF Categories** list on the right will become enabled. Scroll down to see all the Income Tax return Form 1040 Schedule C (Profit or Loss From Business for a Sole Proprietorship) line items. Click on **Sched C Legal and professional fees**. In the gray box at the bottom you should see a brief description of this item as well as that this is currently line item 17 in the income tax form Schedule C as shown in the following screenshot:

Many of the tax preparation software have support for a standard data format known as the **Tax Exchange Format (TXF)**. These files have a file extension .txf. As TXF is an accepted standard for saving tax data in financial software, most income tax preparation software will import TXF files.

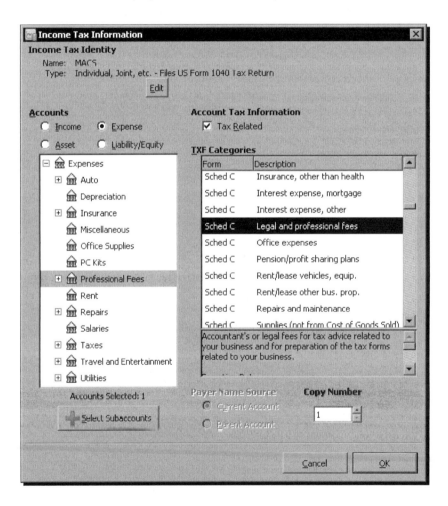

5. Click **OK** to complete the mapping of this account. Go ahead and map other accounts in the same way.

6. Back in the GnuCash main window (also known as the Accounts Tree window) click on the down arrow on the column name line. Select **Tax Info** from the list. You should now see an additional column in the Account Tree showing the Schedule C mappings for each account as shown in the following screenshot:

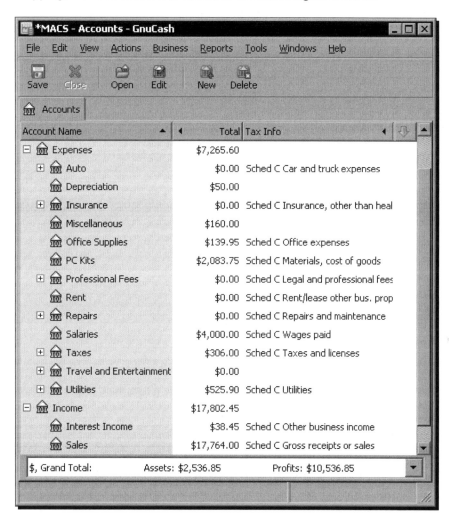

What just happened?

How does a small business in the US calculate income tax? Someone who is totally unfamiliar with the US **Internal Revenue Service (IRS)** might say something like, "Well, run the Income Statement also known as the **Profit & Loss (P&L) Statement**, attach it to your tax return, and pay tax on whatever is the net income for the year." Someone like a Martian who just landed on earth. A Martian who is looking for trouble.

> We are not giving you tax advice. We are trying to get you up to speed with using GnuCash for your business accounting. The examples we provide are intended to be illustrative. Regarding what type of business entity is suitable for your business, which form and schedules to use for your tax returns, and what specific items will go into which line item in the schedule, you should seek the advice of an accountant or a tax consultant.

This brings us to a point where we cannot help but say something in defense of the IRS. Ok, give us a minute while we work up the nerve to say it to this group of small business owners. Most of you use part of your home for business purposes. Most of you use your personal cars and trucks for business purposes. Some of you may not even have a separate bank account or a separate credit card for your business. What is Travel and Entertainment expense for one may be Sales Promotion expense for another and Business Development expense for a third. So, how are the good people at the IRS supposed to figure out what is the true revenue, expenses, and taxable income of any small business?

The answer to that question is Schedule C. To avoid wading through all these different terms, and assessing taxes of all businesses in an equitable manner, IRS has standardized things. Every business is required to report their income, expenses, cost of goods sold, vehicle expenses, and other expenses in Schedule C of Form **1040**. This is for sole owner businesses. Partnerships and Corporations are required to use other standard forms with their own schedules.

> The calculation from Schedule C showing the net profit of the business not only determines your income tax but pretty much forms the basis for your self-employment tax as well.

Pay your dues and demand services

As a civic minded citizen, I know you are as anxious to pay your fair share of taxes as the next person. In turn, of course, you are equally demanding when it comes to the delivery of services from your government. On the other hand, you want to make sure that you are not overpaying taxes either.

Don't leave out any income and expense accounts unmapped

It is in your best interest to make sure that none of the expense accounts are left unmapped to Schedule C, unless you have a specific reason for doing so, such as claiming a mileage rate instead of reporting car expenses. If you do, you will unnecessarily leave out on legitimate business expenses and over-report income and pay higher taxes on it. On the other hand, the IRS doesn't want you to leave out any income account either. So, make sure that you map all of your income and expense accounts to Schedule C.

Good bookkeeping and maintaining source documents such as receipts and vehicle logs will help you to account for business expenses and make sure that you are not overpaying taxes.

Pop quiz – filing tax returns

1. Partnerships file income tax returns using which form to IRS?
   a. 1065
   b. 1120
   c. 1120S
   d. 1040

2. What is the format of the file suitable for importing into tax preparation software?
   a. TXT
   b. TFX
   c. TXF
   d. TAX

Have a go hero – ensuring all business expenses are included in tax return

Create a list of your expenses accounts that are not mapped to Schedule C. Double check that they all have a valid reason why they are not mapped.

Creating income tax schedule report and TXF export

Accounting software is one of the tools that can help you manage and control your business effectively. As we outlined earlier, you want to make sure you meet sales targets, keep expenses under control and watch cash flow carefully. This is what you will be doing on a day-to-day basis and this tool should help you do that. So, you will set up your accounts to help you do that. However, IRS wants you to file your tax returns by following their template.

You need to find a way to meet your business goals and at the same time get the numbers for IRS ready without a lot of manual effort. That is where GnuCash comes in. Using the **Income Tax Information** window you can map your existing accounts to provide you with the necessary 1040 Schedule C numbers aggregated in a convenient way.

Time for action – getting the numbers for tax returns

Let's say that it is time to prepare your annual tax returns. We will see the steps we have to go through to output the numbers needed for your tax return software:

1. From the menu select **Reports | Tax Schedule Report/TXF Export**.

2. In the **Options** dialog's **Display** tab, uncheck **Do not print Action:Memo data** and **Do not print transaction detail**. Now the report will look as shown in the following screenshot:

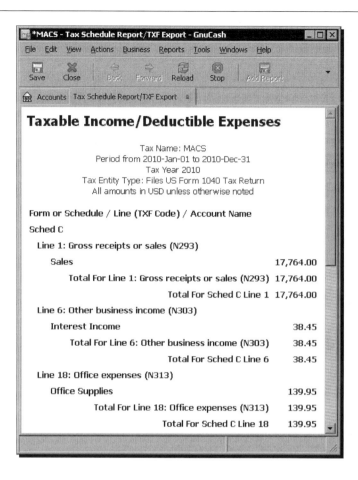

3. Click the **Export** toolbar button and in the **Choose export format** dialog select **TXF** as shown in the following screenshot.

4. Click **OK**. You will get the **Save TXF to File** dialog. Give the file a suitable name such as **MACS2010.txf** and click **Export**.

5. If your accountant asks for transaction details for any account, you can create an account register report for that report alone. With the **Sales** account open, select from the menu **Reports | Account Report**. The report will open as shown in the following screenshot:

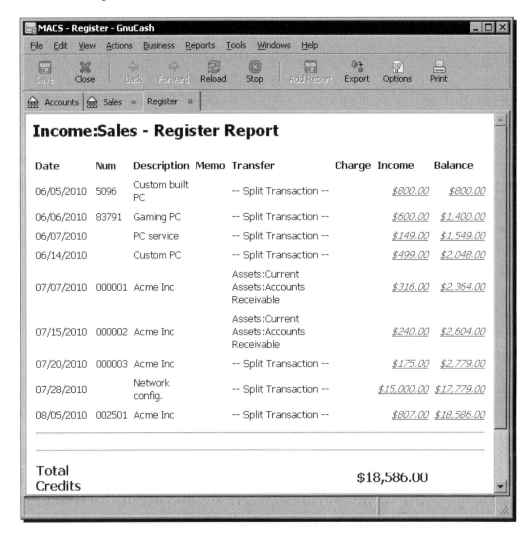

6. You can either print this or export it and save it as an HTML report and send it to your accountant.

What just happened?

Of all the new tricks that small business people need to learn, taxes can be the most difficult. This is partly because the IRS wants you to pay your taxes as you earn rather than waiting for you to file your annual returns. As we said earlier, if you are an employee, your employer handles this part conveniently for you. If you're a small business owner or are self-employed, you must estimate income and self-employment taxes due on your earnings every quarter and make a payment to the IRS. If you postpone this payment until your annual income tax return is due, the IRS will charge penalties and interest if the amount owed is large enough.

> Though estimated taxes are loosely referred to as quarterly, these are due on very specific dates. To avoid penalties, please check with your accountant or tax consultant.

Under some circumstances, you can use your previous year's history of income and earnings to help estimate the current year's tax burden. In others, you have to estimate the current period income.

Keep track of estimated taxes paid

After you start paying estimated taxes, be sure to keep a record of the dates you paid them and how much you paid for each period. If you don't keep accurate records, you may miss one or more of the payments you made. If you pay estimated taxes, be sure to claim credit for them when you file your income tax return. The use of a good bookkeeping system such as GnuCash can make this easier.

Transferring data from GnuCash to Schedule C

While most of the items in Schedule C can be directly mapped from one or more of the GnuCash accounts, some of the line items require special attention.

Cost of goods sold

When you sell a physical product, the cost of the raw materials, components, and labor that are required to make that product are to be grouped under this heading. IRS has specific guidelines on how to value your opening and closing inventory of raw material and components used in making your product. Also, you need to keep separate accounts for wages paid for production workers to be included in here.

Car and truck expenses

If you use your personal car or truck for business use, IRS gives you two different ways to show car and truck expenses. You can choose to account for each and every expense associated with maintaining the car or truck. In this case, you will maintain various accounts for the expenses such as gas, parking, repairs, insurance, and so on. You will map these to the Schedule C as you saw in the tutorial earlier. You will also need to divvy up this cost between personal use and business use in a way that can be backed up with usage records. Alternatively, IRS has standard mileage rates you can opt for. In this case, you will simply have to maintain logs of how many miles you drove your personal car or truck for business use and apply the standard IRS rates. This has to be done in a separate log maintained outside of GnuCash.

Depreciation

Depreciation is another item that is not a simple mapping from a GnuCash account to Schedule C. You need to fill out the appropriate form for computing the allowable depreciation expense that you can charge.

Expenses for business use of home

This is an item that you won't be tracking in GnuCash at all. You need to fill out the appropriate form for computing the allowable expense that you can charge to your business.

Other expenses

Business expenses not included in any of the previous categories will typically go here. However, work with your tax professional to identify and calculate the items that go into this section of Schedule C.

Self employment tax

As we mentioned in the payroll section earlier, you need to pay self employment tax in the US. This self employment tax is nothing but the FICA tax that we saw earlier in the payroll section. Now you are paying the employee contribution as well as the company contribution and so it has got doubled. There are specific rules for calculating these. Therefore, you should take the advice of a tax professional for computing them.

Other taxes

In addition to the Income Tax and Self Employment tax, there may be other taxes applicable for specific types of businesses. One example is heavy highway vehicle use tax. If you use certain highway trucks or buses in your business, you may have to pay a federal highway motor vehicle use tax. There may be other such federal, state, county, and local taxes as well. Consult your tax professional about what those are and how to set up GnuCash Expenses accounts, for example, to keep track of specific expenses.

Manual entry or TXF import?

Next comes the task of getting these numbers from GnuCash to your income tax preparation software, such as Intuit TurboTax in the US. You can use the .txf file saved from GnuCash and import it into your tax prep software and save time entering data into the tax prep software for your income tax return.

On the other hand, if your tax filing software doesn't support TXF import, or you find it convenient to transfer the numbers manually, you can follow that route as well.

Options for printing the Tax Schedule Report

As we saw earlier, you can choose to print transaction detail, if needed in the **Tax Schedule Report**. When you print the transaction detail, you will find that the **Notes** column also prints.

Pop quiz – exporting income tax data

1. Where will you find the menu item to export income tax data?

    a. **File | Export | TXF Export**

    b. **Edit | Tax Report Options | TXF Export**

    c. **Reports | Tax Schedule Report/TXF Export**, then click on the toolbar button **Export**.

Have a go hero – filling out Schedule C

Print the **Tax Schedule Report** and fill out a draft version of Schedule C for review by your accountant or tax consultant.

Setting up sales tax tables

Sales tax is an unusual transaction. The money that you collect does not belong to your business. It is government money. However, you are obligated to collect and pay it to the government on the due date. In general, you will be collecting sales tax only if you are selling to the end customer.

Time for action – setting up sales tax tables

We will set up tax tables for a jurisdiction that has separate taxes for the state, county, and town. Once the tax tables are setup, you can use them to charge the applicable taxes on invoices.

1. Prerequisites: Make sure you have three sales tax accounts **VA Sales Tax**, **Fairfax Sales Tax**, and **Vienna Sales Tax** of type **Liability** and with **Liabilities** as the **Parent Account**.

2. From the menu select **Business | Tax Tables**.

3. In the **Tax Tables** dialog, click the **New** button in the **Tax Tables** pane. In the Name field, enter **VA-Fairfax-Vienna**. Enter **4.00** in the **Value** field, select **VA Sales Tax** in the **Account** field drop down, and click **OK** as shown in the following screenshot.

4. That accounts for the state sales tax. We now have to add the County and Town taxes.

5. Click the **New** button in the **Tax Table Entries** pane and add the **Fairfax Sales Tax** of 1.00% and **Vienna Sales Tax** of 0.50%. After adding these, your tax table should look as shown in the following screenshot:

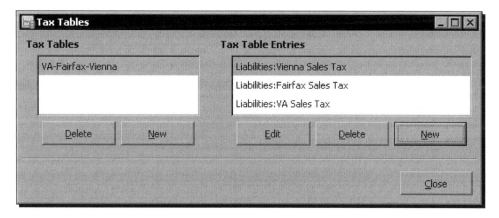

9. Click the **Close** button and make sure that your work is saved.

What just happened?

In some jurisdictions in the US, there may be three separate **sales tax** rates applicable – one for the State, another for the County, and a third one for the Town. In Virginia, for example, the State charges 4% and Fairfax County charges 1% for a total of 5% Sales Tax. For some items, there may be separate rates for the towns of Vienna and Herndon. While some of these are combined and collected in one place, that may not always be the case. You may have to pay it to the three different jurisdictions separately.

 Sales tax is a liability. Your business collects sales tax from your customer and you are obligated to pay it to the appropriate jurisdiction – State, County, or Town – within the required date. So, make sure you set up these tax accounts of type **Liability** with **Liabilities** as the **Parent Account**.

Tax table

We are simply using Virginia as an example and trying to show the worst case scenario, where you have to collect three different taxes and pay them to three different tax jurisdictions separately with supporting statements. Please check the applicable law in the jurisdictions where you do business.

Tax on tax

There are some jurisdictions that charge a local tax on top of the total of the base price and the federal or state sales tax. This tax, naturally, has to be computed as a compounded tax or tax on tax. In Canada, for example, the province of Quebec applies **Provincial Sales Tax (PST)** to the sum of base price and **Goods and Services Tax (GST)**.

For example, if an item is subject to 5% GST and 7.5% PST, then you will set up your tax tables as follows:

- GST 5%
- PST 7.5% on (base price + 5% GST) = 7.875%

The following diagram will help illustrate the concept of a tax on tax better.

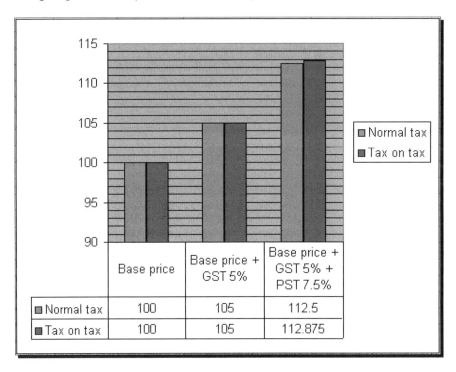

	Base price	Base price + GST 5%	Base price + GST 5% + PST 7.5%
Normal tax	100	105	112.5
Tax on tax	100	105	112.875

Thus, when you sell a product, say with a base price CAD 1000, if you apply this tax table, there will be a total of 12.875% charged combining the GST and PST for a total invoice price of CAD 1128.75 to the customer.

Pop quiz – setting up tax tables

1. How many different taxes can be combined in one tax table?

   a. One

   b. Two

   c. Three

   d. Any number

Have a go hero – charging compounded sales tax

Assume you are doing business in the province of Quebec in Canada. Set up a tax table to charge GST and compounded PST on the lines that we described earlier.

Applying sales tax to invoices

Now that you have the tax tables all set up for the jurisdictions where you do business, when the time comes to create the invoices, you can simply choose from the available tax tables.

Time for action – charging sales tax on sales

Let us take an example where we are selling an item for which all three taxes are applicable:

1. In the **Edit Invoice** window, you will see a column for **Tax Table**. From the dropdown list select the **VA-Fairfax-Vienna** tax table. Make sure the column marked **Taxable?** Is checked and **Tax Included?** is not. You will see that the appropriate tax is calculated and applied.

2. In some jurisdictions, some of the costs are not taxable. For example, in Maryland, delivery charges are not subject to sales tax. Add a separate line item for delivery charges in the invoice and uncheck the **Taxable?** column.

3. Once you have verified all entries, make sure you **Post** the invoice as shown in the following screenshot:

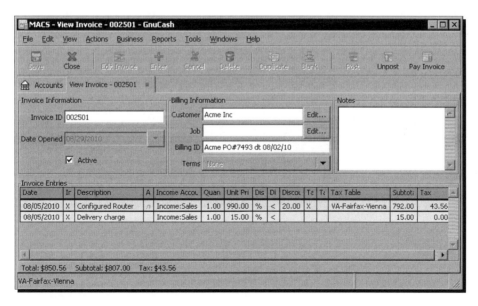

4. Showing individual tax items on the invoice: If you are required to show individual taxes separately in the invoice, you can do that in GnuCash. From the menu select **Reports | Business | Printable Invoice**. Select the invoice that you would like to print.

5. Open the **Report Options** dialog using the **Options** toolbar button. In the **Display** tab you will see a checkbox **Individual Taxes**. Check that to see the separate tax line items displayed separately as shown in the following screenshot:

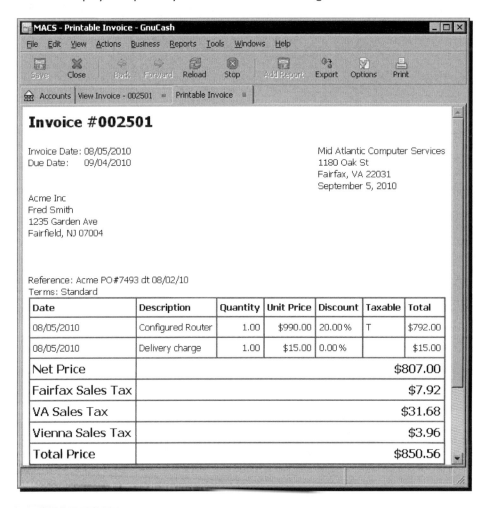

6. When the time comes to pay the sales tax, you need a statement of all the sales tax collected by you during the period to attach to your sales tax return. With the **VA Sales Tax** account register open, from the menu select **Reports | Account Report**. The report will appear as shown in the following screenshot.

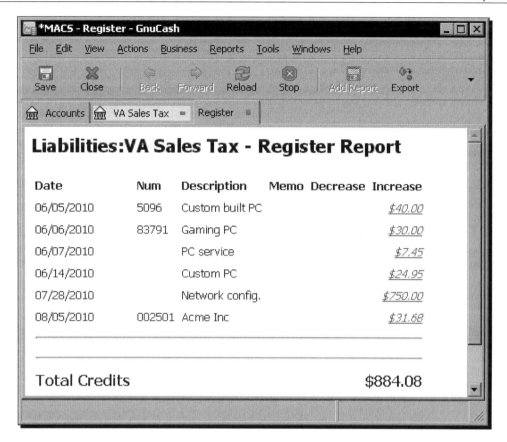

What just happened?

We were able to create sales tax tables according to the applicable law in our jurisdiction. While preparing the invoice, we were able to apply the appropriate sales tax on the line items where tax is applicable. We were able to print invoices showing the separate tax line items, if needed. At tax time, we were able to create a report to enclose with the tax return.

Take a moment to read this statement. Sales taxes in the US are due and payable when the merchandise is given to the customer or when the work is performed, not when payment is made. Did that make you pause? It should have. If it didn't, I am probably flying too fast for you. I should slow down and let you catch up. If you are offering credit terms to your customers, and if you don't collect before tax payment is due, you will be paying the tax from your pocket. It is on top of the credit that you have extended to your customer, effectively delivering a double whammy on your cash flow. Other countries may have different rules.

Pop quiz – applying tax tables to invoices

1. Can you apply more than one tax table to an invoice?

    a. Yes

    b. No

    c. Under certain conditions

Have a go hero – showing individual taxes on the invoice

Create an invoice, apply the tax table that you created earlier for the province of Quebec in Canada, and create a printable invoice that shows the individual taxes, GST, and PST, separately on the invoice.

Summary

We learned a lot in this chapter about tax matters.

Specifically, we covered:

- ◆ Creating mapping between GnuCash accounts and Schedule C: You will set up GnuCash accounts to help run your business on a day-to-day basis effectively. However, at tax time, you need to be able to create the tax returns quickly. This mapping is a convenient way to get that output.

- ◆ Manual or electronic transfer of data into your tax return software: We saw how to get the numbers needed for the tax return in a report that can be entered into your tax return software manually. We can also export this data in a standard format and import into the tax return software.

- ◆ Setting up sales tax tables: We saw different ways of setting up tax tables to follow the law in different jurisdictions.

- ◆ Applying sales tax to invoices and submitting sales tax returns: We saw how the sales tax can be applied on the invoice. We also saw how to create reports to attach to our sales tax returns.

Now that we've covered the stressful tax issues, we're ready to look at ways of making use of GnuCash to handle some routine administrative tasks to make your life easier, which is the topic of the next chapter.

9
Printing Checks and Finding Transactions

"...when is the easiest time to get a firm grip on accounting? During the start-up stage! The start-up stage is perfect for learning accounting due to the minimal number of transactions occurring." – from a website about accounting for entrepreneurs.

In every office there is always someone who is handy at finding, fixing, and organizing things. Fax machine toner needs to be replaced? Call Joe. Cannot find the five year old contract? Joe will know where to look. Copy machine jammed? Where is Joe?

What if a handy helper is free? Such as GnuCash. GnuCash can find things, fix things, and organize things. Of course, GnuCash can be handy only with your bookkeeping and accounting things, but then, at least you can be sure that one aspect of running your business is taken care of. That should be a big relief, considering that financial management and control is one of the most important aspects of running a business.

In this chapter we shall learn the following:

- ◆ How to search and find a transaction or a set of transactions.
- ◆ **Printing checks**.
- ◆ Adding **account codes** to accounts.
- ◆ How to check and fix transactions, if some of the splits are accidentally not imported or deleted.
- ◆ How to use the **financial calculator** provided by GnuCash for calculating loan and mortgage payments.

So let's see how we can make use of the features of GnuCash to organize, find, and fix things.

Finding transactions

When you start entering transactions, things are easier to find. You have very few transactions covering a short period. However, if your business is transaction intensive, or you have data for a longer period, you may find yourself spending more time in searching for transactions. GnuCash provides a number of features to organize, winnow, and find the very specific transaction or set of transactions that you are looking for.

Time for action – searching for a transaction

You are looking for a transaction during the month of August for Acme for which you issued a check which has not cleared yet. Let us see how you can find this one transaction among the thousands you may have in your books.

1. From the menu select **Edit | Find**. The **Find Transaction** dialog opens. **Description contains** is the default. Enter **Acme** in the value field.

2. Now you want only transactions in August. Click the **Add** button. Another line will be added to the **Search Criteria** pane. Select **Date Posted is on or after** and **08/01/2010**. Click **Add** again. Select **Date Posted is before or on** and **08/31/2010** as shown in the following screenshot:

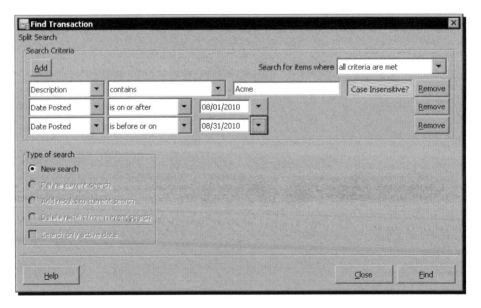

3. Click **Find**. You will now get a **Search Results** window showing all the transactions with **Acme** in the **Description** field during the month of August.

4. However, we need only the transactions that have not cleared. With the **Search Results** window open, go ahead and select **Edit | Find** again from the menu. Now you will find that **Refine current search** is selected by default in the **Type of search** pane.

5. Select **Reconcile** and then **is**. By default the **Not Cleared** button will be clicked. Leave that as it is, as shown in the following screenshot:

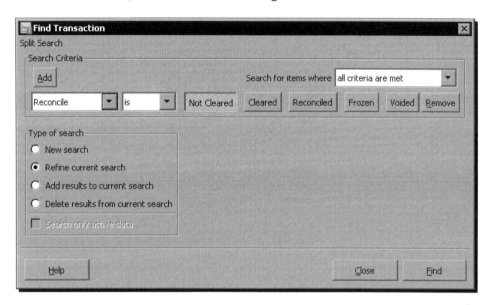

6. Click **Find** to see only the not cleared transactions in the **Search Results** window.

What just happened?

In the preceding example, we found the transaction that we were looking for in two steps. In the first step, we used multiple **Search Criteria**, and in the second step, we further winnowed our **Search Results** by refining further.

Sorting transactions

Mom was always right. If you were searching for something all over your home, she would say, "Go, organize your room. I am sure you will find it there." A place for everything and everything in its place. That was her motto. How can you not find something when you did that? Not that it remained so for long.

Similarly, it is much easier to find something in a sorted list than in a jumbled one. Sorting is nothing but rearranging your list in a particular order. So, let us first see whether we can make your search problem easier by sorting the transactions. First open the account register that you want to sort. Then from the menu **View | Sort By....** The Sort dialog will open and show that the transactions are sorted by **Standard Order** as shown in the following screenshot:

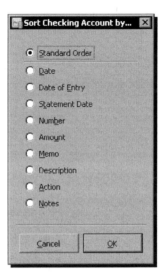

What is the **Standard Order**? The standard sort order for the account register is by **Date** first, then by **Num**, then by **Date of Entry** (this **Date of Entry** field is not visible in the **Account Register** window, nor is there any way to make it visible) and finally by **Description**.

However, now that you are in the **Sort** dialog, you can change it to sort by **Amount**, **Description** or any of the other fields available there.

> There is no way to change the sort order for an account register from ascending to descending or vice versa. However, if you do need to sort transactions in ascending and descending order, you can do that in the **Transaction Report**. The **Transaction Report** lists transactions just like the account register and it can do sorting of transactions and has ascending and descending sort options.

When you change the sort order, you will notice that the balance in the balance column is not recalculated based on the new order. It will continue to show the balance on that date.

Sorting transactions within a day

If you would like to sort the transactions within a day, add numbers into the **Num** column, and GnuCash will use that to sort the transactions within a day. As we pointed out earlier, the **Standard Order** for an account register is first by **Date** and then by **Num**. For example, you might find that a withdrawal shows up ahead of a deposit, resulting in a negative balance as shown in the following screenshot:

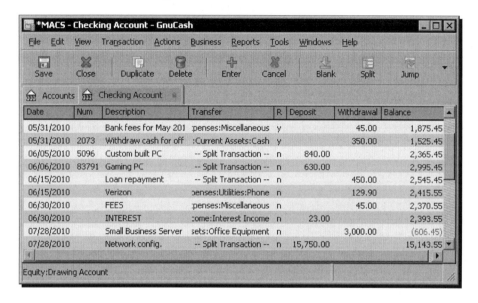

Maybe you are not too happy with that. Now if you add **Num** values to the two transactions within the same date, you can sort them the way you want them. By doing this you have moved the deposit ahead of the withdrawal, so that there is no negative balance in your account any more, as shown in the following screenshot:

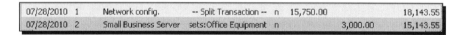

Instead, if you strictly want the transactions to be sorted chronologically, you can put in a number showing time, for example, in the **Num** column.

Filtering transactions

With the account register open, from the menu, select **View | Filter By....** The **Filter** dialog will open. You can now filter by a date range or one or more statuses.

> It is not possible to save filter settings. However, you could leave the account register open, when you quit GnuCash. When you start GnuCash next time, the account register will open, with the previously set filter settings.

Unlike in the case of sort, when you filter transactions, you effectively eliminate the extraneous transactions that you don't want to be distracted with. However, there are only limited filtering options in GnuCash.

> If you suddenly find that some transactions appear to be missing, in an account register window that you left open, don't panic. You probably set a filter and forgot to remove it when you were done. Like the young Casabianca, who stood on the burning decks of the ship obediently following the instructions of his father and perished with the ship, GnuCash will remember and follow your instructions obediently until you change them. Select from the menu **View | Filter by...** and check **Show All**. The transactions that you thought were lost, and were having nightmares about, will all come flooding back.

Viewing and sorting all transactions

If you want to view all transactions, regardless of which account register they are in, and sort them, there are three different ways of doing it in GnuCash:

- **Transaction Report**: From the menu select **Reports | Transaction Report**. Make sure you select all accounts and all children as well.

- **Find Transaction**: You may recall that we covered a way to get all items in the Find dialog – by selecting **matches regex** and entering a single dot (**.**) in the value field. On clicking **Find** you will get a **Search Results** window with all transactions. You can then sort it, as needed.

- **General Ledger**: From the menu select **Tools | General Ledger**. You will see all of the transactions, just like in an account register. You can then sort them in the same way as you would sort an account register.

The **Transaction Report Sort** options allow you to select a **Primary Key** as well as a **Secondary Key**. Also, you can select **Ascending** or **Descending** for both. So, for example, you can sort by Account Name as the Primary Key and then sort by **Amount Descending** within that. This will show all transactions in each account with the larger amounts on top. However, in the **Search Results** window and the General Ledger, you can only select one sort key and you don't have the **Ascending** or **Descending** options. Try them all and pick whichever suits the task at hand.

Find transactions FAQ

Here is a list of frequently asked questions about the find transactions process and our answers:

◆ Q: I have used **Edit | Find** to generate search results of transactions matching a particular text. How do I print it?

    ❑ A: You cannot print directly from the **Search Results** window. However, you can create a report from it and print that. With the **Search Results** window open, select **Reports | Account Report** from the menu. You will see the search results in the form of a report. Now you can click the toolbar **Print** button or **File | Print Report** to print it.

◆ Q: I am trying to filter my checkbook transactions by the payee on checks. I would like to filter on the **Description** field.

    ❑ A: There is no filter option for that. Instead, go to the **Find Transaction** dialog, set **Description contains** as the name of the payee and click **Find**.

◆ Q: I would like to know if there is a way to see all the transactions for a given day.

    ❑ A: From the menu select **Tools | General Ledger**. You will see all the transactions regardless of account. You can now filter and sort this, as needed.

◆ Q: How do I use the **Account** option in the **Find** dialog?

    ❑ For example, let us say you would like to see all the transactions in **Office Supplies** and **Miscellaneous** together in one report. In the Find dialog select **Account** and **matches any account**. Then select both **Office Supplies** and **Miscellaneous** in **Choose Accounts**. Now when you click **Find** you should see transactions from both accounts.

◆ Q: How do I use the **All Accounts** option in the **Find** dialog?

    ❑ A: For example, let us say you would like to see all rent payments you made by cash. Select **All Accounts** and **matches all accounts**. Then select both **Cash** and **Rent** in **Choose Accounts**. Now when you click **Find** you should see only **Rent** payments made from the **Cash** account.

◆ Q: How do I use **Add results to current search**?

    ❑ A: After you have completed one search, you can use this feature to do a second search and add those results to the first one. The advantage is that you will have the results of two different searches in one **Search Results** window. You can then sort it, filter it, or create a report from it.

◆ Q: How do I use **Delete results from current search**?

    ❑ A: This works in a fashion similar to the one above. After you have completed one search, you can use this feature to do a second search and delete those results from the first one.

Find customers, invoices, and so on

Find Customer, Invoice, Vendor, Bill, Employee, and Expense Voucher – all of these use the same basic dialog that we have been studying so far for finding transactions. So, once you are familiar with how to search for and find transactions, you will be able to apply the same techniques to find any of these as well. For example, from the menu select **Business | Customer | Find Invoice** to search for invoices as shown in the following screenshot:

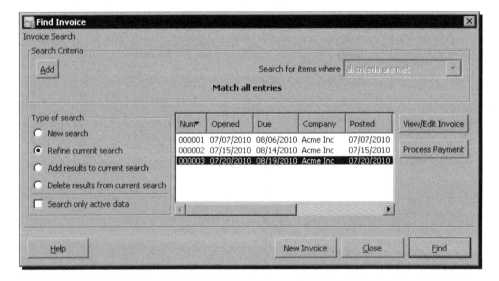

Pop quiz – filtering transactions

1. You cannot filter transactions by which one of the following attributes?

    a. By amount range

    b. By date range

c. By cleared status

d. By reconciled status

Have a go hero – searching for transactions

Find all transactions that have either **Acme** or **Zebra** in the description.

Printing checks

Printing checks makes check writing easy for you and minimizes scope for errors by getting the data for printing from your books of accounts. It also gives a professional appearance about your business to the recipients.

Time for action – printing checks

Let us look at two examples of printing checks. For testing purposes, we are going to print them on plain paper or, preferably, on a copy of your check sheet. When printing real checks though, you will be using pre-printed 3-to-a-page checks or Voucher checks, which have one check and a voucher in one page. In the first test, we will print a single check with address. In the second, we will print three checks in one go.

1. Prerequisite: Please make sure that you have entered the transactions for which you want to print the check in the account register first.

2. Open the account register that you want to print from. In this case, open the **Checking Account** register. Make sure the transaction for which you want to print the check is selected. The cursor should be on that transaction and that line should be highlighted.

3. Select from the menu **File | Print Checks...**. The **Print Check** dialog will open. Select **Quicken/QuickBooks (tm) US-Letter** in the **Check Format** dropdown list. Make sure **Check Position** is **Top**, if not already so. Make sure **Date Format** is **US (12/31/2001)**, if not already so.

4. In the **Address** pane, the name will be pre-filled. Fill out the other address lines manually.

5. Please note that the **Checks on first page** field is disabled indicating that you can print only one check at a time as shown in the following screenshot:

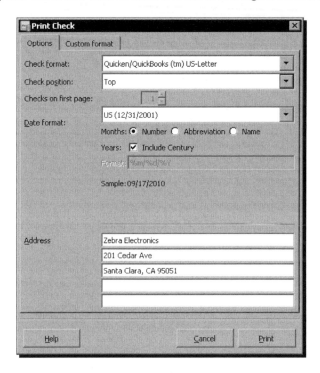

6. Check everything and click **Print**. The print output should appear as shown in the following screenshot:

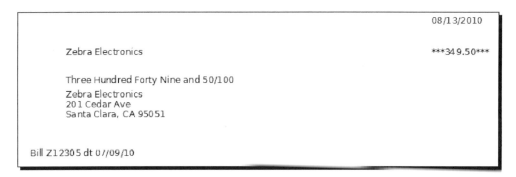

7. Compare the printed page with the check sheet and make sure that the printed text is properly aligned. If you are using plain paper, you can put the printed sheet behind the check sheet and hold them against a light to check the alignment. Checks are available with or without lines printed. Order what works best for you.

8. Printing multiple checks in one go: To print multiple checks in GnuCash you need to do a search to find the transactions you wish to print. Let us say that you have three checks to print for Zebra Electronics. Now that you are familiar with searching, go ahead and get those three payments in the **Search Results** window.

9. With this window open, invoke **File | Print Checks....** Now the magic will happen and the **Checks on first page** field will be enabled. Select the **Quicken(tm) Wallet Checks w/ side stub** in **Check format** and change the **Checks on first page** field to **3** as shown in the following screenshot:

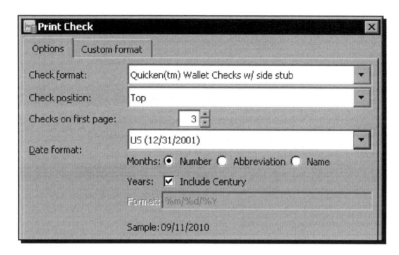

9. Check everything and click **Print**. You should see that all three checks print in one go.

What just happened?

We did say that cash flow management is an important part of running a business successfully, and that you should control your cash outflows very carefully. However, that doesn't mean that you don't issue any checks at all. That will be counterproductive. Remember, we also said that you have to pay your bills on time in order to maintain good credit scores? It is good to know how to print checks, for those rare occasions when you do want to make a payment.

As we saw in this tutorial, checks are printed in GnuCash primarily from the account register.

Printing Memo on checks

Checks usually have a place for a Memo. You might want to write the Account Number, Policy Number, Loan Number, and other such cross reference information there. This **Memo** field serves as important reference information, especially if the check gets detached from the accompanying statement that shows what that payment is for.

With the account register open, from the menu select **View | Double Line**. You will now see an extra line for each transaction and a **Notes** field below the **Description** field. Add whatever information you want to print in the **Memo** field of the check in this **Notes** field.

Also, as we saw in this tutorial, you do get options to select a check format and change the date format.

Printing one check at a time on a 3 check sheet

If you are using 3 checks to a page sheet, there are two ways of printing one check at a time:

1. After printing each check, you can tear it off. Next time when you print, send the smaller page through the printer again for the next check. Always leave the **Check Position** as **Top**. The printer will print, starting at the top of the page, as if it has a full sheet.

2. Alternatively, you can send the already printed check through with the rest of the full sheet and you can set the **Check Position** as **Middle** or **Bottom** setting, as the case may be.

If you are printing a small number of checks and need to send them out as soon as you print them, you may prefer the first option.

Printing address

The following two **Check Formats** allow you to print an optional address:

◆ Quicken/QuickBooks US-Letter
◆ Voucher Check 3-part US-Letter

When you select either of these **Check Formats** in the **Print Check** dialog, the Address pane will become enabled. The name of the payee will be populated by the system from the selected transaction. However, you have to enter the address manually.

Printing multiple checks

If you invoke **File | Print Checks...** from an account register, you will only be able to print a single check at a time for the one selected transaction.

To print multiple checks in GnuCash, as you saw in the tutorial above, you need to do a search to find the transactions you wish to print. However, please note that all the transactions in the **Search Results** window must be from a single account, such as the **Checking Account**. Otherwise, it will cause an error. So make sure you have transactions from a single account, for each invocation of printing, to avoid this error.

Custom check format

If none of the standard formats are suitable for your purpose, you can create a custom check format and save it for your use. However, this is painstaking work and be prepared for several trial print runs to get it just right. Here is a brief outline of how to create a custom check format.

In the **Check format** field, select **Custom** and switch to the **Custom format** tab. You will now find that all the fields are enabled.

The **Custom format** tab has a line across the tab dividing it into a top pane and a bottom pane. The top pane allows you to position individual fields in the check. It contains two columns to enter in the x and y co-ordinates of the field position on the check. Positions in the Custom Check Format entry area are specified horizontally with an x value of 0.000 at the left edge of the check with x increasing to the right. Vertically y values start with 0.000 at the top edge of the check with y increasing as you travel down.

The bottom pane allows you to position the entire check correctly on the page. The **Translation** field is the distance from the top left corner and the **Rotation** field rotates the check clockwise by the **Degrees** entered. The **Units** field in the bottom pane specifies the units used in all the x and y fields in the entire tab. You can choose from Points (same as Pixels), Inches, Centimeters, and Millimeters as shown in the following screenshot:

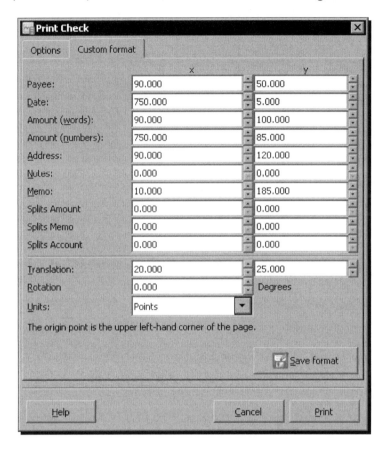

Make sure you save the custom check format and give it a name of your choice. Then it will appear as an additional selection in the **Check format** field.

Printing receipts

GnuCash doesn't have a way to **print receipts** for payment received. However, if what your customer needs is a record of having made a payment, you can offer the following alternative.

From the menu, select **Reports | Business | Customer Report**. In the **Options** dialog select the customer and put in a date range. You will see a record of invoices and payments during that period. You can print this report and give it to the customer. Unlike a simple receipt, this report has the added advantage that it shows current balance and serves as a reminder to the customer for any payments still due. If your customer expresses frustration asking you why they are being reminded about the next payment when they are asking for a receipt for this one, you can always blame it on your quirky accounting software. Neat!

Pop quiz – printing date format in a check

1. The **Print Checks** menu is available only from which window?

   a. **Account Tree** window

   b. **Account Register** window

   c. **Transaction Report** window

   d. **View Invoice** window

Have a go hero – printing a voucher check

In printing a check, change the date format to use dash as the separator – for example, 09-19-10.

Numbered accounts

Streets typically have names, right? Some cities have numbered streets. In Washington DC, for example, the North-South streets are numbered. In the NW part of the city, you have First Street at the US Capitol going up to 50th Street, on Massachusetts Avenue, past the Embassies, all the way up to near the Maryland state line.

GnuCash gives you the best of both worlds. You can have account numbers in addition to names.

Time for action – assigning numbers to accounts

Let us see an example of how to assign account numbers using the Renumber Subaccounts feature of GnuCash.

1. Make sure the **Account Tree** window is on top. Select one of the parent accounts, say, **Expenses**. From the menu select **Edit | Renumber Subaccounts...**. Enter **4** in the **Prefix** field and select an **Interval** of **5** as shown in the following screenshot:

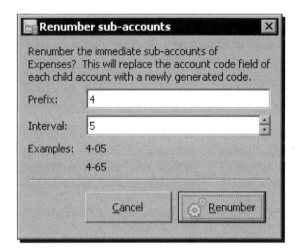

2. Click **Renumber**. You will find that GnuCash has renumbered all the subaccounts of this parent account.

3. Next you can select, say, **Auto** and renumber all its subaccounts.

4. However, you will find that the top-level account, namely **Expense** has not been numbered. You have to number this manually. Click on the **Account Code** field on the **Expense** line. The field will become a textbox allowing you to edit it. Enter the number **4** as shown in the following screenshot:

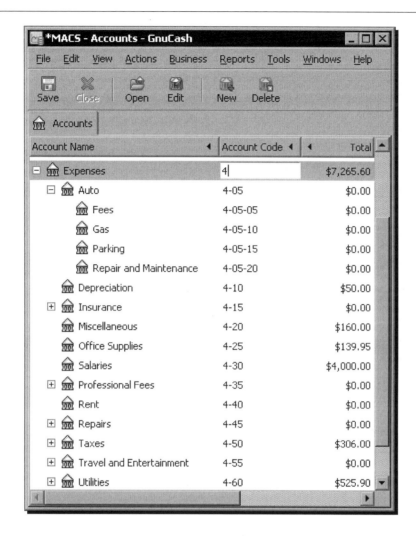

5. Now you can tab out of that field and make sure to save your changes.

What just happened?

Who said that numbered accounts are for dictators and spies? You can have them too. No, these are not for stashing away your ill-gotten or clandestine money from prying eyes. We are talking about assigning numbers to your GnuCash accounts.

Why account numbers?

You may want to have account numbers for the following reasons:

♦ You find it convenient to organize a large group of things by number rather than by name.

♦ You attended an accounting course and numbers were recommended.

♦ You have been using a chart of accounts with account numbers for some time and you find it easier to follow the same system.

♦ You want to arrange your accounts in a different order and giving them a number and sorting by the numbers is the way to do that.

♦ You have an unduly large number of accounts and you find it difficult to handle them by names alone.

In addition to using the account numbers to sort in the Account Tree itself, you also have the option of selecting it as a sort field in several reports.

Keep a provision for future additions

As you saw in the tutorial, it is a good idea to increment by five or ten when assigning account numbers so that you can insert new accounts in between at a later date, if needed, without having to change any of the existing ones.

An example account numbering system

Some people have found it convenient to follow a four-digit account numbering system as follows:

♦ 1000: Asset Accounts. What you own.

♦ 2000: Liability Accounts. What you owe.

♦ 3000: Income Accounts. Sales.

♦ 4000: Direct Expense Accounts. Typically, what you will report under Cost of Goods Sold.

♦ 5000: Indirect Expense Accounts. Other overhead expenses.

  ❑ 5100: Repairs

  ❑ 5200: Professional Fees

  ❑ And so on.

♦ 7000 - 8000 Non-Operating Accounts (Equity, interest income, and so on).

Then the individual accounts will have numbers such as 5205: Legal Fees, 5210: Accounting Fees, and so on. However, please note this system requires you to enter the numbers by hand. You won't be able to use the **Renumber Subaccounts** feature to automate it.

 The **Transaction Report** allows you to sort transactions by Account Code.

Rectify over-invoicing

Let us say that you created and posted an invoice. Later you discovered that you over-invoiced due to an error. Accountants deal with this by issuing what they call a **credit note**. You can think of a credit note as the opposite of an invoice. GnuCash doesn't have a way to issue a credit note.

However, you can go back to the original invoice, unpost it, and modify it as follows. Add a new line to the invoice to show the correction amount on the side opposite to that of the sales. Now post the invoice again. This method has the following advantages:

- The amount was directly amended in the original invoice. This will make sure all the reports are correct.
- If you adjusted the original invoice amount, you would get the same result. However, you will not have any record that the invoice was created and sent and later adjusted with a credit note.

Sales refunds

Your customer bought a product from you and paid for it. Subsequently they came back to you and said that they were not happy with all or some part of the product. You have offered to rectify or replace what they are not happy with. However, they are insisting on a refund. Customer satisfaction is a key motto of your business and you have decided to refund the money.

Sales refund is the reverse of a sale. When you made a sale, you increased **Sales** and increased the **Checking Account** bank balance. Now you have to make an entry that decreases both. Also, for easy reference, you may want to add a note to the original invoice that a refund was made. Remember, you will have to **Unpost** it, add the note and **Post** it back again.

Purchase refunds

What happens if you return an item back to the store after you bought it and entered the transaction in the books? You later found that it was not the right item or you were not happy with the quality. Of course, if you got a full cash refund, the easiest way of fixing it would be to delete the original transaction, as if you never bought it in the first place. This approach will work in the case of credit card transactions where the store reverses the transaction fully. However, it is possible you have already accounted for the transaction in the previous month or quarter and you don't want to reopen those transactions and reports.

In the case of a **purchase refund**, you should make a transaction that is the opposite of a purchase transaction. When you buy an item for cash, you will reduce **Cash** balance and increase **Office Supplies** expenses. Now that you have returned the item and got a cash refund, you can make an entry increasing **Cash** balance and decreasing **Office Supplies** expenses.

Check & Repair

As we described in detail in the section on transactions, all GnuCash transactions have matching splits. For example, if you create an entry for an expense, there will be a matching reduction in cash or bank balance or an increase in the amount you owe in a credit card, depending on how you paid for that expense. If you delete an expense, the matching payment entry will also get deleted. Thus, GnuCash tries to keep transactions balanced at all times with matching splits. However, sometimes these entries can go out of balance. How come? The following are some of the ways this can happen:

- You migrated from another accounting software to GnuCash and you imported all the transactions into GnuCash. Due to errors in importing, one split got imported successfully, while the other didn't.

- You imported transactions from your bank or credit card accounts into GnuCash. Due to errors in importing, one split got imported successfully, while the other didn't.

After doing any of the preceding, or if you notice that one split of a transaction seems to be missing, you can get GnuCash to repair it. How? From the menu select **Actions | Check & Repair**. If you do this from the **Accounts Tree** window, you will get options to **Check & Repair** an **Account**, **Subaccounts**, or **All**. If you are in an account register, you will get options to **Check & Repair** a **Transaction** or **All Transactions**. Choose whichever you are trying to repair. However, please note that this feature was built for earlier versions. Currently you may not find the need to use this feature that often.

The Check & Repair process is a quiet operator. It won't show you any message to indicate that it has completed its work, and whether there were any errors that were fixed or that there were none. It works silently.

Pop quiz – editing account codes

1. Which one of the following is not a valid window for editing account codes?

    a. **Edit Account** dialog

    b. **New Account** dialog

    c. **Account Tree** window

    d. **Open Subaccounts** window

Have a go hero – sorting by account code

Create a **Transaction Report**, display the **Account Code** field in it and sort it by **Account Code**.

Financial calculator

The Financial Calculator in GnuCash should have been called a Loan Repayment Calculator or Mortgage Payment Calculator, because that is what it does.

Time for action – calculating mortgage payments

You are planning to borrow $30,000 from the bank towards the purchase of a truck for your business. You will be paying it off fully in three years in 36 equal monthly payments. The bank has told you that the interest **APR (Annual Percentage Rate)** is 9.5%. You asked and found that the APR will be compounded monthly at the end of the month. You want to calculate and see what the monthly payment will be before heading to the bank for finalizing the loan.

1. From the menu, select **Tools | Financial Calculator**. The **Financial Calculator** window will open with a sample calculation already filled.

2. Change the **Present Value** to **$30,000**, **Interest Rate** to **9.50%**, **Payment periods** to **36**, and **Future Value** to **0.00**. Clear the **Periodic payment**. As soon as you clear one of the fields, the **Calculate** button will become enabled. Click it.

3. The **Periodic payment** will be filled with an amount in parentheses. This is the equated monthly installment. The **Payment Total** at the bottom of the right pane will also be recalculated as shown in the following screenshot:

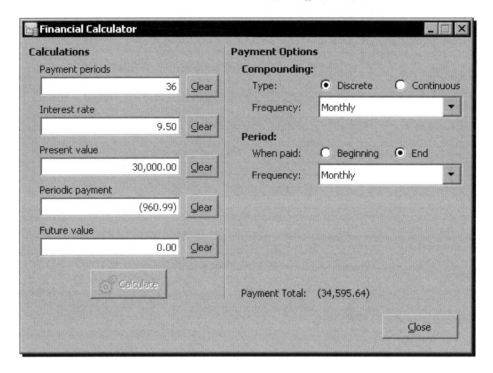

What just happened?

The GnuCash Financial Calculator is used to calculate **loan payment** and **mortgage payment** by applying compound interest. It provides a way of entering the amount you wish to borrow, the interest or Annual Percentage Rate (APR) applicable, the repayment period and calculates the **Equated Monthly Installment (EMI)** payments to pay off the entire loan. Alternatively, if you know your capacity to pay and the repayment period, you can calculate the maximum amount you can borrow to keep within that limit.

Simple calculations in GnuCash

As we saw earlier, you can enter calculations in any amount field in the account registers. GnuCash will do the calculation for you and put the result in that field

Some banks compound interest once a month, while others may compound continuously. Most banks will ask you to pay at the end of the month. This calculator allows you to set any of those options.

Pop quiz – calculating mortgage payment

1. You want to pay off the entire loan. Which amount should be set to zero?

    a. Present value

    b. Future value

    c. Payment Total

    d. Periodic payment

Have a go hero – maximum borrowing limit

Looking at the cash flow projection, you find that your business can only afford to pay $500 per month. Assuming a three-year repayment period, calculate the maximum amount your business can borrow.

Summary

We learned a lot in this chapter about using GnuCash to find, fix, and organize transactions.

Specifically, we covered:

◆ Finding transactions: We learned that sorting is often the first step to finding transactions and learned how to do sorting. Then we went on to filtering out transactions that we are not interested in so that we can home in on the ones that we want. Finally, we studied a variety of ways to search for that needle-in-the-haystack elusive transaction.

◆ Printing checks: We looked at how to print checks in standard formats including how to print address and memo on the checks as well as how to print multiple checks in one go. We also briefly covered how to create and save a custom format, if the standard ones don't work for you.

◆ Numbered accounts: We saw why you might want to give numbers to your accounts and how to go about doing that.

◆ We saw how to check and fix transactions, if some of the splits are accidentally not imported or deleted.

◆ Loan and mortgage calculator: We also saw how to use the custom calculator provided by GnuCash for calculating loan and mortgage payments.

We also learned what to do if your client asks for a receipt for payment, how to correct over-invoicing, and how to handle sales and purchase returns.

Now that we've learned about the handy ways to use GnuCash, we're ready to see how to use GnuCash for nonprofits – which is the topic of the next chapter.

10
Adapting GnuCash for Non-profits and Personalizing

"Support groups may want to spend the year creating gift quality artwork in a co-op art class to sell at a holiday bazaar. Families can host a bake sale and present a spaghetti dinner in order to boost attendance. A gift wrapping table and live performances of music are nice additions to a holiday fundraising programs"-excerpts from a website providing fundraising event ideas for non-profits.

Non-profits, by definition, are not trying to earn a buck for their owners or shareholders. So, bookkeeping and accounting for a **non-profit** should be easier than for a business, right? "Au contraire, mon ami", as the fictional Belgian detective Hercule Poirot, might say.

Non-profits receive their funding from many different sources such as donations from the public, grants, investment income, fundraising, membership fees, and non-monetary contributions of goods. They also receive contributions in the form of hours and expertise, known as "in-kind" contributions.

Some of the donations, grants, and other funds provided to non-profits are tied directly to specific programs. This makes it obligatory on the part of the non-profit to apply those funds only to those specific programs. In addition, common expenses such as rent and salaries must be allocated to each funded program so that the accounts of that program can be prepared separately and sent to that grant provider or to those donors. Although the income statement and balance sheets include the same main categories for a non-profit as for a commercial business, being able to obtain detailed program level totals is a vital necessity.

You may recall the accountant's lingo that we referred to earlier. Well, there are also dialects within that lingo. This type of accounting is known as **"fund accounting"** in the particular dialect that non profit accountants speak.

Also, many non-profits tend to depend on fundraising events, seasonal campaigns, and other such events. If you are the treasurer or another office bearer of a non-profit, you would like to account for the costs and income of each such event separately so that you can help decide whether these are providing returns in proportion to the effort put in and whether to repeat them again. If these expenses and income are buried in the overall annual income and expenses, such valuable analysis cannot be done and objective decisions cannot be made.

In this chapter, we shall cover:

◆ Adapting GnuCash for maintaining the accounts of smaller non-profits.

◆ Setting preferences in GnuCash and personalizing it to suit your specific needs.

◆ Protecting your data from unauthorized access and backing up your data to safeguard it from data loss or corruption.

So let's get on with it...

No separate non-profit version of GnuCash

Before you start using GnuCash for a non-profit, you should know that there is no GnuCash version specially created for non-profits. We are going to stretch the business features of GnuCash to suit the needs of a non-profit. As a result of this, you may find the following issues, among others.

When you create transactions or run reports, you may find that 'Donors' are called 'Customers', 'Pledges' are called 'Invoices', and other such anomalies.

Also, as we said earlier, GnuCash is suitable for small businesses. By the same token, GnuCash may suit the needs of only small non-profits. Walk through the steps we have outlined and satisfy yourself that it will meet your needs, before taking the plunge.

Bookkeeping for non-profits

As we said earlier, accounting and bookkeeping for a non-profit is harder than that for a for-profit organization. Let us work through a few examples so that we can be better prepared for the different types of situations that we will encounter in a non-profit.

Time for action – using GnuCash features for non-profits

Let us take a few scenarios of accounting challenges that are more commonly found in non-profits and see how best to leverage the features of GnuCash to meet those requirements:

1. Non-profit scenario 1 - Income/Expense for an event: You are the treasurer for the non-profit, Save Our Souls (SOS). During the month of November, SOS plans to run a Holiday Fundraising event of buying Poinsettias and Wreathes and distributing them to the local community. You would like to track the income and expenses for the event separately, so that you can create a report showing how the event did financially.

2. Prerequisites: Set up a new account hierarchy for SOS. You can use the **Business Accounts** as a starter.

3. Create a new account - the **Account Name** should be **Holiday Fundraiser**, **Account Type** should be **Income**, and **Parent Account** should be **New top level account**.

4. Create another new account **Income** of type **Income** with **Holiday Fundraiser** as the parent.

5. Create two new accounts **Poinsettias** and **Wreathes** of type **Expense** with **Holiday Fundraiser** as the parent.

6. Enter the cost of a truckload of Poinsettias and half a truckload of Wreathes and the transportation and loading costs in the appropriate expense accounts. As the stock gets sold, make income entries on a weekly basis. At this point, your account tree should look as shown in the following screenshot:

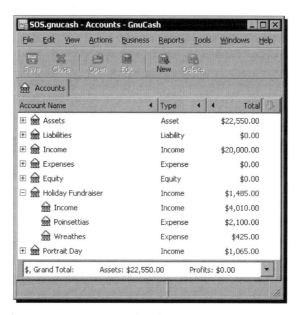

7. From the menu, select **Reports | Income &Expense | Income &Expense Chart**. In the **Report Options** dialog **Accounts** tab **Clear All**, select the **Holiday Fundraiser** account and Select **Children**.

8. In the **Display** tab, select **Show table**.

9. In the **General** tab, select the **Start Date** to be Nov 1 and the **End Date** to be Nov 30 and the **Step Size** to be **Week**.

10. Change the **Report name** to **Holiday Fundraiser** and click **OK**.

11. You should now see the **Income**, **Expense**, and **Net Profit** by week, both in chart form and in tabular form. Note that this is for each week and not cumulative.

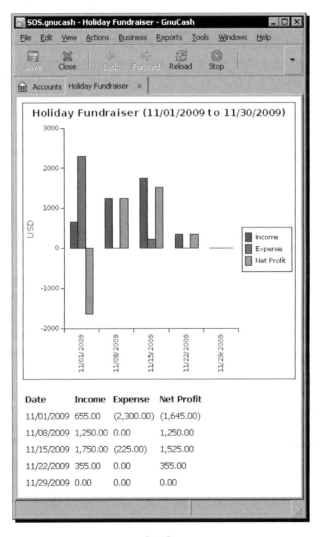

In the previous chart, net profit is arrived at by subtracting the expense from the income. If the income is more than the expense, there is a net profit. If, on the other hand, the expense exceeds income, there is a loss, which is shown in the net profit column in parenthesis.

What just happened?

In this tutorial, we were not only able to account for the income and expenses of one event separately, we were also able to perform further break-out analysis of those numbers. This is helpful to make important decisions such as:

♦ Whether the event is profitable enough to run it again.

♦ Whether there are other event options you have that are more profitable.

♦ If you are going to run the same event, are there improvements you can make regarding the ordering of supplies, scheduling of delivery, negotiating payment terms, pricing that can help improve profitability and cash flow.

Donors and members

Some non-profits largely depend on fee paying members for their income. Others may have donors who donate services, money, and goods. There are two ways of setting up donors and members in GnuCash:

♦ Each donor as an income account: Under the top level account **Income**, you can have **Donations** as a subaccount and each donor as a separate income account. This method may work if you have a handful of donors.

♦ Each donor as a customer: On the other hand, if you have a large number of donors, you may find it easier to create each donor as a customer. If you need reports on individual donors, you can run the **Customer Report (Reports | Business | Customer Report)** and select that donor in the **Company** field. Another advantage of this approach is, when you obtain a pledge from a donor, you will be able to raise an invoice and show this amount as a receivable for tracking purposes.

Keeping funds for projects separately

As we said earlier, non-profits often have a need to account for funds for special projects separately. Let us see an example of how this can be done.

Time for action – allocating funds for projects

Non-profit scenario 2 – Keeping funds for projects separately: SOS is planning to add a new wing to the building for community healthcare. You are receiving donations specific to the building project and you want to keep the funds separately, even though you don't want to open a separate bank account for that purpose.

1. Create a new account **Funds for building new wing** of the type **Bank** and with **Current Assets** as the **Parent Account**. This will show up as a sibling to **Checking Account**. Now, when you reconcile the Bank balance, you have to reconcile with the total of **Checking Account** and **Funds for building new wing**, as shown in the following screenshot.

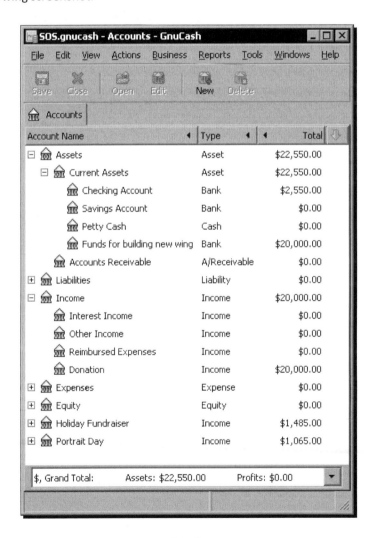

What just happened?

Ideally, you might want to create a separate bank account for such projects. In this case, you were able to achieve the same results without going through the extra cost and effort of opening another bank account.

Getting overall Income Statement

Even though you might keep Income/Expense for an event separately, as we saw in Non-profit scenario 1, or keep funds aside for a project separately, as we saw in Non-profit scenario 2, you may still need the Income Statement for the organization as a whole. You might need this for your annual report, tax returns, audits, or for a variety of other such purposes.

Time for action – getting overall Income Statement

1. Getting overall Income Statement for the non-profit: Even though you are keeping separate Income and Expense accounts for events as well as keeping the funds for building the new wing separately, you still need the overall Income Statement for the non-profit for tax returns, audit, annual report, and other purposes.

2. From the menu, select **Reports | Income&Expense | Income Statement**. In the **Report Options** dialog, in the **Accounts** tab, you will find that all Income and Expenses accounts have been selected by default. In the **General** tab, make sure the start of the year and end of the year are selected. Click **OK** to see the **Income Statement** for the entire year covering all accounts, as shown in the following screenshot.

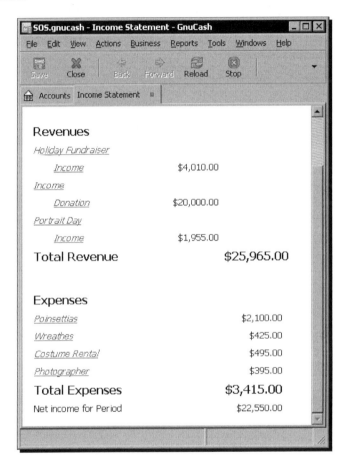

What just happened?

Non-profits tend to work with a lot of volunteers and some of them may be occasional volunteers. This is another reason why it is harder to do bookkeeping for a non-profit. Keeping track of expenses and paperwork is a huge challenge with a transient workforce. Ask any accountant of a non-profit. And, while you are talking to them, ask whether a non-profit is allowed to make a profit. Of course, you should be prepared for a sudden shift into the accountants' lingo and, especially, the non-profit dialect. How would you know you are there? When you hear profits being referred to as surplus.

Yes, non-profits are allowed to make a profit, except it is called a surplus now. Not just allowed, but encouraged to generate a surplus. Only then the non-profit can ensure its survival and growth, and be in a position to deliver whatever services the non-profit set out to deliver to more of its target population. However, the surplus cannot come out of unrelated business income. In which case, not only the IRS may want its cut, but also the tax exempt status may be at risk as well.

Making reports presentable

As we pointed out earlier, when you run reports, you may find that 'Donors' are called 'Customers' and Pledges' are called 'Invoices' and other such anomalies. Thus, even though you may get the right numbers, you may find that the labels and headers are not right. You should plan to export the reports to HTML, open it in your favorite spreadsheet program and change these, as needed, before printing and distribution. However, please note that only the tabular report can be exported, not the chart.

Receivables

Let us say your process is that you get pledges of donation from donors first and later they make the actual payment. When you get the pledge, you can invoice them and show the amount as receivable. Later, when they pay, you can process the payment. Similarly, at the time grants are awarded, you are unlikely to receive the money. You can book that into a receivable account. You may have to do a lot of paper work and follow other processes to receive payments. Also, you may receive these payments in many installments. You can keep showing partial payments received against the original invoice you created at the time of the grant award.

Handling multiple grants from the same foundation

When you receive multiple grants from the same foundation, you can make use of a feature of GnuCash called Customer Jobs. Each grant can be treated as a job. This approach will allow you to get a separate report for each job. This will allow you to account for each grant and the corresponding expenses separately from other grants from the same foundation. However, be aware of the limitation that there is only one job report. Please check and make sure this report will meet your needs before jumping in.

Multiple sets of books

If your programs have special requirements such as stringent reporting or the need to be grouped differently or require program level accounts to be maintained for audit purposes, you may want to consider maintaining separate GnuCash accounts for each program.

If you decide to use multiple sets of accounts, you will have the following options:

- ◆ In the first approach, you may decide to maintain a set of accounts for the organization as a whole and separate books for the major programs that require separate accounting. This will involve duplication of work, because transactions have to be entered once in the organization's account and again in the applicable program.

- ◆ In another approach, you can choose to account for program-specific transactions only in that program. Only non-program specific transactions would be entered into the organization's book of accounts. However, there will be some number of cross charges. Also, to arrive at the overall organization's financials, you have to consolidate all of these accounts in a spreadsheet, outside of GnuCash.

Non-profit accounting FAQ

Here is a list of frequently asked questions about using GnuCash for non-profit accounting and our answers:

- ◆ Q: The non-profit for which I am the treasurer has a large number of members. We want to send invoices to them twice a year for membership fees. Is there a way to generate invoices in bulk?
  - ❑ A: No, invoices can only be done one at a time in GnuCash. You may have to rely on an external program to generate invoices in bulk, using the mail merge capability of a word processor such as OpenOffice.org Writer or MS Word.

- ◆ Q: Will I be able to create budgets for events and run budget vs. actual reports?
  - ❑ A: Yes, as we saw in *Chapter 7, Budget: Trip Planner for your Business*, GnuCash allows you to create several budgets and save them. If you need to create a budget for an event or a project, you can do that. Then, when you create the budget report, you can select only the accounts pertaining to that event or project.

◆ Q: I need to have a Donor ID in order to keep track of pledges and donations from individual donors. How can I do that?

    ❑ A: You can set up separate accounts for each donor and give an Account Code for each account. However, the better option would be to set up each donor as a customer. As we saw earlier, GnuCash will automatically generate an ID for each customer. Alternatively, you can assign your own ID.

Pop quiz – creating a separate account for an event or a project

1. What should be the Parent Account for creating a separate group of accounts for an event or a project?

    a. New top level account

    b. Placeholder account

    c. Event account

    d. Project account

Have a go hero – creating a set of accounts and a budget for an event

SOS is planning to organize a Portrait Day by hiring a professional photographer for a day and renting a variety of period costumes and props. Set up a separate set of accounts for the event and create a budget for it.

Personalizing GnuCash

Everyone has their own unique working style. And, if you can arrange your desk and your screen to suit your specific style, you can be more productive. Let us see what preference settings are available in GnuCash to allow you do that.

Time for action – getting your work environment just right

When you work in GnuCash, you find that you have to keep several windows open at the same time. Also, you don't need the Summary Bar and Status Bar for now. You want to hide them to minimize clutter and free up screen real estate. It will also be convenient if the tabs have unique colors so that you can find them quickly and easily. Let us see how you can accomplish all that.

1. From the menu, select **Edit | Preferences**. The **GnuCash Preferences** dialog will open. This is where you set most of your preferences.

2. In the **Windows** tab in **Toolbar Style**, select **Icons Only**. Check **Show close button on notebook tabs**. Select **Tab Position Left**, as shown in the following screenshot:

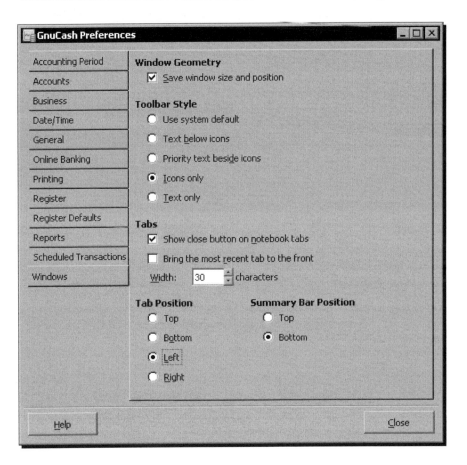

3. Click **Close**.

4. While most of the settings are available in the Preferences dialog, some of the personalization has to be done from other menu items. In the **View** menu, uncheck **Summary Bar** and **Status Bar**.

5. In the **Account Tree** window, right click on **Checking Accounts** and select **Edit Account**. Click on the long **Account Color** button. The **Pick a Color** dialog will open, as shown in the next screenshot. Click on the black line on the outer ring and drag around to a bright green color. Click and drag the small black circle in the inner triangle to make that green color darker.

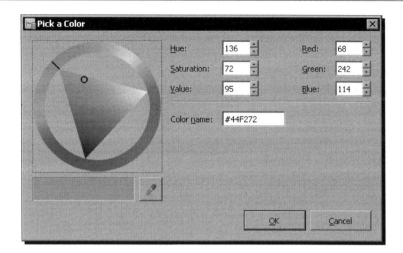

6. Click **OK**. Now you should see the GnuCash window personalized to your specific style of working and to your taste, as shown in the following screenshot:

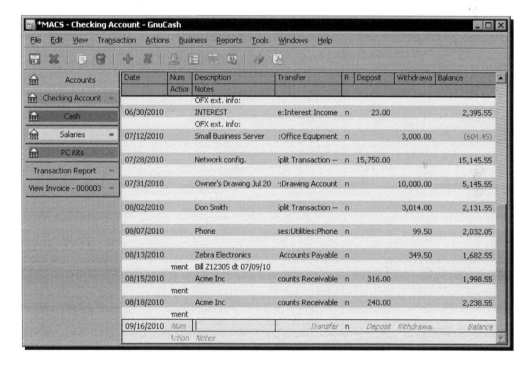

What just happened?

Arranging your workspace to suit your working style, at a minimum, helps reduce distractions. And, at best, it can help improve your productivity. People have different approaches to arranging their workspace. Some get a good chair and arrange it in such a way that they can sit for hours without pain or discomfort. Others play relaxing music. Some add a lush green indoor plant in their office while others need a whiteboard for outlining their thoughts.

In the same way, you can customize and personalize GnuCash to suit your working style.

 The **Edit | Preferences** settings are applicable per user. If you have more than one GnuCash application, the selections you make here will apply to all of those applications. However, if you have another user, your business partner or an associate, even though they may be working on the same application, they can have their own preference settings.

While most of these settings are accessible from the **Preferences** dialog, there are others that can be changed from other menu items.

 GnuCash is eager to act on your command. There is no **OK** button in the **GnuCash Preferences** dialog. As soon as you change a setting, you can see it take effect. When you are done, use the **Close** button to close the dialog.

GnuCash preferences

Here are some of the preference settings and the result of that setting. This is not intended to be an exhaustive list of settings. This is intended to provide additional detail, where needed, beyond what is available in the pop-up tips. Feel free to try out various options to see how you can use these preferences to suit your working style.

 What does a preference do?

For many preferences, you can pause the mouse over the preference setting in the **GnuCash Preferences** dialog and a pop-up tip will appear with details of what that setting will do.

Accounting period:

Preference setting	Result
Start Date and **End Date**	Many businesses in the US tend to have quarterly sales and other business targets. So, for much of the quarter, a setting of **Start of this quarter** and **End of this quarter** will work. Soon after the quarter has ended though, you will be doing a lot of catching up with the end of the quarter sales and expense postings as well as running reports. For example, at that time, you can change the settings to **Start of previous quarter** and **End of previous quarter**.

Business:

Preference setting	Result
Tax Included (Invoices)	Whether taxes are included by default in entries on invoices. This setting is inherited by new customers and vendors.
Notify when due	Lets you set whether you want to be notified when a bill will soon become due.
Days in advance	How many days in the future to warn about bills coming due.
Tax Included (Bills)	Whether tax is included by default in entries on bills. This setting is inherited by new customers and vendors.

General:

Preference Setting	Result
Display "tip of the Day" dialog	You can turn off the option to display the **Tip of the Day** dialog on start-up.
Show close button on notebook tabs	Adds a small close icon on each tab, to make it easier to close the various tabs.
Compress files	This option determines whether the GnuCash data file will be compressed or not. If you have a large file, you can use this option to save space.
Auto-save time interval	You can set how often you want GnuCash to save changes. If you set this to zero, there will be no auto-save.
Retain log files	This option lets you select how long log files should be retained. You can choose **Never**, **Forever**, or **For** and then the number of days.

Online Banking:

Preference Setting	Result
QIF Import – Show Documentation	Shows more detailed help as you step through the QIF importer.
Generic importer – Use bayesian matching	This option will let GnuCash learn new matching rules based on your manual mapping a transaction to an account. It applies to all importers except QIF.
Match display threshold	The minimal score a potential match must have to be displayed in the match list. Higher values will tighten the matching.
Auto-add threshold	A transaction whose best match's score is in the red zone (above the display threshold, but below or equal to Auto-add threshold) will be added by default. Please refer to the *Electronic reconciliation* section in *Chapter 4, How Not To Get Lost in the Transactions Jungle*.
Auto-clear threshold	A transaction whose best match's score is in the green zone (above or equal to Auto-clear threshold) will be cleared by default. Please refer to the *Electronic reconciliation* section in *Chapter 4, How Not To Get Lost in the Transactions Jungle*.
Commercial ATM fees threshold	If the ATM machine adds a small transaction fee, GnuCash will still be able to match it to the transaction, as long as the difference is below this threshold. For example, if you withdrew $100 from an ATM machine, you may have entered that amount in GnuCash. However, the bank will add the ATM transaction fee and show $103. If you set the ATM fees threshold at $3 or above, this will still be matched automatically and will not need your manual intervention.

Other preference settings

There are some other preferences that can be set elsewhere outside of the **GnuCash Preferences** dialog. We will cover those next.

Set a color to each account tab

In addition to the preferences you can set from the **GnuCash Preferences** dialog, as we saw in the tutorial, you can set a color to each account tab from the **Edit Account** dialog.

In the **Pick a Color** dialog, click the eyedropper and click the color anywhere on your screen to select that color.

No, there is no way to set the color of the report tabs. They are destined to remain in the default gray color.

Resize columns in the account register

To resize columns in the **Account Register** window, you grab the border between the column headers with the mouse, click on it, and stretch the column to the size you want. However, the **Description** column is a tricky one. It is designed to always auto-fill to fit the window size. So, you cannot just reduce the size of the **Description** column because as soon as you let go it will then resize itself to fill the screen. If you want to reduce the size of the **Description** column, you should first stretch the other columns until the horizontal scrollbar appears. At this point, you will be able to reduce the **Description** column back to the full size of the window.

Leaving windows open

As we pointed out earlier, one of the major customizing features in GnuCash is to leave the windows that you need open when you exit GnuCash. When you launch GnuCash again, all of these windows will be recreated with any options and settings that you had selected.

Summary Bar and Status Bar

As we showed in the tutorial, you can opt to show or hide the **Summary Bar** and the **Status Bar** from the **View** menu.

The **Summary Bar** displays balances for the opened account type at a glance. Usually accounts display today's account balance, any balance for future dates, a balance for cleared items, and a reconciled balance.

The **Status Bar** is very useful when you are not sure what a menu item does. When you open the menu and pause on the menu item, it displays more explanation about what that menu item does. It also shows a progress bar when opening or saving a GnuCash data file or generating reports.

Pop quiz – setting your preferences

1. By default, GnuCash opens reports in the same window in a separate tab. How do you make reports open in a new window?

    a. From the **Reports** menu.

    b. From the **Business** menu.

    c. From the **GnuCash Preferences** dialog **Reports** tab.

    d. From the **File** menu.

Have a go hero – setting more of your preferences

At the time of starting GnuCash, you will normally see a **Tip of the day** dialog. Change your preference settings to turn this off.

Protecting your data

As the wise man said, the moment of acceptance that valuable data has been lost forever brings with it a determination to never again operate without a reliable backup. However, we don't want to go there. Let us see what we can do to avoid getting to that moment.

 The tutorial and screenshots in this section are based on GnuCash running on Windows XP.

Time for action – backing up your data

You are going to make a backup of your accounting data in a removable media from your office computer and store it at your home location. Your goal is to be able to restore your books of accounts, if your business computer is stolen or damaged entirely.

1. Prerequisites: Please keep a USB flash drive handy to make a backup copy of files and folders.

2. Find the directory where you created your books of accounts and find the main accounts file. In our case, the file we need is MACS (with the .gnucash extension or without any file name extension). When viewed in Windows Explorer, it will appear as shown in the next screenshot.

3. Make a copy of this MACS file on your USB flash drive.

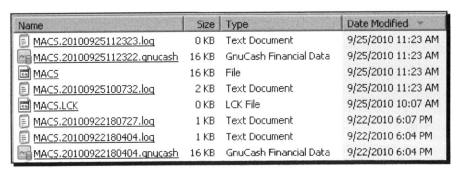

Name	Size	Type	Date Modified
MACS.20100925112323.log	0 KB	Text Document	9/25/2010 11:23 AM
MACS.20100925112322.gnucash	16 KB	GnuCash Financial Data	9/25/2010 11:23 AM
MACS	16 KB	File	9/25/2010 11:23 AM
MACS.20100925100732.log	2 KB	Text Document	9/25/2010 11:23 AM
MACS.LCK	0 KB	LCK File	9/25/2010 10:07 AM
MACS.20100922180727.log	1 KB	Text Document	9/22/2010 6:07 PM
MACS.20100922180404.log	1 KB	Text Document	9/22/2010 6:04 PM
MACS.20100922180404.gnucash	16 KB	GnuCash Financial Data	9/22/2010 6:04 PM

4. Next, find your Documents and Settings folder. Here you will find a folder with your username. Open this folder and you will find folders named .gconf and .gnucash, as shown in the next screenshot.

5. Copy these two folders also onto the USB flash drive.

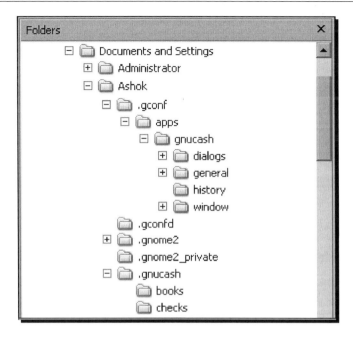

6. Take this USB flash drive with you when you go home.

What just happened?

How often should you backup your accounts? That depends. That depends on how much disruption your business can tolerate. That also depends on whether you have the stomach for putting in the extra work needed to recover from such a crisis. And quick enough so that your customers won't know about it and your business won't be impacted. If you are a superman or superwoman, who has all the source documents well organized and who can pull an all-nighter to catch up with transaction entries for a month, then you can afford to backup once a month. However, ordinary mortals, like you and me, should plan on more frequent backups.

Backing up

Which files should you backup?

1. Backup your main data files that contain the bookkeeping entries, for each book of accounts. In our case, the file is simply called MACS (with the `.gnucash` extension or without any extension). Any time you're working and the MACS file is lost or corrupted, all you have to do is bring this file back and open it in GnuCash and you are back in business. Of course, you will have to redo any transactions that you entered since the last backup. However, now that we have agreed on taking frequent backups, there should not be much of that.

2. As we saw in the tutorial, **Preferences** are stored here at `C:\Documents and Settings\<User>\.gconf\`. You should backup this directory as well.

3. Also, as we saw in the tutorial, custom reports, check formats, stylesheets, and so on are saved here at `C:\Documents and Settings\<User>\.gnucash\`. You should backup this directory as well.

Making use of auto save

There are only two kinds of people in this world. Those who want to do things in their own sweet way and their own sweet time and those who believe, "Why should I bark when I have a dog for that very purpose?"

Depending upon which type of person you are, you might want to use **Auto-save** or not. If you belong to the latter type, you will make full use of the GnuCash built-in capability to auto save changes. In the **Preferences** dialog, in the **General** tab, make sure the **Auto-save time interval** setting in the **Files** pane is set to a number other than zero.

Retaining backup files

In the same **Files** pane of the **General** tab, the **Retain log files** setting will let you say for how long the backup files should be retained. However, there are some limitations to GnuCash backups. For one, this backup only takes care of the main account data files. This doesn't backup your preferences, custom report, check format, or stylesheets. Also, the backups are created in the same place as the main accounts file. If your hard disk crashes or, more likely, gets corrupted by a virus, you will lose all the backups along with the main files. So, to extend the above analogy, while GnuCash will do most of the barking, you have to do some. We recommend that you supplement the retain log files with the following steps, at a minimum:

◆   Move backups to another physical location frequently. For example, you can make a backup on a removable media such as a USB flash drive and take it home, as we saw in the tutorial. Alternatively, you can make a backup on a network drive or on one of the online storage services, if you use one.

♦ When you do the above, make backups of your `.gconf` and `.gnucash` directories as well.

Let us see what happens when you do a manual save or auto-save kicks in. Each time a data file is saved, a backup copy will also be saved with the extension `.gnucash`. This backup file is a complete copy of your previous data file, and the filename format refers to the data file, year, month, day, and time of the backup. For example, the filename `MACS.20101001203512.gnucash` indicates this is a backup copy of the file MACS saved in the year 2010, Oct 1, at 8:35:12 p.m.

In some older GnuCash documentation, you may see some references to replaying the `.log` files to recover transactions lost due to a crash or power failure. However, this is not recommended. The `.log` files do not serve any purpose and can be safely ignored.

If you have set the retention period to 30 days, GnuCash will automatically delete any `.gnucash` and `.log` files that are older than 30 days. If you want to keep the files for a longer or shorter period, you can change this in the GnuCash preferences.

Sometimes the loss or corruption of data may be self-inflicted. You may mess up the data accidentally or otherwise and find that it is easier to start over than try to unravel what you did. The backup files will come in handy in these instances as well.

Restoring from a backup file

To restore from a backup file, simply open the .gnucash file with the date and time to which you wish to return. After you open it, be sure to save this file under a different name.

Password protection

GnuCash does not have a password protection feature. How can you protect your accounts data from being accessed by other people, if your computer is shared? There are two ways of protecting your files from being accessed by unauthorized users:

♦ Using the Operating System (OS) features: Windows XP, Vista, and 7 allow you to set up user accounts with password protection. For example, here is a tutorial on how to password protect Windows XP from eHow (`http://www.ehow.com/how_6930539_password-protect-windows-xp.html`). This way you can decide which files you want to share and which ones you do not. Also, you can give occasional users 'guest' access, so that they cannot view unauthorized files or damage files accidentally or otherwise.

◆ If you need more robust protection, you can look at third-party file system encryption solutions, including some open source ones such as **TrueCrypt** (`http://www.truecrypt.org`).

Pop quiz – creating a backup

1. What are the three things that should be backed up?

   a. The `main accounts` file, the `log` file, and the `.gnucash` file.

   b. The `log` file, the `.gconf` folder, and the `.gnucash` folder.

   c. The `main accounts` file, the `.gconf` folder, and the `.gnucash` folder.

   d. The `main accounts` file, the `stylesheet` folder, and the `check format` folder.

Have a go hero – restoring from a backup file

Try and restore from a backup file the main accounts as well as the preferences and custom reports and stylesheets.

Summary

We learned a lot in this chapter about non-profit accounting using the business features of GnuCash.

Specifically, we covered:

◆ Non-profit accounting: Non-profits have special needs to maintain accounts for each event, project, or program separately. We saw how we can stretch the features of GnuCash to meet those needs.

◆ Personalizing GnuCash: We saw how to set preferences in GnuCash so that you can arrange the environment to suit your needs.

◆ Protecting GnuCash data: We covered backing-up and restoring data as well as options available for password protection.

Now that we've learned about backing up GnuCash data, we're ready to venture into importing data as well as exporting it – which are the topics of the next chapter.

11

Data Import/Export: Use your Phone to enter Expenses

"Ever come back from a business trip with a purse or wallet full of receipts and notes scribbled on napkins and no clear recollection of which expense was for what? No more forgetting your cash expenses, no more half-day expense entry sessions." – extracts from a website reviewing expense tracking services.

You want to avoid tax hassles. You want to stay within budget. However, keeping on top of expenses seems to be a struggle. There are only so many hours in a day. You know that falling behind on recording your expenses in the books will only make matters worse. You have set a specific time aside to deal primarily with record keeping. You know that this will make tax time easier and quicker for you. You know that this necessary function of a business is so crucial to the success of your business that you cannot put it off.

But when you do, sit down and start entering expenses and pulling the receipts together, you find that it takes longer than expected. Much longer. This time can be more usefully spent on things that matter such as meeting with prospects and making deals. Is there any way to make it shorter?

Yes, there is. Capturing expense data while on the road is by far the most effective way to stay on top of business expense reports. There are three major reasons why this will save you time:

1. You are capturing expenses closer to the point of transaction – before you misplace the receipts and, more importantly, before other crises come in and make whatever happened yesterday feel as if it was in a previous life and on another planet.

2. While you are on the road, you are often waiting. Waiting for a flight, waiting for your prospect to show up for lunch or waiting between meetings. This is a great way to get stuff done and fill those waiting times with tasks that will actually save you more time later.

3. Many phones come with a camera these days. If you have one of those, you can take a snap of the receipt as well. If you misplace the receipt, which seems to happen more often than you would like when you are on the road, you have a digital copy as backup. However, check with your accountant or tax consultant whether you are required by IRS to keep your paper receipts as well.

While this is true of mobile employees in general, it is a lot more applicable to small businesses for the following reasons:

◆ As a small business owner, partner, or employee, you tend to wear many hats and try to get a lot of things done while you are on the move.

◆ Smaller businesses tend to buy as needed a broader range of items than larger ones.

◆ Too many small business owners tend to mix and mingle their personal and professional expenses. Even if you are a sole proprietor, you should keep your business and personal expenses separate. This will help come tax time when you need to separate your business expenses. You can do this a lot more effectively if you capture expenses closer to the scene of the action.

Oh, by the way, this approach may also satisfy the IRS requirement to maintain "contemporaneous records" of business travel, entertainment, and other expenses. How much more "contemporaneous" can you get? Check and confirm with your accountant or tax consultant.

In this chapter, we shall:

◆ Learn how to use your mobile phone to capture expenses close to the scene of the action.

◆ See how to migrate data from another accounting software to GnuCash.

◆ Export data from GnuCash for a variety of reasons.

So let's take a closer look at the ways in which this can be done.

Saving expense data in your smartphone and uploading to your PC

Smartphones may look small, but they have a lot more power these days than PCs of yesteryear. More importantly, that is what you are carrying while on the road. You can use it to capture expense data closer to the scene of the action and later sync or upload to your PC when you get back to the office. The trick is to save it in a format that doesn't require you to jump through hoops to get that data into your bookkeeping software. We will see how in this tutorial.

Time for action – using a smartphone to save expense data

Let's say that you have expenses saved in your smartphone in a spreadsheet application. You would like to import these transactions into GnuCash.

1. Prerequisites: A smartphone with a spreadsheet application. You have saved a few cash transactions in the spreadsheet application.

2. Connect your phone to your PC and upload the spreadsheet file. You can upload to any popular spreadsheet of your choice such as OpenOffice.org[4]Calc or Excel[2] or Google Docs[3].

3. Open the spreadsheet in your PC and save the data in a **CSV (Comma Separated Values)** format. OpenOffice.org Calc and Excel will you give you an option in the **Save As** dialog to choose a type. Google Docs has a Download As CSV option for its spreadsheet.

4. When you have completed the preceding step, you should have a file named expenses.csv in your PC with the saved data.

 Make sure that you delete the header, if there are any in the spreadsheet, before saving the data in CSV format. If there is a header in it, when you import into GnuCash, you will see an error such as **Date column could not be understood**.

5. Prerequisites: Make a backup of your GnuCash accounts data file first. Please refer to the *Backing up* section in *Chapter 10, Adapting Gnucash for Non-profits and Personalizing*.

6. Prerequisites: From the menu, select the **Edit | Preferences, General** tab, **Files** pane. Set **Auto-save time interval** to **0** (Do not save automatically). This will give you the option of closing GnuCash without saving, if the data import runs into any problems, and start over.

7. In GnuCash from the menu, select **File | Import | Import CSV/Fixed Width....** In the **Select an CSV/Fixed Width file to import** dialog, find the folder where you have saved the expenses.csv file, select it, and click **Import**.

8. The **Import CSV/Fixed Width File** dialog will open. In the date format, select **m-d-y**. Below that, you should see the **Select the type of each column below** pane showing your data. Click on **None** in the header for the first column. A drop-down list will appear. If that is your date column, select **Date**. For the amount, select **Withdrawal** because these are all expenses. Similarly, select the type of each column, as shown in the following screenshot:

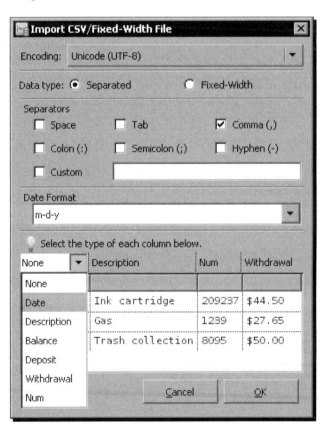

9. Once you have completed selecting the type for all the columns, click **OK**. The **Select Account** dialog will open to let you select an account for the source of funds. Select the **Cash** account under **Current Assets** in **Assets** and click **OK**. The **Generic import transaction matcher** dialog will open, as shown in the following screenshot:

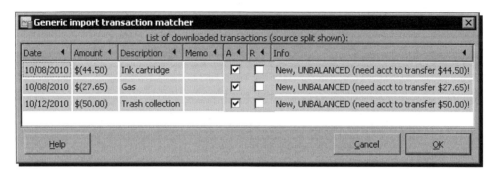

10. All the lines are yellow to show that none of them have been matched with an account. Double-click on the first row. The **Select Account** dialog will open again to let you select a "use of funds account" for that line. Select the **Office Supplies** account under **Expenses**, as shown in the following screenshot.

11. Click on **OK**. That line will turn green and the **Info** column will be updated to show the selected account, as shown in the following screenshot:

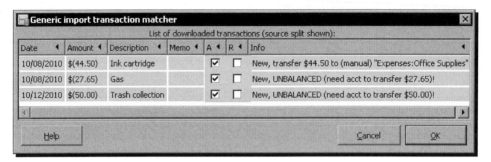

12. Continue double-clicking on each yellow row that has the text "need account to transfer" to select the matching use of funds account. Once all rows have turned green, click **OK** to complete the import.

What just happened?

1. What data should you enter into the mobile phone spreadsheet application? Not a lot. As you saw, GnuCash can only import four columns. So, this is all you need:

   ◆ Date

   ◆ Description

   ◆ Amount

   ◆ Receipt number

Leave the safety door open

Before importing, we recommended turning off the automatic save. If you run into any problems while importing, you can exit without saving and restart from where you were before the import. Now that you have completed the import successfully, don't forget to turn Auto-save back on.

As you saw in the tutorial, while you can map the use of funds to different accounts for each transaction, the source of the funds account is a single one. What if you are paying cash, by check, as well as by credit card, for different expenses? In that case, you need to create separate files for cash, check, and credit card so that each will go into its matching account.

There are two ways of saving expense data in your mobile phone and uploading to your PC.

If you have a smartphone with an application that can edit a spreadsheet, you can enter and save the data in the spreadsheet and sync with your PC or upload to your PC. Then you can **import** that into GnuCash, as you saw in the preceding tutorials.

However, if you don't have a spreadsheet application, you can use a note-taking application. If you use a note-taking application, the data you enter should look like the following:

10/8/2010,Ink cartridge,209237, $44.50

10/8/2010,Gas,1239, $27.65

10/12/2010,Trash collection,8095, $50.00

When you use a note taking application, please follow these guidelines:

- ◆ As you see in the preceding example, each field should be separated by a comma, a semicolon, or a colon. Whichever punctuation you select as the separator, just be consistent throughout that file.

- ◆ Make sure you click the *Enter* key at the end of each transaction so that the next transaction starts on a new line.

- ◆ The $ sign is optional. If it is convenient for you, enter it. Otherwise feel free to leave it out.

- ◆ Do not use any commas, or other separator such as semicolon or colon that you chose, within the description.

- ◆ Once you have successfully uploaded the file to your PC, make sure to change the filename extension to CSV before attempting to import into GnuCash.

Pop quiz – separating transactions by type of payment

1. How do you make sure that transactions paid in cash, paid by check, and paid by credit card are imported into their matching accounts?

    a. Select the appropriate matching account in the **Select Account** dialog.

    b. Create separate files for each type of payment.

    c. GnuCash will automatically match them by payment type.

    d. Flag each payment as cash, check, or credit.

Have a go hero – archiving the images of receipts

Come up with an archiving system of folders and filenames that will allow you to store the images of receipts so that you will be able to find them, when needed.

Sending data through an expense tracking service

If you don't have a mobile phone that can handle a spreadsheet or a note-taking application, is there another way to capture expenses at the scene of the action? Yes, there is, but it requires a third-party expense tracking service. Let us look at an example.

Time for action – using an expense tracking service to get data into GnuCash

Let's say that you have selected an expense-tracking service, set up an account with them, and registered your mobile phone to send text (also known as SMS) messages. We will walk through the steps to transmit your expenses through such a service to your GnuCash account

1. You have lunch with a client. After lunch, send a text message "Lunch with Jon Smith of ABC Systems 79.50". You buy an accessory for your office PC. You send a text message "Wireless adapter 24.95". On the way to the store, you pay toll. You send a text message "Route 267 toll paid in cash 4.50". Whoa, not so fast, not while still driving! Yes, we did say that you should capture the transaction close to the scene of the action. But not that close. It is acceptable if you reach wherever you are trying to reach safely and then send the text message.

2. Once a week or whatever is the convenient frequency for you to attend to these matters, you can log into the web account of the expense-tracking service.

3. View a report of the expenses for the week or any other selected period. You can quickly check whether everything looks in order. Some of the services will allow you to add notes to the expenses as well.

4. You can then go ahead and import the expenses to your PC as a CSV file or a QIF file, whichever option is available.

5. Prerequisites: Make a backup of your accounts data file first.

6. Now you can follow the appropriate tutorials in this book to import the CSV or QIF file into GnuCash.

What just happened?

If you don't have a mobile phone that can handle a spreadsheet or a note taking application, don't despair. There is no necessity to rush out and spend a pile of money on a smartphone either. Not unless you are looking for a reason anyway to justify to your spouse why you are buying a fancy toy. We will show you an alternative way to capture expenses.

However, please note that this cannot be done from your phone to your PC and GnuCash directly. You need to sign up for a third-party **expense tracking** service. There are several on the market. Some of these are paid services and others are free at present. Please evaluate your options and satisfy yourself that there is business value in doing this and the associated costs, if any, are acceptable before taking the plunge.

For importing notes

If you want to import notes, use the QIF format. The CSV format doesn't have the capability to import notes.

Selecting an expense tracking service

Here is a list of some expense tracking services:

◆ **xpenser** (`http://xpenser.com/`)

◆ **Expensify** (`https://www.expensify.com/`)

◆ **iXpenseIt** (`http://www.ixpenseit.com/`)

There are several other such services. While evaluating and selecting an expense tracking service, you might want to look into the following aspects:

◆ Most of the expense tracking services will allow you to export CSV. However, if you need QIF export, look for that.

◆ Some services allow you to submit receipts using your mobile phone's camera.

◆ These services will provide multiple ways to send a message, namely, text (SMS) message, e-mail, IM, or Twitter messages. See what works for you and verify you can use that with the service.

◆ Some services allow you to send the message even through a voice call. If you need that feature, look for that and also test that feature to see how effective it is in transcribing your voice calls.

◆ Some services also have features to track mileage as well as currency conversion. If you need these extra services, look for those as well.

Last but not least, cost is always a consideration for a small business. Look for a free service, even if some of the bells and whistles are not available. Once you start using the service, you can evaluate the business value of some of the advanced features and determine whether you need those.

Pop quiz – importing a CSV file

1. While importing expenses, when you map the CSV fields, you will map the amount field to which of the following:

    a. Balance

    b. Deposit

    c. Withdrawal

    d. Total

Have a go hero – adding notes to transactions

Add notes to transactions by editing the transaction using the web interface. This will allow you to provide justification to the IRS, for example, which client you met over lunch and what business was discussed. Export that to QIF format. After importing the transaction into GnuCash, confirm that the notes were imported successfully.

Migrating to GnuCash from other accounting software

You make an effort to select the right software and try and stick to it. However, business requirements change and you have a business to run. Let us say you find that your existing software has become a financial burden or is not allowing you or your team to be effective. You want to find practical ways to work around such limitations. You can't be like the person with a hammer for whom everything looks like a nail. You have to choose the right tool for the right job. And if your requirements change, you may very well have to change the tool. And find a way to transition into the new tool which brings us to one of the main reasons for importing.

Let us say that you are using another financial accounting software today. Perhaps you are uncovering the layers of hidden costs or that it is overkill for the size and complexity of your business or that it forces you to pay for upgrade whether you want to or not. After extensive evaluation, you have decided to migrate to GnuCash. Let us see an example of such a migration in this tutorial.

Time for action – migrating to GnuCash from other software

Let's say that your transaction data is in Quicken Home & Business. You want to migrate this to GnuCash. We will first walk through the steps of performing this migration. Then we will analyze the pros and cons of such a migration:

1. Prerequisites: You have already exported the data from Quicken. You have a set of QIF files. While exporting, please remember that you can have only one category per file.

2. Prerequisites: Create a new account hierarchy in GnuCash first. Save it with the name CAMS.

3. Prerequisites: Make a backup of the CAMS file. If you want to fine tune your migration, you may have to restart from this backup file a couple of times.

4. Prerequisites: Set the following preferences. In the **General** tab's **Files** pane, set **Auto-save time interval** to **0**. This means data is not saved automatically. If there are any problems, this will allow you to exit without saving and start over. In the **Online Banking** tab, the **QIF Import** pane, check **Show Documentation**.

5. To start the import, select from the menu **File | Import | Import QIF**. You will see the QIF Import information dialog. It will show that only when you click Apply at the end of the series of steps the data will be imported. Click **Forward**.

6. The **Select a QIF file to load** dialog will open. Click **Select** and find the folder where you have stored the QIF files. Select the first file to import and click **Import**. Click **Forward**.

7. You will see the **QIF files you have loaded** dialog showing the file you have loaded, as shown in the following screenshot:

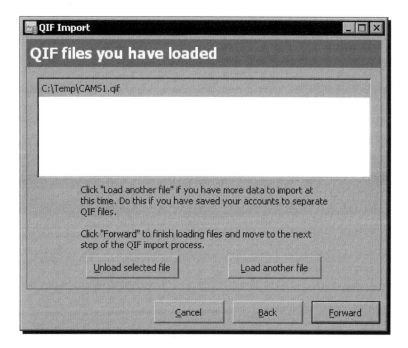

8. Click the **Load another file** button and load the next file. Continue until you have loaded all the files in your set. Once you have loaded the last file, click **Forward**.

9. You will see the **Accounts and stock holdings** dialog telling you that many new accounts will be created if it cannot find a match. Click **Forward**.

10. The **Match QIF accounts with GnuCash accounts** dialog will open, as shown in the following screenshot:

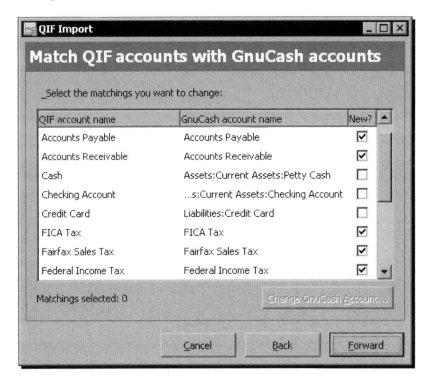

11. If you find that some of the matching is not right, you can click on that line. The **Change GnuCash Account...** button will become enabled. You can click that and select a different GnuCash account as a match. If some of the transactions end up in the wrong account, you can individually edit those transactions to the right account, after the import. Click **Forward**.

12. You will see the **Income and Expense Categories** information dialog. Click **Forward**.

13. You will see the **Match QIF accounts with GnuCash accounts** dialog again. Click **Forward**.

14. You will see the **Payees and memos** information dialog. Click **Forward**.

15. The **Match payees/memos to GnuCash accounts** dialog will open. Click **Forward**.

16. The **Enter the QIF file currency** dialog will open. **USD (US Dollar)** will be selected by default. Click **Forward**.

17. GnuCash will import the data into a temporary staging area. You may see the progress bar briefly. The **Update your GnuCash accounts** dialog will open. This dialog has the all important **Apply** button that will actually import the data into GnuCash. Click **Apply**. You should now see the **Account Tree** window with all the imported transactions, as well as any newly created accounts, as shown in the following screenshot:

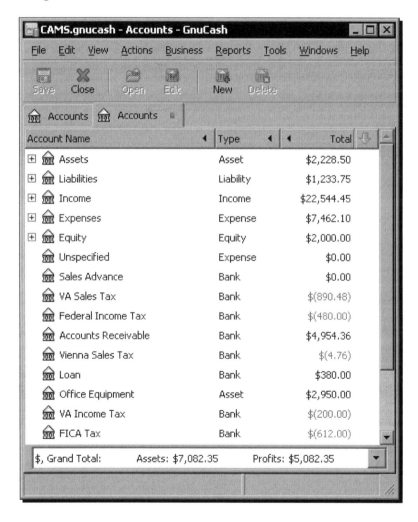

18. Once the transactions have been imported successfully, don't forget to **Save**.

What just happened?

Now that you have seen the steps for performing one such migration, let us look at the different ways of handling such a migration and their pros and cons.

 GnuCash can only import transactions. It can also create the account tree under some circumstances. However, you will have to enter other data such as customers, vendors, scheduled transactions, and so on manually.

Migrating data is not easy

Migration of accounting data from one software to another is a difficult process for the following reasons:

- The extent of support for exporting data varies not only from one software to another, but also from one version to another.

- There is not a single common data standard across different accounting software.

- In the absence of a well defined format or process, you are left to research and try out various ways until you find one that works.

- You may have to locate, evaluate, and use third-party open source, freeware, or commercial software tools for converting from one data format to another.

- After importing, you have to rearrange your account tree.

Keeping in mind these difficulties, you may be able to meet your business requirements by archiving the old data and starting a fresh implementation of GnuCash.

First consider a fresh start on GnuCash

The best time for archiving your old data and implementing GnuCash afresh is the beginning of the year. So, plan on continuing to use your existing software till the end of the current year. Side by side, you can keep working on trying out GnuCash with sample transactions and tweaking your account tree to better suit the needs of your business based on what you have learned about what works and what needs to be improved. Then when the New Year rolls by, you can implement GnuCash and finish up the previous year's transactions in your existing software and archive it.

Business case for migration

We list some circumstances, as examples, that may justify putting in the effort to perform a migration of the old data from your existing accounting software to GnuCash:

- ◆ You started on another application a few months ago and want to switch to GnuCash for whatever reason.

- ◆ There are compelling business reasons why you cannot wait till the end of the year and you have to switch in the middle of the year.

- ◆ You have to have reports comparing the same period in prior years and they must be run in the same software so that your comparisons are apples to apples.

- ◆ You are evaluating GnuCash. Migrating is the shortest route to get some real data in for a quick evaluation.

- ◆ Your older application will not work on the newer operating system you are upgrading to. So, archiving is not a viable option for you.

At the end of all this assessment, if you are convinced that you have a strong business case for attempting to migrate, take a deep breath, roll up your sleeves, and get ready to get your hands dirty:

- ◆ You will be required to do web research to see what other people in your situation have done, what worked for them, what didn't, and what are the gotchas to look out for.

- ◆ You will search for, find, evaluate, and select format conversion tools. Some of them may be open source or freeware and others may be commercial software.

- ◆ You will have to back up your data and run several trials to select the process that gives the best results.

If you are tech savvy, that is great. If not, take your "trusted techie" out for lunch. This may be a friend, cousin, consultant, or a fellow small business owner you have an informal mutual cooperation agreement with. At some point, if you run into trouble, you may need to call in the troops. You can also get help in the **GnuCash User Forum** (`http://gnucash.1415818. n4.nabble.com/GnuCash-User-f1415819.html`). Search the forum first to see whether your question has been already asked and answered. If not, post a new message clearly stating what system you are using, what you are trying to do, which step failed, and what the specific error is. And, of course, don't forget to thank the volunteers who not only provide great software but are very prompt to respond to users' questions as well.

Migrating from Excel[2] and OpenOffice.org[4] Calc

You are using a spreadsheet to maintain your accounts. These are getting more complicated over time and seem to be requiring more and more of your time. It now appears burdensome to keep track of your accounts through this manual method. You have also come to the conclusion that your business could benefit from modern accounting software features such as bank reconciliation, scheduled transactions, sales tax, income tax statements, and check printing.

You have two options to import that data into GnuCash:

- ◆ Save as CSV and then import into GnuCash.
- ◆ Convert to QIF using a freeware Excel to QIF converter, such as **XL2QIF** (`http://xl2qif.chez-alice.fr/xl2qif_en.php`) and then import it into GnuCash. For converting from Calc, you can try a converter like Calc to QIF (`http://xl2qif.chez-alice.fr/calc2qif_en.php`). One advantage of using QIF is that GnuCash will create your accounts automatically from the information in the QIF files. The QIF format will also import the **Notes** field in addition to the **Description** field.

Make a trial import with each option and see what works best for you.

Migrating from Office Accounting[2] (formerly Office SBA[2])

Microsoft Office Accounting was formerly known as **Office Small Business Accounting** (**Office SBA** for short). It allows you to export the data to an Excel file. Once the data is in an Excel file, you can follow the same process as outlined in the section on migrating from Excel.

Migrating from Quicken Home & Business[1]

The level of difficulty of migrating from Quicken[1] depends largely on whether your version of Quicken allows you to export to a QIF file.

Your version of Quicken allows you to export to a QIF file

If your version of Quicken allows you to export to a QIF file, then you have the following direct path to bringing that data into GnuCash:

- ◆ Export your transactions from Quicken to a QIF file.
- ◆ Import the resulting QIF file into GnuCash.

An additional advantage of this approach may be that you can export the entire file and its categories in one pass.

Your version of Quicken does not allow you to export to a QIF file

If your version of Quicken does not allow you to export to a QIF file, then you can try the alternative approach below:

- ◆ Create a report of each Category.
- ◆ Save or print to file the report to a spreadsheet format. You may have to rename the print to file report from PRN to CSV.
- ◆ Convert the data to QIF format using a freeware or commercial tool.
- ◆ Save the newly created QIF file.
- ◆ Repeat the above steps until you have saved all of the accounts you want to import into GnuCash.
- ◆ Use the GnuCash import QIF feature to import all the saved QIF files in a single import step.

After the import is completed, you can rearrange your accounts so that they are all subaccounts of the five main accounts namely, assets, liabilities, income, expenses, or equity. You can do this from **Edit Accounts** by changing the **Parent Account**. If there is no equity account you can create one.

Migrating from QuickBooks[1]

QuickBooks doesn't support exporting to QIF format. Instead, it allows export to the IIF format. So, you have the following options to export data from QuickBooks:

- ◆ Export to IIF and then convert it to CSV.
- ◆ Another approach that has worked for some people is as follows. Create a report of the transactions. Print the report but use the print to file option. Set the file type to Excel before printing. Rename the extension of the resulting file from PRN to CSV.

Then you can either import the CSV data directly or convert the CSV to QIF using a freeware or commercial tool.

Exporting FAQ

Here is a list of frequently asked questions about exporting from other accounting software and our answers:

- ◆ Q: I can't find the **Export** menu item under the File menu. Help!
  - ❑ A: In some of the software, in order to export, you must be in single user mode and have Owner, Office Manager, or Accountant access privileges.

◆ Q: Even after changing my role and trying single user mode, I am not able to find a way to export. What now?

❑ A: You may have to create reports and save them to QIF or Excel format.

◆ Q: I have created a report. However, there is not a way to save it to QIF or the Excel format.

❑ A: In some of the software, you have to print to file. In order to do this, print the report. However, select print to file and choose the appropriate format. When you go through this route, you may have to rename the extension of the resulting file from PRN to CSV.

Importing FAQ

Here is a list of frequently asked questions about migration to GnuCash and our answers:

◆ Q: I am trying to import a QIF file. I get an error message saying "QIF file load failed:File does not appear to be a QIF file". What could be wrong?

❑ A: Make sure the file you are trying to import is a QIF file.

◆ Q: My QIF import appeared to go well. The transactions seem OK. However, my account tree is all messed up. Should I start over?

❑ A: In migration, your primary goal is to get the transactions into GnuCash. If that is successful, there is no need to start over. You can rearrange the account tree by editing each account and changing its **Parent Account**, as needed.

◆ Q: In the QIF file, I made sure to export a 'memo' field, but that is not to be found in GnuCash after import. What do I do now?

❑ A: That will be imported into the **Notes** field, which is normally not visible in the GnuCash account register. You can select the **View | Double Line** mode to see this.

◆ Q: What is the best way to handle split transactions?

❑ A: You can leave split transactions, such as loan repayments, which have both interest and principal, in the **Imbalance** account. After the import is completed, you can open the **Imbalance** account and edit each transaction to send it to wherever it belongs. In short, you can use the **Imbalance** account as a To-Do list.

◆ Q: I was able to export from Quicken only one category at a time. Now I am left with a number of QIF files. What is the best way to import them?

  ❑ A: If you have multiple QIF files, make sure to import them all together, in one run. Otherwise you will find duplicate transactions or mismatched transfers.

◆ Q: Can I use the importer to create an empty account hierarchy?

  ❑ A: No, the QIF Importer cannot import an empty account tree. It is designed to import transactions. As part of importing transactions, it will create the accounts necessary. However, you cannot use it to import an empty account hierarchy alone.

Pop quiz – format suitable for creating accounts

1. Which of the following formats will not only import the transactions, but also create the matching accounts?

   a. QIF

   b. CSV

   c. IIF

   d. OFX

Have a go hero – migrating from Excel to GnuCash

Find, evaluate, and select a freeware Excel to QIF converter tool. Use this tool to migrate your accounting from Excel to GnuCash. List what benefits this approach has over saving as a CSV file and importing that.

Exporting data from GnuCash

You may want to export transaction data from GnuCash for a variety of reasons. Let us look at some examples.

Time for action – exporting data from GnuCash for migration and other purposes

Let us say you are trying to migrate to another accounting and bookkeeping software. That software requires either a CSV file or a QIF file for importing. In this tutorial, we will see how to create a CSV file of all the transactions in GnuCash:

1. Prerequisites: Make a backup of your accounts data file first.

2. From the menu, select **Reports | Transaction Report**. Open the **Report Options** dialog and unselect **Totals**, **Subtotals**, **Account Name**, and **Secondary Keys**, leaving only the main headers other than the transactions. The **Transaction Report** will now appear as shown in the following screenshot:

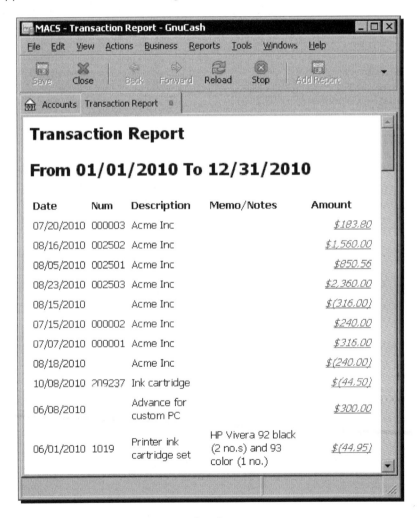

3. From the menu, select **File | Export | Export Report** to export that report as an HTML file.

4. Open this HTML file in your favorite spreadsheet program.

5. Delete all the header rows, leaving only the transaction data. Select the amount column. Change the format so that the 1000 separator comma is removed. Save this file first in the spreadsheet format. Then, save the same spreadsheet as a CSV file.

What just happened?

You may find that you want to **export** data from GnuCash for a variety of reasons:

- ◆ You have to send accounting data to your accountant. However, your accountant doesn't use GnuCash. In the chapter on reports earlier, we showed you how to create a report and export it to a spreadsheet to send to your accountant.

- ◆ Another important use for data export is in TXF Export for creating tax schedules for enclosing with your Income Tax returns to the IRS. We have covered those already in an earlier chapter.

- ◆ You want to start again from scratch but want to keep the same account hierarchy without any of the transactions. You can do this by selecting from the menu **File | Export | Export Accounts**. This will export only the account hierarchy into a separate file.

Let us look at migrating from GnuCash to another accounting software in greater detail in the next section.

Migrating from GnuCash to other accounting software

You may want to migrate from GnuCash to another accounting package for a variety of reasons:

- ◆ You are not happy with the features, or the lack thereof, of GnuCash. This is understandable. As we said earlier, GnuCash doesn't have a payroll module, it doesn't have an inventory module or **Point of Sale (POS)** capability or integration. Also, GnuCash is not a multi-user software. If you need any of these features, you are better off looking for something else.

- ◆ You have outgrown GnuCash. Congratulations! Hopefully GnuCash was helpful in some little way to help your business grow. As we said earlier, GnuCash is suitable only for small businesses. If you have outgrown that, naturally, you should look for a suitable bookkeeping and accounting software that can handle the needs of your current and future needs.

There are two ways to get all of the data out of GnuCash for migration:

◆ As we showed In the tutorial, you can create a Transaction Report covering all the transactions in GnuCash and then save it to a spreadsheet and from there to a CSV file.

◆ Alternatively, **GnuCash to QIF** (`http://gnucashtoqif.sourceforge.net/`) is an open source project that takes the GnuCash account file and converts it to a QIF file. Remember to save the GnuCash accounts file without compressing it, before running this program. This can be done from the menu **Edit | Preferences | General** tab, **Files** pane, and uncheck **Compress Files**.

Pop quiz – creating a Transaction Report with all of the transactions

1. How do you create a Transaction Report with all of the transactions, after selecting all the Accounts and Subaccounts in the Accounts tab of the Report Options dialog?

   a. In the **Report Options** dialog, in the **General** tab, select **All**.

   b. In the **Report Options** dialog, in the **Display** tab, select **All**.

   c. In the **Report Options** dialog, in the **General** tab, select **Start Date** to be the same as your earliest transaction or earlier and the **End Date** to be the same as your last transaction or later.

   d. In the **Report Options** dialog, in the **Sorting** tab, select **All**.

Have a go hero – converting a GnuCash fileto a QIF file

Download the conversion tool developed by the open source project for converting GnuCash accounts file to a QIF file. Use that tool to take your GnuCash accounts file and convert it to a QIF file.

Summary

We learned a lot in this chapter about importing transactions into GnuCash as well as exporting transactions from GnuCash.

Specifically, we covered:

◆ Using your smartphone: We looked at two different formats in which you can save the transactions in your smartphone and then sync it or upload it to your PC and then import that into GnuCash.

- Using a third-party expense tracking service: We learned how to make use of a third-party expense tracking service to send transactions and then bring them into GnuCash.

- Migrating from other accounting software to GnuCash: We covered the various formats and processes available to migrate from other accounting software to GnuCash.

- Exporting transactions from GnuCash: We saw that there were two ways available to export transactions out of GnuCash.

Now that we've covered all of the features that will be of use to most normal users of GnuCash, we're ready to look at some of the advanced features of GnuCash – which is the topic of the next chapter.

[1]QuickBooks, Quicken and Quicken Home & Business are registered trademarks of Intuit Inc.

[2]Excel, Office Accounting and Office Small Business Accounting (SBA) are registered trademarks of Microsoft Corporation.

[3]Google Docs is a registered trademark of Google Inc.

[4]OpenOffice.org is a registered trademark of Sun Microsystems Inc.

12
Application Integration and Other Advanced Topics

"Thinking of your firm's current planning cycle, how important is each of the following goals? The top 3 answers were: 1. Improve integration between applications. 2. Reduce IT costs. 3. Use information technologies to improve innovation." – from a recent survey of small medium businesses.

You run a small business. You don't mess with fancy software that is overkill for the size of your business. However, you do leverage technology to keep costs down and, more importantly, to provide quicker and better service to your customers. Providing customized service at lightning speed is the name of your game. That is your strength. That is your unique value proposition. That is where the big boys cannot even begin to touch you. You are constantly looking for ways to provide customized service and ways to speed it up. In addition to GnuCash, you use a few other applications to run your business. However, you find that your team is often copying and pasting data from one system to the other. It is probably OK if this has to be done once in a while. However, if it is done often, it wastes time, frustrates people, and leads to mistakes, expensive mistakes, such as shipping a product to the wrong address.

What you are looking for are inexpensive ways to transfer data from one system to another. For most of the data, if you can sync up once a week, that should be enough. For some types of data, you may need to do it once a day. This data sync up from one application to another is what goes by the fancy name of **Application Integration**. You can get scripts written and scheduled to run weekly or nightly; that will keep the data among these applications in sync. However, in the past, you were frustrated by the limited ability of GnuCash to export data, but not anymore. Say "Hello" to GnuCash's new feature to export to a SQL database. You can get all of the data from GnuCash in convenient ways that can be used with popular querying and reporting tools.

Once you get GnuCash data into databases, you can not only query the data and use it for application integration, but you can also create highly customized reports and charts using third-party software as well.

In this chapter, we shall:

◆ Learn how to export the GnuCash data into popular database formats.

◆ Use popular query tools to extract the data we need from the database.

◆ Use popular reporting tools to create custom reports and charts.

◆ Create application integration to import this data into other applications.

◆ In addition, we shall also learn how to handle foreign currency transactions in GnuCash.

◆ Use the Customer Job and Vendor Job features of GnuCash.

◆ Learn special actions such as voiding a transaction, adding a reversing transaction, and year-end closing of books.

◆ Learn about inventory management and mileage tracking.

So let's get on with it...

These tutorials assume a certain level of proficiency

This chapter assumes a certain level of proficiency.

◆ We assume that you can find, evaluate, select, and install software, such as ODBC drivers, and configure them.

◆ We assume that you are proficient in one of the two leading office applications –OpenOffice.org or Microsoft Office.

◆ Unlike the GnuCash tutorials so far, which were not only step-by-step but also provided additional tips and pointed out pitfalls along the way, the third-party software tutorials will be illustrative, because these are out of the scope of this book.

If you are not that familiar with these, you might want to spend some time doing some self-study tutorials, or get help from a knowledgeable person. While we show the use of OpenOffice.org for the query and Microsoft Office for the custom reports and charts, you can stick to the one you are most comfortable with.

Using OpenOffice.org Base to query data

As we said earlier, you can use the GnuCash data exported into a SQL database for creating custom reports and charts as well as for application integration. But first, we will see how to export the GnuCash data into SQL databases as well as how to use popular tools to extract the specific data you need from the exported data.

Time for action – using popular office software to query GnuCash data

We are going to do two things in this tutorial. First we are going to export the GnuCash data into a **SQLite** database. **SQLite** is a popular open source database that is being used behind the scenes in many well-known applications. It is possible that you already use SQLite, though you may not even be aware of that. As a prerequisite to the next step, get an ODBC driver for SQLite3 (`http://www.ch-werner.de/sqliteodbc/`) or a similar one and install it on your PC. This ODBC driver enables client applications such as OpenOffice. org Base to connect to databases such as SQLite3 as long as both support the **ODBC (Open Database Connectivity)** standard. After exporting the GnuCash data into SQLite3 database, we are going to use OpenOffice.org Base[1] to connect to that exported database and run a query to extract specific data of interest to us.

1. Select from the menu **File | Save As.... The Save As... dialog will open.** Click on the **Data Format dropdown** and select **sqlite3** as shown in the following screenshot:

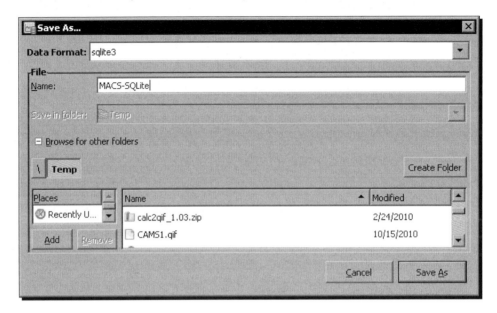

2. Click the **Save As** button. Select the folder where you want to save this and give it the file name MACS-SQLite. It will be saved as `MACS-SQLite.gnucash`.

3. Prerequisites: In order to connect to this SQLite3 database from OpenOffice.org and other applications, you need an ODBC driver. As mentioned earlier, evaluate, select, download, and install an ODBC driver for SQLite3.

4. Once the ODBC driver is installed, you are ready to set up a **DSN (Data Source Name)**, for this database so that you can connect to it from OpenOffice.org and other such applications. In Windows XP select **Control Panel | Administrative Tools | Data Sources (ODBC)**. Windows Vista and 7 should be similar.

5. The **ODBC Data Source Administrator** dialog will open. In the **System DSN** tab, under **System Data Sources** select **SQLite3 Data Source** click **Add** and the **Create New Data Source** dialog will open. Select **SQLite3 ODBC Driver** and click **Finish**.

6. The **SQLIte3 ODBC DSN Configuration** dialog will open. Enter **Data Source Name** as MACS and for **Database Name** click **Browse** and find the **MACS-SQLite.gnucash** file that you saved from GnuCash. Click **OK**. You should see a new System DSN created with the name **MACS** as shown in the following screenshot:

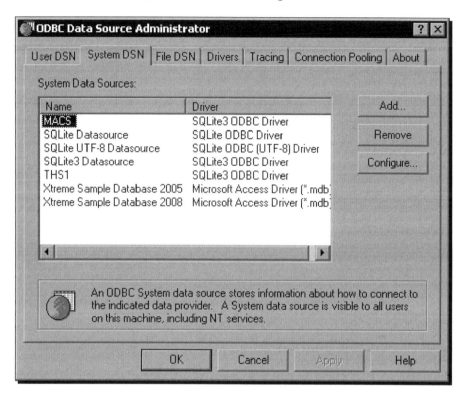

7. Prerequisites: Make sure you have OpenOffice.org installed in your system. This tutorial, as well as the screenshots, is based on the OpenOffice.org version 3.2 running on Windows XP. If you have a different version or are on another operating system, please look for equivalent steps.

8. We are planning to use OpenOffice.org Base, which is the database application. Launch OpenOffice.org and under **Create a new document** click on the Database icon. You can also select from the menu **File | New | Database**. The Database **Wizard** will open, as shown in the following screenshot:

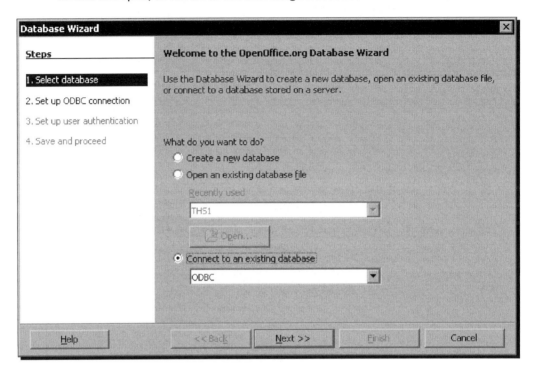

9. Select the **Connect to an existing database** option, select **ODBC** in the drop-down list, and click **Next >>**.

10. The second step in the database wizard is to **Set up a connection to an ODBC database**. Click on the **Browse** button in the **Name of the ODBC data source on your system** field. The **Data Source** dialog will open. Now that you have already set up an ODBC DSN, you should see **MACS** in that list, as shown in the next screenshot. Select **MACS**.

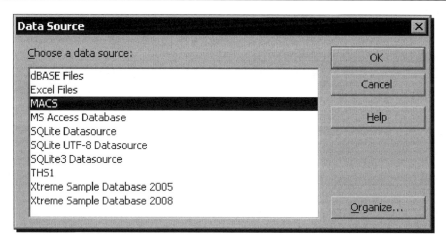

11. Click **OK** to launch **OpenOffice.org Base**.

12. Click **Queries** on the left pane. Click **Create Query in design view....** The **Add Table or Query** dialog will open. Select **accounts** and click **Add**. Similarly add **splits** and **transactions** tables.

13. Select from the menu **Insert | New Relation....** The **Join Properties** dialog will open. Make an inner join from the **accounts** table **guid** field to the **splits** table **account_guid** field. In the same way, create another inner join from the **splits** table **tx_guid** field to the **transactions** table **guid** field.

14. Drag the **name** field from the **accounts** table and drop it into the **Field** list below. Similarly add **description** and **post_date** from the **transaction** table as well as **value_num** from the **splits** table.

15. We want only transactions from the Checking Account. In the **Criterion** line under **name**, type **Checking Account** and tab out. OO Base will add single quotes.

16. We want them ordered by amount, with the largest amount first. In the **Sort** line under **value_num**, select **descending** from the drop-down list.

17. Now click the **Run Query** button to see the results of the query duly filtered and sorted, as shown in the following screenshot:

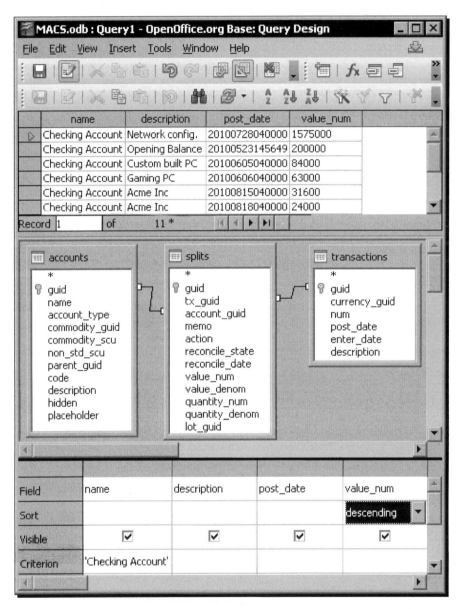

18. Don't forget to save the query for future use.

What just happened?

"OK, I was able to export the GnuCash data into a SQL database, connect to it from OpenOffice.org, and run the query successfully. Great! But when I look at the result, I don't seem to have achieved anything useful. Tell me again, why am I jumping through all these hoops?" Well, that was just a means to an end, not the end in itself. No wonder you were underwhelmed. In the next couple of sections, we will look at creating custom reports and charts as well as application integration. All of those will require very specific data. These queries will supply that specific data to them.

In the preceding tutorial, we looked at a small sample of data from three of the tables. We were able to get the specific data we wanted, filter out unwanted data, and order the data the way we wanted it. There are a total of about two dozen tables and you can do plenty with those, depending on what business problems you are trying to solve.

 Getting access to GnuCash's data can sometimes feel like a "Fortunately, Unfortunately" Improvisation Exercise. Fortunately, you have access to all of the GnuCash data. Unfortunately the data is raw and you have to work at formatting it to make it presentable and usable.

Which databases?

In addition to SQLite3, GnuCash Export to SQL database gives you the option to export to the following popular open source databases as well:

- MySQL: In the **Save As** dialog, you should select **mysql**.
- PostgreSQL: In the **Save As** dialog, you should select **postgres**.

SQLite3 has a small footprint and does not need a lot of memory, disk space, or processing resources. On the other hand, if you are looking for a more robust and heavy duty database, you might want to consider MySQL or PostgreSQL. Depending on your business need and familiarity, you might want to choose one of these options for your custom reporting, query, and application integration needs.

Pop quiz – GnuCash default data format

1. When you simply click **Save**, GnuCash saves in its default data format. What is GnuCash's default data format?

    a. `xml`

    b. `gnucash`

    c. `sqlite3`

    d. `csv`

Have a go hero – formatting the GnuCash raw data

As you can see, the **post_date** and **value_num** fields display the raw data stored by GnuCash. Format these fields to be more presentable and usable.

Using MS Excel to create reports and charts

Next let us look at how to create reports and charts using another popular spreadsheet – Microsoft Office Excel[2].

Time for action – connecting from Excel to create reports and charts

You are going to create your Monthly Expenses report and also display it as a chart. This will give you the flexibility to extend reporting and charting capability beyond what is available in the canned GnuCash reports.

1. Prerequisites: Make sure that you have saved your MACS accounts as a SQLite3 database from GnuCash.

2. Prerequisites: Make sure that you have Microsoft Office Excel installed on your system. This tutorial and the screenshots are based on Excel 2003 running on Windows XP. If you have a different version or another operating system, then please look for the equivalent steps.

3. Prerequisites: In order to connect to this SQLite3 database from Excel, you need an ODBC driver. Make sure you have installed an ODBC driver for SQLite3 and created an ODBC DSN to the exported GnuCash accounts file.

4. While you are in a new worksheet in Excel, from the menu, select **Data | Import External Data | New Database Query…**. The **Choose Data Source** dialog will open.

5. You will see the **Databases** tab in the **Choose Data Source** dialog showing a list. Now that you have already set up an ODBC DSN, you should see MACS in that list. Select it and uncheck the **Use the Query Wizard to create/edit queries**, as shown in the following screenshot:

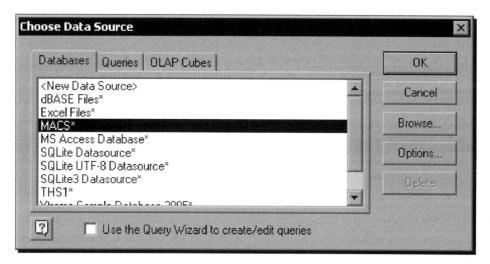

6. Click **OK**. The **Microsoft Query** application will launch with the **Add Tables** dialog open. Select **accounts** and click **Add**. Similarly, add **splits** and **transactions** tables as well.

7. You will find that the **guid**s in the three tables are joined, which is incorrect. You can click on each join and click **Delete** to remove these joins. From the menu, select **Table | Joins…** to open the **Joins** dialog. Now create the two joins, as shown in the next screenshot.

8. Drag and drop the four columns in the Data pane, as shown. We want the **transaction description**, not the **account description**. Click the **Query Now** button to retrieve data, as shown in the following screenshot:

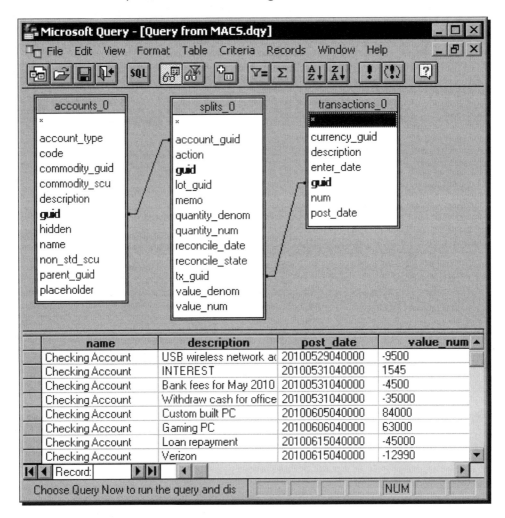

9. Once the data looks OK, select from the menu **File | Return Data to Microsoft Office Excel**.

10. You will get the option of putting the data in a worksheet or creating a pivot table. The pivot table feature is well suited for presenting summarized data as well as for cross tabulations and is available in most spreadsheet applications. Choose to create a pivot table. This will help you to do the monthly report.

11. As we cautioned you earlier, the GnuCash raw data needs to be formatted to be made presentable. For example, the **value_num** field needs to be divided by the `value_denom` field to arrive at the amount.

12. You can then copy the data from the pivot table into a worksheet and format it as $ to create the report and chart, as shown in the following screenshot:

Account Name	May	Jun	Jul	Aug	Sep	Oct	Grand Total
Garbage collection	$50.00	$50.00	$50.00	$50.00	$50.00	$50.00	$300.00
Gas	$27.65	$27.65	$27.65	$27.65	$27.65	$27.65	$165.90
Internet	$99.50	$99.50	$99.50	$99.50	$99.50	$99.50	$597.00
Loan	$380.00	$380.00	$380.00	$380.00	$380.00	$380.00	$2,280.00
Miscellaneous	$45.00	$115.00	$55.00	$100.00	$85.00	$300.00	$700.00
Office Equipment	$59.50	$40.00	$29.50	$15.00	$200.00	$500.00	$844.00
Office Supplies	$95.00	$44.95				$44.50	$184.45
PC Kits		$1,185.25		$898.50		$1,400.00	$3,483.75
Phone	$129.90	$129.90	$129.90	$99.50	$95.00	$95.00	$679.20
Salaries	$2,500.00	$2,500.00	$2,700.00	$2,700.00	$2,700.00	$2,700.00	$15,800.00
Total	**$3,386.55**	**$4,572.25**	**$3,471.55**	**$4,370.15**	**$3,637.15**	**$5,596.65**	**$25,034.30**

What just happened?

Though we didn't walk you through the preceding tutorial step-by-step, rest assured you can create such reports and charts without writing a lot of custom code. However, you do need proficiency with spreadsheets to get your reports and charts just right.

Oh, by the way, looking at the MACS monthly expenses chart, here is a quick friendly tip. The expenses seem to be running out of control. Unless the business of MACS is booming and has consciously decided to spend more money to gear up for better execution, MACS should take a close look at what is happening on the expense side and get that under control. No wonder they said that a picture is worth a thousand words.

Other query and reporting tools

In OpenOffice.org Calc, you should be able to view the ODBC DSN created for the SQLite3 database from **View | Data Sources**. You should also be able to view queries saved in OpenOffice.org Base and execute the queries and retrieve data. Data Pilots are the OpenOffice.org Calc equivalent of pivot tables. You can access them through **Data | Data Pilot | Start...**.

In addition, there are a ton of other query and reporting tools available in the market for SQLite3, including open source, freeware, and commercial tools. Moreover, when you add the tools available for MySQL and PostgreSQL as well, the options are extensive indeed. Depending on your business needs and familiarity, evaluate the options available out there and pick what will work for you and your team.

Pop quiz – understanding GnuCash fields

1. When you look at the tables, you can understand some of the things better that we said earlier about accounts, transactions, and splits. The memo field is stored in which table?

    a. accounts

    b. transactions

    c. splits

    d. none of the above

Have a go hero – changing the report frequency

A monthly report is probably OK for a large business. However, for a small business, a month feels like an eternity. You can't afford to wait that long to take corrective actions. Change the report to make it a Weekly Expense report.

Application integration

As we said earlier, the goal of application integration is to enter data once and reuse it multiple times across different applications, as needed. In order to achieve that, we should be able to export the data we need from one application and import it into other applications.

Time for action – exporting contact information from GnuCash

Let's say that you have a contact management system to keep track of customers, prospects, and other contacts. You find that you are entering all the customer contact information in one system and then either re-entering or copying and pasting all of that information again in the other application. You want to avoid this by entering the data in one application and then exporting from that application to import into the other application. This will avoid duplicate work and the possibility of errors.

1. Prerequisites: Save the GnuCash MACS data in the SQLite3 format. Connect to it from OpenOffice.org Base, create a query to pull the customer contact information including contact name, address, and phone number, and save the query as **Query1.**

2. Launch OpenOffice.org Calc and from the menu, select **View | Data Sources.** You should see all data sources available in the left pane.

3. You should see **MACS** in that list. Click on the **+** sign to expand it and expand the Queries again by clicking on its **+** sign. You should see the **Query1** you earlier saved in OpenOffice.org Base. Click on **Query1** and you should see the data in the right pane. This will serve as a preview to make sure that is the data you want to export.

4. Drag **Query1** and drop it on cell A1 of the spreadsheet below, as shown in the next screenshot.

5. Now that the data you need is in a spreadsheet, you can save this as a CSV format file.

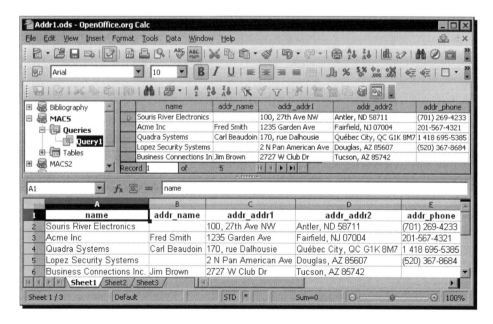

6. You can now import this CSV format file into your contact management system.

What just happened?

Is GnuCash the only application that you use to run your business? Not likely. While each business is unique, it is likely that you use one or more of the following types of applications.

- Shared Address Book, Contact Management, or CRM (Customer Relationship Management) System.
- Point of Sale (POS) or Inventory Management System.
- Payroll or Time Keeping System.
- Other systems: Cash flow management tool, Expense, Receipt, Time, and Mileage Tracking Systems, Online Invoicing Service, Document Management System, and so on.

While you are still going to have to work within the limitations of what data each of these applications will allow you to import, your options have improved significantly with the availability of export to the SQL database feature in GnuCash.

Export any data

We covered what data you can import into GnuCash and in what formats, extensively in another chapter. You may find that there are lots of limitations in what data you can import into GnuCash. However, your ability to export data out of GnuCash has gone up dramatically by using this new Export to SQL database feature. You can export and extract all and any data that is in GnuCash.

Pop quiz – contact info stored in GnuCash

1. GnuCash doesn't have a field for which of the following contact info?

    a. E-mail address

    b. LinkedIn username

    c. FAX number

    d. Twitter username

Have a go hero – extracting other data from GnuCash

Following a similar approach, export the vendor contact data from GnuCash and import that into your contact management application.

Foreign currency transactions

Most of the time, you manage your business in USD. However, businesses are becoming global, even small businesses. Occasionally, you have the need to enter into a contract designated in a foreign currency or you travel overseas on business and pay your bills in a foreign currency. On such occasions, it is good to know how to account for it in GnuCash.

Time for action – invoicing and receiving payment in Canadian dollars

You worked hard to pursue a prospect in Canada, Quadra Systems. Finally, after tough negotiations, you have landed the contract. This is a great start and you can feel it in your gut that there is huge potential for you with this client, if you execute well. The contract is designated in Canadian Dollars (CAD) and so you need to gear up to invoice in CAD and receive payment in CAD.

1. Create a new income account with the name **Sales (CAD)**. In the **Security/currency** field, click on **Select...** and the **Select Currency** dialog will open. Select **CAD (Canadian Dollar)** from the Currency drop-down.

2. Create a new **Accounts Receivable (CAD)** account. Select the **Security/currency** as CAD and the **Account Type** as **A/Receivable**.

3. You need a holding account to show the payment received in CAD, until it is converted to USD. Create a new bank account named **Holding Account (CAD)** under **Current Assets**. Select the **Security/currency** as **CAD** and the **Account Type** as **Bank**, as shown in the next screenshot. You should create this GnuCash account, regardless of whether or not you have a bank account designated in CAD.

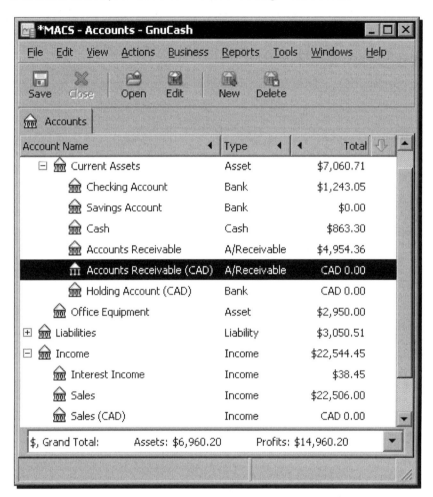

4. Remember your contract is in CAD not in USD. Create an invoice for CAD 9,950. Select the newly created **Income:Sales (CAD)** account as the **Income Account**, as shown in the following screenshot:

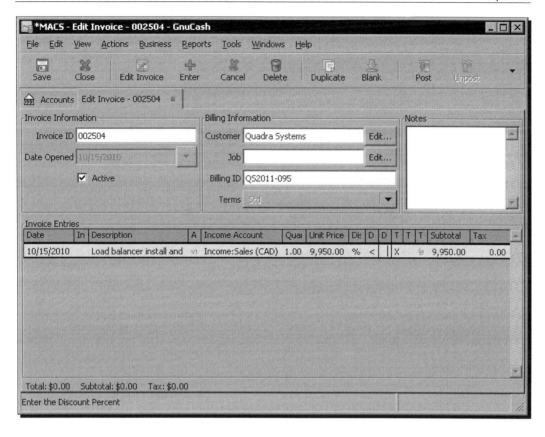

5. Click **Post**. Make sure the **Post to account** is your newly created **Accounts Receivable (CAD)** account.

6. Go to your **Accounts Receivable (CAD)** account and make sure that it shows an amount of CAD 9,950.00 receivable from Quadra Systems.

7. Now you have received the payment. Go to **Business | Customer | Process Payment**. Select the **Customer** and **Invoice** and enter the CAD received in the **Amount** field. Select **Accounts Receivable (CAD)** in the **Post To** field, and select **Holding Account (CAD)** in the **Transfer Account** field, as shown in the following screenshot:

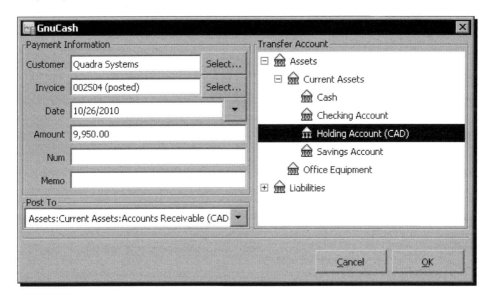

8. Open your **Holding Account (CAD)** and make sure that it shows a balance of **CAD 9,950.00**.

9. Next, you have to manually transfer this amount from this holding account to your USD bank account and apply the exchange rate that your bank gave you on the day of conversion. With the cursor on the transaction in the **Holding Account (CAD)**, select from the menu **Actions | Transfer...**. (Note: The cursor position is very important for this step.). The **Transfer Funds** window will open. Enter the **Amount** and **Description** in the **Basic Information** pane. The **Holding Account (CAD)** will be selected as the **Transfer From** account already. Select your **Checking Account** as the **Transfer To** account. As soon as you do that, the **Currency Transfer** pane below will be enabled. You know the exact amount in USD that your bank credited to your account. So, check the **To Amount** radio button and enter that amount. GnuCash will calculate and show the Exchange Rate for your ready reference, as shown in the following screenshot:

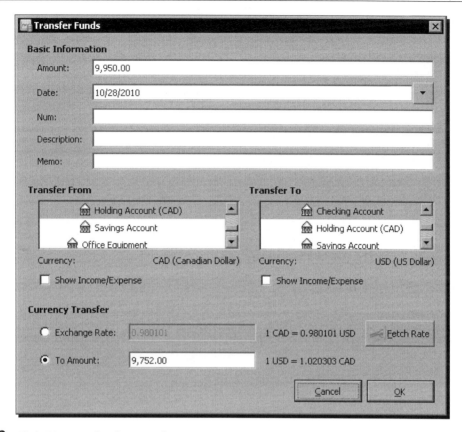

10. Click **OK** to make the transfer.

11. You will also have to manually apply any fees charged by your bank. There are two ways of doing this. You can either apply this as a split in the transfer transaction you did previously or you can create a separate transaction for this, whichever is convenient.

What just happened?

Even though your client paid in CAD, you suddenly found that a USD credit showed up in your bank account. This way of recording an implied transaction using the **Holding Account (CAD)** makes sure there is clarity in exactly what happened here. Even though there is no real **Holding Account (CAD)** at the bank, it is true that the amount came in as CAD from your customer to your bank and your bank sold the CAD and bought USD to credit your account, and your bank charged you a fee for providing this service. All of that is well represented in this method of accounting.

Please note that your Accounts Receivable account and the Holding account must be in the same currency as that of the invoice. If, for example, you invoice in three different currencies, you need three sets of those accounts.

Credit card charged in foreign currency during overseas travel

Let us say you travelled to Europe on business. You are presented with a hotel bill in Euros. You pay it with your credit card. Until the transaction hits your card account, you won't know what exchange rate the card company applied. Waiting until that happens is not a good option either. How will you enter that transaction in USD? Here is one way of doing it in GnuCash:

◆ Check the going exchange rate and calculate the USD equivalent.

◆ Create an entry in your credit card account for this amount and add ****PROVISIONAL**** at the end of the transaction description.

◆ Optionally, you can also add the EUR value of the hotel bill in the description.

◆ Once the transaction hits your statement, you can go back and correct the transaction that you created earlier with the actual USD amount. At the same time, you can remove the ****PROVISIONAL**** from the description.

This way, you are creating a timely entry and also making sure the correct value ends up in your books.

Foreign currency transactions FAQ

Here is a list of frequently asked questions about foreign currency transactions and our answers:

◆ Q: I have to post a transaction between a USD account and a foreign currency account. How do I enter the two different currency values or apply an exchange rate?

□ A: One way of doing it is using the **Transfer Funds** window, as we showed in the previous tutorial. The other way is to right-click on the transaction and select **Edit Exchange Rate**. The **Transfer Funds** window will come up. However, this second method may not work in some cases. If that happens, you can use the first method as a fall back.

- Q: My contract is designated in USD and my foreign customer pays in equivalent EUR, based on the current exchange rate. However, when the amount is received by my bank and they apply the exchange rate, there is always a currency gain or loss. Where do I record this currency gain or loss?

  - A: You need to manually add the currency gain or loss as a split to the transaction. You cannot do that from the **Transfer Funds** dialog.

- Q: How do the reports work when I have accounts in different currencies?

  - A: Reports convert the amounts from accounts in other currencies into USD. In the **Report Options** dialog, in the **Commodities** tab, the **Price Source** defaults to **Average Cost**. However, you can change it to **Weighted Average**, **Most recent**, or **Nearest in time**. **Nearest in time** will use the conversion rate closest to the date of the report and **Most recent** will use the conversion rate closest to today.

Pop quiz – entering the exchange rate

1. For a foreign currency transaction, which one of the following is not the right way to enter an exchange rate?

    a. From the menu, select **Actions | Edit Exchange Rate**.

    b. From the menu, select **Actions | Enter Exchange Rate**.

    c. From the menu, select **Actions | Transfer...** to open the **Transfer Funds** dialog.

    d. Right-click the transaction and select **Edit Exchange Rate**.

Have a go hero – exchange rate, currency loss, and the bank fee

Create a foreign currency transaction that takes care of the exchange rate, currency gain, or loss, as well as the bank fee.

Other handy tips and tricks

In this section, we will look at some handy tips and tricks of GnuCash that you may need occasionally.

Customer jobs and vendor jobs

Most of the time, you will be able to work with customer-level reports. However, sometimes you may be doing multiple contracts for a single customer and you may be working with entirely different sets of people for each contract. You will find it more convenient to see reports for each contract separately.

Time for action – grouping invoices for each contract separately

Let us say you want to set up a contract as a separate job for a customer, so that you can see reports for that contract alone separately. This is done in GnuCash with a Customer Job.

1. From the menu, select **Business | Customer | New Job...**. The **New Job** dialog will open. Enter the **Job Number** and **Job Name**. In the **Customer** field, select the customer from the list of customers. Also enter a **Billing ID**, as shown in the next screenshot. Click **OK**.

2. Now that you have created the job, go ahead and create a couple of invoices. In the **New Invoice** dialog, you must first select a **Customer**. As soon as you do that, you will find that the **Job** field becomes enabled. Select the job to which that invoice belongs.

3. Now you are ready to create job level reports. From the menu, select **Reports | Business | Job Report**. Open the **Report Options** dialog and in the **General** tab, click the **Select** button next to the Job field. The **Find Job** dialog will open.

4. In the first field, **Job Name** will be selected by default. In the second field, change **contains** to **matches regex**. In the third field, enter a dot (.). Click **Find**.

5. A list of jobs will appear. Select one of the jobs and click **Select**.

6. Now you will be back in the **Report Options** dialog with a job selected in the **Job** field. Click **OK** to see the **Job Report**, as shown in the following screenshot:

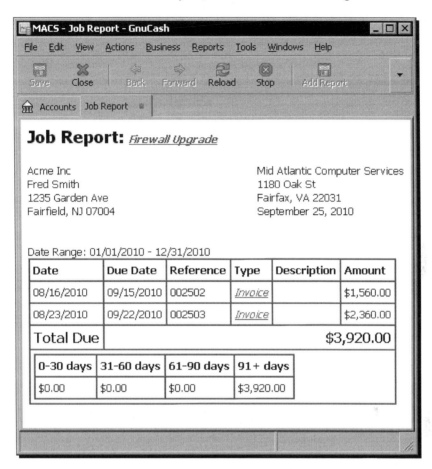

What just happened?

As we said earlier, businesses can use this feature if they are doing multiple jobs for the same customer and would like to view reports of invoices for each job separately. We also saw that non-profits require event, project, or program-level accounting and reports. This feature will come in handy to meet these requirements.

 However, please note that GnuCash has only one job report at present. Please proceed after confirming if that is adequate for your needs.

Vendor jobs

In a similar manner, vendor jobs are used to group multiple bills from a single vendor. The use of the vendor jobs feature is optional. This feature is useful when you have given multiple contracts or projects to the same vendor, and would like to view the reports for a single contract or project separately.

Special actions

There are some treatments to transactions that you may need once in a while. Voiding and adding a reversing transaction belong in this category, as is closing the books. We will briefly see when you might need them and how to apply them effectively.

Voiding a transaction

Let's say, you issued a check to a vendor. As usual, you promptly posted the transaction in your books. The vendor found that the check was issued for the wrong amount, or you discovered that you issued it for the wrong amount. You then asked the vendor to return the check and issued a new check for the correct amount.

Now the question is what to do with the transaction entered earlier. One option is to delete it. Another option is to edit the transaction with the new amount and check number. Either of those actions will make it go away as if the transaction never happened. However, it is possible that you may need to revisit what happened for a variety of reasons.

GnuCash provides you with a more elegant option to handle this situation. The first check issued was an incorrect transaction, but the transaction did happen. You printed the check and sent it to the vendor. To represent this correctly in your books, GnuCash allows you to void the transaction in the register. With the cursor on that transaction, select from the menu **Transaction | Void Transaction**. GnuCash will pop a dialog asking you to enter a **Reason for voiding transaction**. The status column in the register with the header **R** will change to **v**. Voiding changes the amount of the transaction to zero but keeps a record of it in the register. Voided transactions can be viewed easily in the register at any time to remind us of adjustments we made in the records. This will preserve the history.

There is another reason why voiding is a better option. It is not uncommon that you later discover why you wrote a check for that amount in the first place. GnuCash gives you the option to resurrect the transaction. With the cursor on that transaction, select from the menu **Transaction | Unvoid Transaction**. Come back transaction, all is forgiven!

When do you void a transaction?

You void a wrong transaction to undo a mistake that actually happened in the current accounting period.

You can see only voided transactions by filtering the transactions using the **Filter By** dialog and the **Status** tab.

In the **Filter By** dialog, you will see a checkbox marked **Frozen** in the **Status** tab. This status is currently not in use. You can ignore this.

Adding a reversing transaction

Let's say, you issued a check to a vendor. As usual, you promptly posted the transaction in your books. You forgot all about it. Months went by and you closed the accounts for that year. You are now in the New Year and you have just found out that the vendor didn't cash that check at all.

Now the question is what to do with the transaction entered in the previous year. Deleting and editing the old transaction are not valid options because you have closed the accounts for the previous year.

GnuCash provides you with a more elegant option to handle this situation as well. GnuCash allows you to reverse the transaction in the register. With the cursor on that transaction, from the menu, select **Transaction | Add Reversing Transaction**

It will add a transaction that has all the opposite entries to the selected transaction, so that the net effect is fully cancelled out. To reverse a transaction means to turn the transaction around, and nullify its effect in the books.

When do you reverse a transaction?

You reverse a transaction to undo a mistake that happened in a previous accounting period that is now closed. You discovered it now, but you cannot reopen the closed accounting period. So, you make the reversing entry in the current period.

Year end closing

Let us fast forward to the beginning of the New Year. You have completed maintaining your small business accounts in GnuCash successfully for the first year. At the time of starting the New Year, you are wondering what the best way to start the New Year is. With GnuCash, we give you three options:

◆ In the first option, using the included close books feature creates a couple of transactions that zeroes out the income and expense accounts and adds an entry in the equity account to show the surplus or the deficit. You can do this by selecting from the menu **Tools**   **Close Book**. Unfortunately, you then have to avoid those records whenever you run any reports, and this is a problem that you have to deal with every time you run reports.

◆ In the second option, when a year is completed, you can leave that file, start a new file with the same account tree, and start entering transactions of the new year. This way, you will have one file for each year. Your transactions are nicely packaged into small manageable files of one year each, right? However, this approach has the following limitations:

  ❑ You have to create opening balance transactions for all your accounts, manually.

  ❑ It prevents you from estimating initial budget amounts, based on past transactions.

  ❑ It prevents you from running any long-term reports on your financial data.

◆ The third option is to continue the transactions of the new year with the same data file that has the transactions of the previous year. When you create the reports, you can choose the starting and ending dates. You can also run year-to-date reports for the current year. You won't have the limitations listed in the second option.

Pick whichever option works for you and also run it by your accountant.

Inventory management

Inventory management has the following essential characteristics:

◆ Inventory is an asset. It doesn't become an expense until it's used or sold.

◆ The loaded cost of an item may include, in addition to its basic cost, associated costs such as shipping costs.

◆ You may be buying different batches of an item at different prices, and keep using them, as and when you need them. You have to decide on a costing policy of how to expense them – **first-in first-out (FIFO)**, **last-in first-out (LIFO)**, or average. There may be IRS guidelines about what options are available to you.

GnuCash doesn't have an inventory management module. If your small business has inventory, here are some possible ways to handle it:

◆ If your business has a large inventory, by number or by volume, or you have heavy transactions, you may want to consider an open source inventory management application such as **tracmor** (http://www.tracmor.com/) or a commercial one.

◆ If you have a smaller number of items and you have a modest number of transactions, you may be able to manage with a purpose-built spreadsheet template.

◆ If you have only a handful of items and infrequent transactions, you may be able to make do with your own tables in a spreadsheet.

At the end of each month or each week, as the case may be, you can simply transfer the expenses into the appropriate expense accounts and adjust the asset value to match. The inventory management application or the spreadsheet provides the break up details of how the GnuCash entries were arrived at.

Mileage tracking

If you are using your vehicle for both personal and business purposes, IRS requires you to keep an actual record of destination, miles travelled, and business purpose. Estimated or approximate miles are not acceptable. So, you need some way of recording this level of detail. GnuCash doesn't have a special module for this. There are a variety of products and online services, called trip books or mileage-logging services, available that will help you to record and store this information. Some of the expense tracking services will also allow you to keep track of the mileage using your mobile phone. Please refer to the *Selecting an expense tracking service* section in *Chapter 11, Data Import/Export: Use your Phone to Enter Expenses*.

Once a month, you can accumulate the miles in a report or a spreadsheet and make an entry in GnuCash showing the amount, after applying the applicable IRS mileage allowance. Preserve the spreadsheet or report to provide break-up details of how the GnuCash monthly entry was arrived at. Check with your accountant or tax consultant first whether this is adequate in case of an IRS audit.

Pop quiz – finding all jobs

1. In the **Find Job** dialog, what values will you enter to get a list of all the jobs in the system?

    a. **contains** and **all**.

    b. **matches regex** and a (.) dot.

    c. **does not match regex** and a (.) **dot.**

    d. **contains** and a (.) dot.

Have a go hero – setting up vendor jobs

Set up a job for a vendor, create bills for that job, and create a job report.

Summary

We learned a lot in this chapter about exporting GnuCash data to a SQL database and using that data.

Specifically, we covered:

- Export data from GnuCash in popular SQL database formats: We learned the benefits of this feature and the various ways in which we can use this data.

- Query the exported data using popular tools: We looked at ways of using popular tools to query this data.

- Create custom reports and charts using popular tools: We looked at ways of using popular tools to create custom reports and charts from this data.

- Application integration using the exported data: We looked at ways of using the queried data for integration with other applications that you use.

- Handle foreign currency transactions in GnuCash: We saw examples of foreign exchange transactions and how to handle them in GnuCash.

- Customer jobs: We also saw how we can get reports at the contract level for the same customer by utilizing the Jobs feature of GnuCash.

- Special actions: We saw two different ways to undo a transaction, if that becomes necessary at a later point in time. We also saw ways to deal with the year-end closing of books.

- Inventory management and mileage tracking: Though GnuCash doesn't have support for these, we outlined some ways in which you can work around these limitations.

Now that you have learned how to use GnuCash in many practical and hands-on ways, I hope you are ready to start using them for your self-employment, non-profit, or small business successfully, which is the topic of the next chapter in your business or career. Best of luck!

[1]OpenOffice.org, Calc and Base are registered trademarks of Sun Microsystems Inc.

[2]Office and Excel are registered trademarks of Microsoft Corporation.

Pop Quiz Answers

Chapter 1: Getting Started with GnuCash

Pop quiz – understanding accounts

Both transactions and sub-accounts

Pop quiz – understanding account types and hierarchies

1. Debit Card
2. Asset, Liability, Equity, Expenses and Income
3. No

Chapter 2: Transactions – the Lifeblood of a Business

Pop quiz – understanding transactions

1. They must be equal to each other

Pop quiz – navigating GnuCash

1. Account register window
2. Using the Close button

Pop quiz – understanding transactions

1. True
2. Only from the account register.

Pop quiz – using shortcuts to speed up bookkeeping

1. Ex:Au:Re
2. M

Pop quiz – viewing the account register

1. View Double Line

Chapter 3: Fun and eye-opening part - Reports and charts

Pop quiz – viewing standard reports

1. Account Report and Account Transaction Report

Pop quiz – customizing a report

1. Click on the **Reload** button.

Pop quiz – creating stylesheets

1. From the menu select **Edit** | **Style Sheets**.

Pop quiz – saving exported reports

1. `.html`

Chapter 4: How not to get lost in the transactions jungle

Pop quiz – reconciling with a bank statement

1. Ending balance from my bank statement.
2. The transactions that appear on the bank statement.

Pop quiz – reconciling with an electronic statement

1. Fixed width
2. Will add the transaction as new.

Pop quiz – changing the account to import into

1. The account that you previously selected as the account to import into by mistake.

Chapter 5: Repetitive work? Let GnuCash do it

Pop quiz – creating a recurring transaction

1. Select **Frequency Semi-Monthly**.

Pop quiz – triggering scheduled transactions

1. In the **Overview** tab of **Edit Scheduled Transaction** window, check **Notify me when created**.

Pop quiz – using the Scheduled Transaction Editor

1. Set the **Start Date** in the **Frequency** tab of the **Edit Scheduled Transaction** window.
2. phonebill

Chapter 6: Business Mantra: Buy Now, Pay Later

Pop quiz – adding customers and creating invoices

1. Company Name matches `regex` .(dot)

Pop quiz – choosing an account

2. Process payment.

Pop quiz – keeping track of credit purchases

1. Unpost

Chapter 7: Budget: Trip Planner for your Business

Pop quiz – creating a new budget

1. **Actions | Budget | New Budget**
2. Select "Every 3 month(s)"

Pop quiz – calculating payroll

1. A liability of the business to be paid to the government later.
2. Account Type "Liability" and Parent Account "Liabilities".

Pop quiz – charging depreciation on capital assets

1. An expense account.

Pop quiz – setting up a Drawing account

1. Equity account

Chapter 8: Making Tax Times Less Stressful

Pop quiz – filing tax returns

1. 1065
2. TXF

Pop quiz – exporting income tax data

1. **Reports | Tax Schedule Report & TXF Export**. Then click on the toolbar button **Export**.

Pop quiz – setting up tax tables

1. Any number

Pop quiz – applying tax tables to invoices

1. No

Chapter 9: Printing Checks and Finding Transactions

Pop quiz – filtering transactions

1. By amount range

Pop quiz – printing date format in a check

1. Account Register window

Pop quiz – editing account codes

1. **Open Subaccounts** window

Pop quiz – calculating mortgage payment

1. Future value

Chapter 10: Adapting GnuCash for Non-profits and Personalizing

Pop quiz – creating a separate account for an event or a project

1.   New top level account

Pop quiz – setting your preferences

1.   From the **GnuCash Preferences** dialog **Reports** tab.

Pop quiz – creating a backup

1.   The main accounts file the `.gconf` folder and the `.gnucash` folder.

Chapter 11: Data Import/Export: Use your Phone to Enter Expenses

Pop quiz – separating transactions by type of payment

1.   Create separate files for each type of payment.

Pop quiz – importing a CSV file

1.   Withdrawal

Pop quiz – format suitable for creating accounts

1.   QIF

Pop quiz – creating a Transaction Report with all of the transactions

1.   In the **Report Options** dialog, in the **General** tab, select **Start Date** the same as your earliest transaction or earlier and the **End Date** the same as your last transaction or later.

Chapter 12: Application Integration and Other Advanced Topics

Pop quiz – GnuCash default data format

1. Xml

Pop quiz – understanding GnuCash fields

1. Splits

Pop quiz – contact info stored in GnuCash

1. LinkedIn username
2. Twitter username

Pop quiz – entering exchange rate

1. From the menu select **Actions** | **Enter Exchange Rate**.

Pop quiz – finding all jobs

1. **matches regex** and a (**.**) dot.

Index

G

General Journal report 65
GnuCash
about 9, 11, 100
account, creating 21
account, deleting 22
account, renaming 22
account types 23
advantages 27
annual tax returns, preparing 174-177
auto-save changes feature 13, 230
bookkeeping, using for non-profits 212-215
budget 144
business accounts 21
business transactions 35
calculations, performing in 208
chart, viewing 62
Check & Repair process 206, 207
checks, printing 195-197
contact information, exporting from 271, 272
credit card reconciliation 94
Customer Jobs feature 219
customizing 221-224
custom report, creating 67-69
custom report, saving 68, 69
data, backing up 228, 229
data, exporting from 251, 253
data, migrating from Excel[2] 248
data, migrating from Office Accounting[2] 248
data, migrating from Office SBA[2] 248
data, migrating from OpenOffice.org[4] Calc 248
data, migrating from QuickBooks[1] 249
data, migrating from Quicken Home & Business[1] 248
default business accounts, creating 14-18
depreciation 159
donors, setting up 215
electronic reconciliation 87-90
files, selecting for backup 230
Financial Calculator 207
find transactions process, FAQs 193, 194
functions 9, 10
income tax related accounts, setting up 168, 169, 172
income tax schedule, creating 174
installing, on other operating system 13
installing, on Windows 11-13
limitations 28
members, setting up 215
migrating to, from other software 242-245
migrating, to other accounting software 253, 254
mileage-logging services 285
minimal set of accounts 18, 19
Owner's Drawing Account 162
parent accounts 23
payroll 154
payroll entries, making in 154-156
personalizing 221-224
preference settings 225-227
pronouncing 11
recurring transactions 100
register views, changing 54
Renumber Subaccounts feature 202
reports, exporting 75, 76
sales tax, applying to invoices 183-185
sales tax tables, setting up 179
simple transactions 32-34
standard reports, viewing 61, 62
starting invoice number, setting 133, 134
tax features 169-171
top level accounts 23
transactions, filtering 192
transactions, searching 188, 189
transactions, sorting 189-192
transactions, viewing 192
working, with stylesheets 72-74
GnuCash accounts
mapping, to tax schedules 169-171
GnuCash, advantages
accounts file, sharing 27
business 27
personal accounting 27
GnuCash A/R modules
customers 130
invoices 130
jobs 130
process payments 130
GnuCash features
using, for non-profits 212-215
GnuCash file
converting, to QIF file 254

N

O

P

Q

R

Thank you for buying
Gnucash 2.4 Small Business Accounting
Beginner's Guide

About Packt Publishing

Packt, pronounced 'packed', published its first book "*Mastering phpMyAdmin for Effective MySQL Management*" in April 2004 and subsequently continued to specialize in publishing highly focused books on specific technologies and solutions.

Our books and publications share the experiences of your fellow IT professionals in adapting and customizing today's systems, applications, and frameworks. Our solution based books give you the knowledge and power to customize the software and technologies you're using to get the job done. Packt books are more specific and less general than the IT books you have seen in the past. Our unique business model allows us to bring you more focused information, giving you more of what you need to know, and less of what you don't.

Packt is a modern, yet unique publishing company, which focuses on producing quality, cutting-edge books for communities of developers, administrators, and newbies alike. For more information, please visit our website: www.packtpub.com.

About Packt Open Source

In 2010, Packt launched two new brands, Packt Open Source and Packt Enterprise, in order to continue its focus on specialization. This book is part of the Packt Open Source brand, home to books published on software built around Open Source licences, and offering information to anybody from advanced developers to budding web designers. The Open Source brand also runs Packt's Open Source Royalty Scheme, by which Packt gives a royalty to each Open Source project about whose software a book is sold.

Writing for Packt

We welcome all inquiries from people who are interested in authoring. Book proposals should be sent to author@packtpub.com. If your book idea is still at an early stage and you would like to discuss it first before writing a formal book proposal, contact us; one of our commissioning editors will get in touch with you.

We're not just looking for published authors; if you have strong technical skills but no writing experience, our experienced editors can help you develop a writing career, or simply get some additional reward for your expertise.

Drupal E-commerce with Ubercart 2.x

ISBN: 978-1-847199-20-1   Paperback: 364 pages

Build, administer, and customize an online store using Drupal with Ubercart

1. Create a powerful e-shop using the award-winning CMS Drupal and the robust e-commerce module Ubercart

2. Create and manage the product catalog and insert products in manual or batch mode

3. Apply SEO (search engine optimization) to your e-shop and adopt turn-key internet marketing techniques

Joomla! E-Commerce with VirtueMart

ISBN: 978-1-847196-74-3   Paperback: 476 pages

Build feature-rich online stores with Joomla! 1.0/1.5 and VirtueMart 1.1.x

1. Build your own e-commerce web site from scratch by adding features step-by-step to an example e-commerce web site

2. Configure the shop, build product catalogues, configure user registration settings for VirtueMart to take orders from around the world

3. Manage customers, orders, and a variety of currencies to provide the best customer service

Please check **www.PacktPub.com** for information on our titles

Printed in Great Britain
by Amazon.co.uk, Ltd.,
Marston Gate.